Praise for *Enslaved by Ducks*

"All of us who feel a deep emotional connection with animals will respond to this book. As Bob Tarte realizes, there is no drug or therapy as effective as an animal who loves you." —Jeffrey Masson, author of *When Elephants Weep*

"A beautiful, honest, hilarious, and touching book about the subtle and blatant ways animal companions take over our lives. It's impossible to read *Enslaved by Ducks* and not fall just a little in love with Bob Tarte, his charming, heroic wife, Linda, and their menagerie." —Jana Murphy, author of *The Secret Lives of Dogs*

"As the adoring owner or former owner of dogs, cats, parrots, rabbits, and six hundred gallons of saltwater fish, I was utterly delighted with *Enslaved by Ducks*. Bob Tarte profoundly understands and brilliantly articulates the extraordinary connections between humans and animals." —Robert Olen Butler

"If you thought one backyard duck was much like another, wait till you meet the tiny, indomitable Peggy, who laid down her life to save her fellow ducks. What May Sarton did for cats in *The Fur Person*, Bob Tarte does for ducks. And destructive parrots and fierce rabbits and a talking baby starling and a whole house and yard full of demanding oddballs that, by comparison, will make you feel better about your own domestic life."
—Barbara Holland, author of *They Went Whistling*

"I started to read a page and ended up reading the book! . . . As Bob Tarte shows, with animal after animal, it's not enough in the end to provide just the basics of food, water, and shelter; you have to love them like family. And he's right: if you are an animal lover, your bond with animals goes far deeper than just companionship. It really is a way of life." —Marty Becker, D.V.M., *Good Morning America*

"In his hilarious debut, Tarte—a city boy at heart—chronicles how his blissful, animal-free life took an unexpectedly raucous turn when his nature-loving wife decided to share their spacious, early-twentieth-century Michigan farmhouse with a menagerie of furry and feathery friends: a malicious bunny with an appetite for live wires, a homicidal turkey, a horny ring-necked dove, a trash-talking African grey parrot, and more than a dozen other quirky creatures. Though each new animal is wackier and more demanding than the last, Tarte rebels against his urban instincts and learns to love his personal zoo. After reading this delightfully punchy account, you may never look at Fido the same way again."
—*Entertainment Weekly*

ENSLAVED BY DUCKS

by BOB TARTE

ALGONQUIN BOOKS OF CHAPEL HILL

2004

Published by
ALGONQUIN BOOKS OF CHAPEL HILL
Post Office Box 2225
Chapel Hill, North Carolina 27515-2225

a division of
Workman Publishing
225 Varick Street
New York, New York 10014

While the people, places, and events described in the following pages are
real, location and human names have been changed for the sake of privacy.

Library of Congress Cataloging-in-Publication Data
Tarte, Bob.
Enslaved by ducks / by Bob Tarte.—1st ed.
p. cm.
ISBN-13: 978-1-56512-351-9 (HC)
1. Pets—Michigan—Lowell—Anecdotes.   2. Animals—Michigan—
Lowell—Anecdotes.   3. Human-animal relationships—Michigan—
Lowell—Anecdotes   4. Tarte, Bob.   I. Title.
SF416.T37 2003
636.088'7'0977455—dc22   2003057756
ISBN-13: 978-1-56512-450-9 (PB)

10

To my wonderful wife, Linda, who somehow keeps the chaos at bay.

Contents

Cast of Characters

(Listed more or less in order of appearance and by type)

INDOOR ANIMALS

Bunnies

Binky: stubborn dwarf Dutch troublemaker
Bertha: feral Netherland dwarf, captured in suburbia
Bertie: Netherland dwarf, brother to Rollo
Rollo: Netherland dwarf, brother to Bertie
Walter: large-headed Checker Giant, rescued from barn

Parrots

Ollie: ill-tempered brotogeris "pocket parrot"
Stanley Sue: gender-switching African grey Timneh
Dusty: chatty, author-biting Congo African grey

Other Birds

Howard: amorous ring-neck dove
Chester: non-hand-tamed canary
Elliott: feisty canary, successor to Chester
Farley: parakeet senior citizen
Rossy: Ollie's female parakeet suitor
Reggie: Howard's male parakeet suitor
Sophie: demure female parakeet
Tillie: visiting dove
Weaver: special guest starling

Cats

Penny: grey reclusive female, intended as Binky's friend
Agnes: bold outdoorswoman, discovered under bird feeder

OUTDOOR ANIMALS

Ducks

Daphne: Muscovy from auto-parts parking lot
Phoebe: black-and-white Cayuga, smitten by wanderlust
Martha: Blue Swede with ear-splitting voice
Peggy: heroic call duck, protector of Chloe

Chloe: mallard who learned to limp
Blabby and Wing Ding: "smelly" call-duck delinquents
Stewart: Khaki Campbell, brother to Trevor
Trevor: Khaki Campbell, brother to Stewart
Marybelle, Clara, and Gwelda: unexpected mixed-duck offspring
Hector: cantankerous, shoulder-sitting Muscovy
Richie: Richmond Pond foundling
Timmy: unexpected son of Richie

Geese

Liza: lap-sitting African goose, sister to Hailey
Hailey: slightly less-friendly goose, sister to Liza

Turkeys

Hazel: victim of sneak attack
Lizzie: presumed perpetrator of sneak attack
And two that remain nameless

ORDINARY HUMANS

Bob Tarte: put-upon author
Linda Tarte: long-suffering wife to unfortunate author
Joan Smith: sister to victimized author
Rupert Murdoch: nonbillionaire duck breeder
Jacob Lestermeyer: operator of petting zoo/meat market
LuAnne Grady: owner of indoor orphan Green-Winged Teal
Bill Holm: mocking yuppie friend of pathetic author
Marge and George Chedrick: DNR-affiliated animal rehabbers

LETTERED HUMANS

Alanson Benedict, DVM: "So you've been bad-mouthing our
    practice."
Katherine Stallings, DVM: prescriber of questionable ointments
Michael Hedley, DVM: amiable zoo-consultant genius
Alice Colby, DVM: doesn't do turkeys
Owen Fuller, DVM: avian expert extraordinaire
John Carlotti, DVM: made Howard a collar
Carl Glaser, MD: "Do you hear voices?"
Jerold Rick, MD: heartless hippie shrink

Introduction

I SHOULD HAVE KNOWN I was doomed to write a book about our animals. Since they had taken over just about everything else in my life, it was only a matter of time before they commandeered my word processor, too. This began to seem inevitable when I was working on a music column for *The Beat* magazine about a vocal group from Sardinia, and my editor CC Smith asked me, "Are there any animals in it?"

"No, of course not," I protested.

"No parrots or rabbits?"

"Not even a sardine."

"Well, that's a first. Every column this year has had a goose in it or something."

"Not this one," I answered defensively, though I had very nearly written about a goose, but a pang of conscience had stopped me.

Though not quite as frequently as my editor had claimed, animal anecdotes had steadily gnawed their way into my music column over the years. I never could figure out why she allowed them to inhabit a magazine devoted to reggae and international music. I suppose they added texture to *The Beat,* like sand clinging to a strawberry. And they certainly made the other writers look even more expert by comparison.

I had started contributing to *The Beat* back in 1989, when record stores still sold records. When I bought my first CD player, I was

seized by a rare fit of extroversion and penned a letter to the magazine suggesting that someone cover the scant few reggae, African-
music, and world-music albums then available on CD. My letterhead
made the bold claim that I was a writer. I had little experience with
magazines, except for an article on strange coincidences involving
clowns and the number 22 that I had written several years earlier
with a friend for a British paranormal magazine. But CC liked what
I had sent her and christened my CD-review column "Technobeat,"
never suspecting that this would one day become the name for a type
of computer-generated dance music—and never dreaming that I
would one day hand in a story about chasing runaway ducks.

My main difficulty with my new column was a profound ignorance of the international music I was supposed to be an authority
on. But I figured that as long as I concentrated on obscure genres
like Tuvan throat-singing or Finnish Karelian *runo* songs, most
readers of *The Beat* probably wouldn't catch on that I didn't know
any more than they did. To help discourage informed readers who
might expose me, I began leading off my column with an obfus-
cating essay on a nonmusical subject—typically one that presented
me in an unflattering light. A ready subject was my jarring change
of address to a rural setting after thirty-eight years of urban life.

One column described how, just after I had moved from an
apartment in downtown Grand Rapids, Michigan, to a one-hundred-
year-old farmhouse, I was tortured by a sign outside GoFer's restaurant up the road that apparently proclaimed CONGRATULATIONS BOB
TARTE. This troubled me. Who knew I had bought a house? Who
should care? When I pulled into GoFer's parking lot to get a closer
look, I discovered that the sign actually read, CONGRATULATIONS BOB
& TATE. But why the strange confluence of names the week of my
arrival? What person is first-named Tate? And why was fate snicker-
ing at me?

I wrote about my wife, Linda, our vacations to oddball places like Wawa, Ontario, and, increasingly, the animals that started invading our lives. The topic of pets became hard to avoid. One evening I was reviewing a CD by Foday Musa Suso, a musician from Senegal playing the West African *kora* harp. Our rabbit, Binky, had been roaming the living room in search of electrical cords to chew when I fired up the stereo, and the plucked strings of the *kora* unnerved him. He hid behind an overstuffed chair, loudly thumping a hind foot against the floor until I finally turned off the CD.

Subsequent animals cut deeper into my listening hours. Noisy parrots—who were themselves inexplicably sensitive to noise—protested if I played music in the evening while they were soaking up their beauty sleep. Animal concerns eventually restricted daytime listening, too. I needed to keep my ears open for signs of mischief from woodwork-destroying parakeets, or for quacks of distress from an outdoor duck that had fallen afoul of its flock.

I still loved music as much as ever, but it no longer played the same role in my life that it had in the days before I had reluctantly begun accumulating pets. Back when I was still an apartment dweller, if I found myself unavoidably thrown into a social setting with a stranger, I would quickly worm my musical tastes into the conversation.

"We just built a new deck onto our house," a fellow might brag.

"Oh, where do you live?"

"On Bali High Boulevard."

"No kidding!" I'd marvel. "Speaking of Bali, are you a fan of Balinese gamelan music? I just got a really good album of small-ensemble shadow-puppet music."

The relentless onslaught of animals changed all that. The quick dart of a question, "Do you have any pets?" usually led to camaraderie rather than strained silence. Most people owned a dog or cat whose bad habits they were eager to discuss. If the stranger was a harried bird or bunny owner, I immediately considered that person a friend. And if an eye-rolling remark about parrots followed, I would add the friend to my will.

But this newfound love of animals perplexed me. If I had grown up swooning over animals, I could better understand my devotion to them. I was as diffident about my boyhood beagle, Muffin, as she was about the family. She wouldn't endure petting unless a snack was somehow involved. I used to tease her using two of the phrases she knew best, "Go for a ride in the car," which never failed to elicit great excitement, and "Get a bath," which sent her scuttling to her hiding place behind the dining room door. "Muffin," I'd address her brightly, "Go for a ride in the bath?" Her change in demeanor from happiness to confusion delighted me, as did talking to her through the vacuum cleaner hose or calling her over a speaker that carried my voice into the kitchen while I hid in the closet with a microphone.

Oh, those were the days. Now it's our pets that confuse, control, and tease us.

This morning Linda's large African grey parrot, Dusty, blocked my path to the bathroom by squaring off on the linoleum and threatening to chomp my toes. Other times, aiming for a coffee refill, I've been forced to stay out of the kitchen rather than suffer the consequences of a starling drilling his beak into my scalp. At least our ducks and geese live in backyard pens, though trudging outside to fill their plastic swimming pools involves a trip through the basement, where two convalescing turkeys yip pathetically if I don't coo and hand-feed them grain.

Pound for pound, these animals don't add up to much. Dog fanciers with a couple of Rottweilers trump us in terms of sheer biomass. But, when it comes to sheer insistence, even the largest, most unruly dogs—or, for that matter, your average herd of cattle—are no match for our ducks, geese, parrots, parakeets, turkeys, cats, rabbits, and other birds.

And over time, I have found myself thinking of them less as "animals" and more as beings, as little packets of alien intelligence. People who hunt for sport probably never consider the deer or turkey they're about to blast to smithereens as a unique individual. But pat the hunter's hound on the head, idly suggest that one of these days you'd like to bag a dog with a .22, and expect a heated discussion. Viewed from an emotional distance, animals do tend to blend together into an undifferentiated mass, like a crowd of spectators at a football game. Yet even a common-as-mud pet like a parakeet will reveal a vivid personality if you pay close attention. When I was a kid, we kept a parakeet in a cage by itself, tucked away in a corner of our dining room. I regarded it as the essence of dullness. But our three parakeets are radiant souls. Sophie is shy and ladylike. Reggie is mischievous and a copycat. He will flutter to my shoulder only after Rossy has already landed there to nibble on my neck.

Our animals have provided me with the only subject besides music that I've ever felt impassioned to write about. Since CC Smith balked at turning over her entire magazine to the art of trimming rabbit teeth, I knew I needed to explore those weighty subjects in a book. I also wanted to grapple with the unlikely series of events that had changed me into an animal lover. The long, smooth slide from keeping one animal to housing more than two dozen amazes me as much as the fact that I'm willing to expend energy on them. I'm so lazy, I'll take an entire month to clean my upstairs office by shuffling around a few mounds of junk per day. Yet pets have compelled me to perform backbreaking labors that would wake me screaming from a dream.

I also thought that telling the story of Bob and Linda might serve an instructive function. Books about raising dogs and cats are plentiful. Bookstores abound in how-to guides on naming, grooming, potty training, feeding, and deworming felines and canines, as well as narratives of joyful ownership, psychic abilities, and heroic exploits of Fido and Tabby. But when we tried to locate a book on keeping ducks, geese, turkeys, doves, and even rabbits as pets, we came up empty-handed. Instead, we found handbooks on backyard fowl filled with gorgeous photos of breeds alongside helpful sections on butchering. And though the literature on parrots has grown over the last few years, I had to read between the lines to realize that you attach yourself to one of these willful animals at your peril.

I thought, too, that I could use my book to warn about the pitfalls of keeping pets: The bunny with the charming overbite will strip your living room carpet bald. Backyard ducks that supposedly "take care of themselves" require more maintenance than the space shuttle. And the goose you got for free could get sick, and empty your pockets faster than a trip through airport security. I heard experts claim again and again that owning pets reduces stress and might extend your life. I tried to remember that as I dragged a hose out of the basement to fill the ducks' plastic swimming pool in January weather so cold, the snow complained as I stepped on it. I wondered: Who wants to live longer under those conditions? Why didn't anyone warn me?

While these were all good reasons for thinking about writing a book, it took a push from an animal to turn thought into action.

I was struggling to eat a sandwich one Sunday afternoon as Linda returned from a potluck at her church. Sitting in the dining room was out of the question. Our green parrot, Ollie, threw himself into a squawking fit as soon as I sat down at the table to cut my sandwich in half. The African grey parrot, Stanley Sue, countered with a few bright "I want" chirps that degenerated into raucous complaints and bell ringing as I took my first bite. I moved to the living room only to find myself still within Ollie's field of view.

"I'm taking my lunch outside," I said to Linda.

"Well, don't sit out on the deck," she warned. "He can see you through the window."

"That's fine. I won't be able to hear him."

"That's what you think. I could hear him out in my car."

I headed for the backyard, but then I realized that if the ducks and geese knew I was outdoors they would clamor to get out of their pen. My sandwich and I roamed the front yard, eliminated it as too close to the road and the exhaust fumes of passing cars, and settled on a soft patch of grass near the front of the barn, invisible to the turkeys behind it. They would yip like dogs when they saw me, and I wanted to eat in peace. The spot I chose felt safe. A massive fir tree that seemed to double in size every year shielded me from the house. Leaning against the post that supported the satellite dish, I raised my sandwich to my mouth just as our black cat, Agnes, leaped upon my lap from out of nowhere and begged for a taste.

Defeated, I shared my lunch with her. A few minutes later, I trudged into the house, sat down at the word processor, and started thinking about our animals—trying to figure out why I had rearranged my life to accommodate theirs.

CHAPTER 1

Belligerent Binky

After living so long in the city, I felt peculiar at the farmhouse in Lowell. Looking out the window and seeing woods instead of another window disoriented me. So did waking up to songbirds and a shotgun blast from across the river rather than to car horns and a pistol shot from down the street. I had trouble getting used to the well house outside the back door, the hulking wood furnace in the basement, and the wall of brambles beyond the fence. Strange beasts prowled the property by night. Vultures sailed overhead by day. Stanchions in the barn and a rusted-out cattle trough on the edge of the swamp told of other animal residents—all part of the past, I told myself. But my wife-to-be, Linda, had ideas of her own.

Linda couldn't wait to start crowding every surface in the house with knickknacks. The same three-acre plot of land whose flooding riverfront and mysterious boulder heaps intimidated me struck Linda as an unbounded gardening opportunity. But she wasn't so certain about living with me. Her original plan had been to live part time in her northern Michigan cabin. But once we got married a few

months later, she changed her mind. I couldn't even get her to move
out to the barn. Harmony ran rampant. And then we got Binky.

Buying Binky was one of the most pivotal, far-reaching actions
of my adult years, and it's inexcusable that I can't retrace the tortured chain of reasoning that convinced me that having a rabbit
was a good idea. Binky was more than just a bunny. He transformed our house from a pristine, animal-free environment into an
indoor petting zoo. He changed my life forever. When I ponder my
pet-free past, I ask myself not only why I ever agreed to buy him,
but also how a sour dwarf Dutch rabbit with few social skills
ended up embodying an argument for more animals rather than
none.

It was during our first spring together in the house that Linda
lobbied me for a bunny. "Wouldn't it be fun to have a little animal
hopping around the house?" she asked.

"You sort of hop when you walk," I told her. "If you worked on
it a bit, we wouldn't need a rabbit."

"You couldn't find an animal that's less trouble," she insisted. "My
friend Justina has a bunny, and it just hangs out near the clothes
dryer and uses an old towel for a bed."

"Then where will you sleep?" I asked her. But I had learned that
it was useless arguing with anyone as strong-minded as Linda.

Before I met Linda, she had owned a couple of dogs and now
missed having them. A rabbit seemed like an easier alternative. I
knew that a dog had to be walked, bathed, brushed, housebroken,
lugged around in the car, trained to bark rarely, taught not to knock
down the elderly, flea-powdered, dewormed, pooper-scooped,
spayed or fixed, deflected from visitors' crotches, kept away from
fellow dogs, protected from roaming skunks, talked to through a
vacuum cleaner hose, fed, licensed, vaccinated, and generally made
a part of the family pack. The world of a panting, ever-hungry,

free-range hound was also *my* world, while the world of a small caged animal was merely a three-foot cube. So went my thinking at the time.

A visit to my friend Philip's seemed to confirm the trouble-free nature of owning a rabbit. As we sat in his living room, I asked him if he might let his bunny, Drusilla, out of her cage.

"Oh, she's already in here somewhere, probably hiding behind a chair," he said.

As I stood up, I caught the barest glimpse of fur backing into the shadows. Compared to the lap-bounding behavior of a cat or the pet-me persistence of a dog, Drusilla's reticence appealed to me. "Is this all she ever does?"

"She basically has two modes. When she first comes into a room, she'll run all over the place as fast as she can. After that, she just stays in one spot unless you can convince her there's a reason to come out." This sounded ideal. I dismissed as sheer whimsy the caution that came next. "She does have an attraction to electrical cords. I usually unplug anything I'm not using and put the cords out of her reach before I let her into a room. Otherwise, she goes right for the cord and bites it cleanly in two."

"And she doesn't get a shock?"

"Rabbits' mouths are very dry," Philip surmised. "They don't have much saliva, so she doesn't get the same jolt you would get if you tried biting through a lamp cord."

The notion of my acquiring a taste for plastic-coated copper wire was so preposterous, I filed the matter away with Philip's other peculiarities—such as keeping a two-year-old Thanksgiving turkey carcass in his refrigerator's vegetable crisper. Some mysterious agent was undoubtedly putting the guillotine to Philip's appliance cords and pointing the finger at his bunny.

I told Linda about Drusilla's alleged taste for electrical cords.

"My customer Rose has a bunny, and she doesn't have that problem," she said.

"I thought Justina had the rabbit."

"Rose has one, too," said Linda, who ran into all sorts of colorful people in her job as a housecleaner. "He sits on Rose's lap while she watches *Wheel of Fortune*."

"That's my favorite show!"

"I know."

"And the bunny would sit on my lap?"

All at once, the road to bunny ownership seemed as smooth and straight as a good intentions–paved superhighway. But in an attack of poor judgment, we ended up choosing a rabbit that showed signs of being exactly the opposite of what we wanted. To start with, it had never dawned on us to do anything as sensible as research before making our selection. Our assumption was that except for variances in size, a bunny was a bunny. Who would have suspected that different breeds might possess different personalities?

Apparently not the farmer just north of the village of Rockford, who had posted a hand-lettered sign in front of his trailer succinctly advertising RABBITS. To Linda's horror, the farmer raised "meat pen" animals, bred especially for the dinner table. Chastened, she tried another farm down the road that sported similar advertising. This time the rabbits were for sale as pets, but all of them were the French lop variety, a breed whose floor-dragging, excessively floppy ears make it resemble a stuffed-animal designer's notion of a cocker spaniel puppy. Linda favored what she termed a "Cadbury bunny," an alert, upright-ear rabbit. The lop-ear breeder, a man with normal ears of his own, suggested that we attend the annual Easter Bunny Show at North Kent Mall the following weekend.

In my graduate-school days I had visited a San Francisco cat show so chockablock with attractive and distinctive breeds of felines, I left vowing never again to use the vulgar term "kitty." And Linda had encouraged my attendance at craft fairs and antique shows brimming with countless numbers of undifferentiated items and varied things. I imagined that the North Kent Mall Easter Bunny Show would be a combination of these.

Instead, the event was a celebration of vacant real estate. Staggered within a vast aisle of acreage that yawned past joyless, deserted shoe stores were exactly three Bunny Show conglomerations of less than six cages each. The first aggregate held a few miniature breeds like the Netherlands dwarf. It reminded me of a guinea pig with Popsicle-stick ears. Never mind that we would later learn that the breed was considered to be remarkably affectionate. The next batch of cages contained the dreaded French lop, renowned for its gentleness and pleasant nature. We passed it by. On the last cluster of tables were several California-breed "meat pen" bunnies a little too large and salty for our tastes, plus dwarf Dutch bunnies. A judge at the Kent County 4-H Youth Fair in Lowell would later charitably describe the dwarf Dutch breed as "moody." We zeroed in on one of these.

A small bristle-haired boy was petting a midsize, amiable rabbit who was stretched placidly on the tabletop exhibiting no urge to squirm or bolt. Like a cat taking an extended nap, it basked in human companionship. We could not resist stroking the rabbit's back while chuckling at its coloring, which comically suggested black britches and a black head cowl with milk-white fur in between.

"Is this one for sale?" Linda asked excitedly.

"She's the mother," the boy told us without looking up.

"But is she for sale?" I asked. "How old is she?"

"Thirteen months."

Linda and I took a hasty conference. An age of a year and a month seemed elderly by rabbit standards, especially when we'd had our minds set on a blank-slate baby bunny that we could lovingly raise and mold to our wills. A breeder had told us that males make better pets than females, presumably, I realize in retrospect, because their habits of mounting anything that moved and spraying the furniture in tomcat fashion appealed to his darker side. Still, the mother bunny did have the quiet temperament we were looking for. We visibly leaned in her direction.

"These are from her litter," the boy told us, indicating a trio of eight-week-old dwarf Dutches in an adjacent cage. If the mother was friendly and people-loving, surely her offspring would follow suit, we reasoned, forgetting the lesson of Cain.

"That one sure is cute," Linda said.

"Has he seen *Wheel of Fortune*?" I asked.

"You like him?" beamed a round-shouldered man wearing a plaid shirt and a nametag that identified him as Warren. "I favor the Dutches, too," he admitted, and indeed there was a resemblance around the teeth and jowls.

"Can we hold him?" Linda asked.

"Sure," Warren assured us with a doubtful air. No sooner had he unlatched the wire door and slid his hand into the cage than did the docile bunny absently nibbling on the steel spout of his water bottle turn into a churning, clawing, parcel of disdain for human contact. Despite his diminutive size, he packed a wallop via muscular back legs whose sole purpose, honed by eons of evolutionary development, was to propel him forward by kicks. With the practiced dexterity of a juggler, Warren tipped the writhing bundle into Linda's arms, but she could not hold him. Neither could I.

"Are there any other boys?" Linda asked as Warren returned the rabbit to his cage. As soon as his feet touched the cedar-chip bedding, he reverted to a picture of innocence.

Warren shook his head. "All the rest are females."

We weighed our options. The pair of breeders Linda had visited near Rockford didn't have what we wanted, and the notion of seeking out other breeders, visiting the numerous pet shops in our area, or waiting even another instant never entered our minds.

"It may be that he just doesn't know you yet," Warren offered.

"We'll take him!" we essentially shouted.

That man knew how to close a sale. Since we lacked the prowess and body armor to carry our purchase from mall to parking lot, Warren packed our bunny in a sturdy cardboard box. All the way back to Lowell, he scratched and bit the carton in a preview of the carpet-pulling, shoe-destroying, antisocial behavior to come. Within an hour of installing him in our home, Linda had managed to convey our new pet to the couch using an embrace resembling a wrestling hold that restricted his struggles to angry wiggles.

"He just needs to get used to being held," Linda suggested, interpreting my vigorous head-shaking as permission to drop him in my lap.

"Let's give him a few days," I suggested as I fought to restrain his clawing feet.

"See. He's settling down."

"He hasn't any choice. If I loosen my grip, I'll probably lose a hand." But after a few seconds, tremors ceased to rock his body and he started to relax. "Well, maybe you're right," I told Linda, precisely as the rabbit cemented the relationship between us by peeing enthusiastically all over my pantleg and the front of the couch.

In the days ahead, I made a game effort at bonding with Binky, whom we named after the sullen rabbit in Matt Groening's comic strip *Life in Hell.* Mimicking photos of Dian Fossey communing with mountain gorillas, I sprawled across the kitchen linoleum in an unthreatening, welcoming posture as Binky hopped around me obliviously. But I was merely a navigation obstacle. I even brought a pillow into the room, dowsed the lights, and feigned a nap to put him at ease with my presence. Ease wasn't the problem, however, as Binky proved whenever we offered him a banana. He'd be at our side in a flash, front paws resting on our wrist for extra eating leverage. His notion of affection was deigning to share a room with his back to us. When feeling especially generous, he'd allow us to squat behind him and give his head and ears a few brisk strokes. If further intimacy was pressed on him, he'd shake our hands away, hop to a human-free zone across the room, and lick himself where we had touched him.

We wheedled Binky with a fancy water bottle, litter box, and chew toys, fed him tortilla chips and buttered toast, built him an outdoor exercise pen, and allowed him unrestricted run of the house, yet he still displayed what we would come to know as typical rabbit belligerence. We bought him a lavender-colored leash and matching Chihuahua-scaled harness, which he hated, and took him out in our woods for ill-conceived walks that alternated between Binky welding himself to one spot and bolting ahead so quickly, we couldn't keep up. Judging by his attitude, we still didn't spoil him enough. My friend Philip would lavish M&M candies on his bunny, Drusilla. The books on rabbits we'd bought warned us that chocolate was poisonous to them. Drusilla obviously hadn't bothered to read the literature. Whenever Philip wanted to summon her, he'd shake a bag of M&Ms, and she would come running from whatever corner of his apartment she was holed up in. The only thing that rousted Binky from a hiding place was the descent of a human hand threatening to pet him or pick him up.

Binky's breeder, Warren, had handed Linda his business card at the time he had sold Binky to us, inviting her to call him with any problems. It was reassuring that we had an expert on tap, and many were the times that Linda took him up on his offer.

"We're having trouble with Binky not wanting us to pet him," Linda said to Warren on one occasion.

"That's odd," Warren replied. "I've never run into that one before. I just don't know what to tell you."

Another time Linda called him about Binky's habit of gnawing on everything in our house. "I wish I had an answer for you," Warren told Linda, encouraging her to phone again if we had any other concerns. We received an identical answer about Binky's penchant for running in circles around our feet while making a buzzing sound. "Boy, that's really a new one on me," he admitted. We wondered how a person who made a profession of breeding rabbits could know so little about their behavior.

Having never owned a rabbit before, I didn't know how to interact with Binky. I'd expected him to behave not too differently from a cat, to be more curious and attentive to his owners and perhaps less fastidiously self-involved. Dogs are easy to deal with because they are so much like us. With a single word or the arch of an eyebrow, you could shame a dog into curling up in the corner instead of bothering you. Cats aren't as easily dissuaded, but you can at least be sure that they're reacting to the sound of your voice. Under the right circumstances, a string of words will evoke paroxysms of pleasure in a cat, far greater than what could be achieved with the finest canned dinner product. I'd read that bunnies also enjoy being talked to, but Binky gave no outward sign that this was true.

His muteness struck me as eerie. A happy cat will purr. An unhappy dog will whine. Parrots are vocal tracts on legs. But rabbits come into this world and leave it as sonic blank slates, occasionally grunting when they're picked up in a manner offensive to them and, as we later learned, emitting a low buzz when they're sexually stimulated or in an aggressive mode. Making eye contact with Binky was only slightly more rewarding than staring into the shallows of an opaque pond. I knew *someone* was there, some being with a strong personality, but no spark of recognition leaped between us.

Though Binky challenged my communication skills, he was adept at conveying his own desires. Banging his empty water dish against the bars of his cage, he expressed his dissatisfaction with being locked up as unmistakably as Jimmy Cagney in *White Heat*. He was addicted to schedules and loathed changes in his environment. The addition of a Christmas tree in our living room met with his approval, because its boughs gave him a new place of concealment. But when Easter rolled around, and we finally removed the tree, he expressed his outrage by thumping the floor with a hind foot whenever he came into the room and snubbing us for more than a month. On another occasion we had the audacity to shift the position of the couch to accommodate a new floor lamp. Minutes after his evening parole from his cage, Binky snuffled at the new lamp, raised himself on his hind legs, and with a shove of his front paws toppled the interloper.

Binky's narcissism was greater than any cat's. The majority of his nonnapping hours were spent fastidiously grooming himself. Other than that, his favorite out-of-cage pastime was giving electrical wires the licorice-whip treatment and hiding in impossible-to-reach places. He was happiest when combining the two. The AC adapter cable to my pricey Sony shortwave portable ran through a narrow channel between the wall and our platform bed, where I figured it was safe. Elongating his pear-shaped bulk to the requisite two-inch width, he wriggled snakewise down the passageway and clipped the wire into pieces. To curb his appetite for the cables I loved most, I cut a three-foot length from an old extension cord and presented it to him. With all the disdain a rabbit could muster, he plucked it from my hand and with a toss of his head flung it from his sight. Like sharks attracted to transatlantic phone cables on the ocean floor, Binky apparently craved live voltage. He never injured himself pursuing his habit, but our appliances sported numerous bandages.

Binky gave us our first jolt of pet destructiveness. Though his widely scattered poop pellets were inoffensive as such materials go, they presented us with an ongoing maintenance problem. Rabbits, we'd been told, were easy to litter train. And it's true. They gravitate naturally toward a litter box, mysteriously divining its purpose the first time they hop inside. Just as instinctively, they are also keenly set on establishing a presence throughout their territory. Chin-rubbing is one method. Glands on the front of their heads deposit their scent on whatever coffee table, coat stand, chair leg, or human foot they rub against. But when a rabbit, especially a male, is serious about letting others know which lands he claims as his own, bodily functions are most effective. We learned this with Binky, and the lesson was magnified with a later rabbit population in which three males vied to plant their flag in shared territory.

More worrisome, we found, was the front end of a rabbit. Rabbits' teeth grow continuously. Unchecked, the lower incisors rise up in werewolf fashion, while the upper teeth can curve inward until they eventually penetrate the roof of the mouth. Usually, the act of eating grinds down the teeth, and excess length is kept in check by a rabbit's love of chewing any object within reach. To that end, Binky gnawed at our woodwork. He pulled out our living room carpet fibers. He made hors d'oeuvres out of the dust jackets to *Flying*

Saucers from Mars, Flying Saucers and the Three Men, and *They Knew Too Much About Flying Saucers,* three classics of modern science I kept on the bottom shelf of an upstairs bookcase. He decimated shoes, speaker cables, antenna feeds, chair legs, phone lines, computer interconnects, area rugs, record-album jackets, litter boxes, wicker baskets, magazines, and the ribbon cable from our satellite dish.

If an irreplaceable possession was challenging enough to warrant several sessions of intensive gnawing, it would turn into a project with Binky. The degree to which we opposed a project defined his enthusiasm for it. To thwart his will was to energize him. As soon as we'd release him from his cage, he would make a bunny-line for his work site and eagerly resume his labors where he'd left off. Reducing a reference book to paper pulp or chewing the Egyptian motifs off a decorative pillow were favored projects. But his appetite for this line of work paled next to his obsession with gaining access to a hiding place once I had blocked its entrance. One of these was the space between the headboard shelf of our platform bed and the wall it nearly touched. Ensconced in this dark recess, Binky was virtually unreachable. Assuming we even knew he was huddled there, the only way of rousting him was to thrust a cardboard wrapping-paper tube down the crack between bed and wall and blindly whisk it back and forth.

I first tried preventing access to this miserable lair by placing a small suitcase on the floor next to the bed, but he easily nosed it aside. When I wedged it in firmly with the help of a spare blanket, he scuttled over the roadblock. I finally had to cobble together a wall of blankets and boxes arranged around a heavy cushion. Though he was unable to surmount the obstruction, he would not be dissuaded. Day after day he would bolt from his cage and scurry directly to the bedroom, where he'd rake his front paws furiously against the pile until Linda or I finally pulled him away and shut the bedroom door. That only turned his attention to the outside of the door, the sound of his clawing reaching us in the living room.

When you match wits with a rabbit, you cannot win. If the rabbit bests you, you're a fool. If you best the rabbit, you're a fool who's bested a rabbit. This truism sunk in the day I forgot to close the basement door and Binky found the most vexing hiding place of his career. I scoured the usual places for him: behind the washing machine, between the dryer and the sink, beneath the workbench, under the fuel-oil tank, in the hellacious cubbyhole where Linda stored Halloween, Easter, and Christmas decorations, against the wall next to the water heater, in a pile of possibly clean, possibly dirty clothes, and even among the canning jars. The third time I hit the basement to search for him, Binky sat nonchalantly grooming himself in plain view as if awaiting my arrival. When I took two steps toward him, he sauntered to the end of an unfinished run of plasterboard, hopped onto a cinderblock, and disappeared behind the wall.

Just beyond arm's length, he resumed his toilette, oblivious to my cajoling, pleading, and threats. I tried to chase him out with a broom, but that only drove him in deeper. From a step ladder, I poked my trusty wrapping-paper tube down toward him via an opening in the unfinished ceiling, hoping to block his path and force him out into the open. But he was too fast for me. He scuttled down the full length of the wall to the far corner, where I could just make out the shape of his ears with a flashlight. I had no reasonable hope of getting to him.

Common sense told me to wait patiently until Binky tired of this warren that lacked a single chewable wire or until his stomach beckoned him toward his food-stocked cage in the kitchen. But I wasn't in the mood for common sense. I needed to show Binky that a rabbit wasn't the boss of our house.

"Leave him alone," Linda counseled. "He'll come out when he's ready."

"You're absolutely right," I told her, pretending to agree as I followed her upstairs. Then, while Linda was taking a bath, I sneaked back to the basement.

With a small utility knife, I cut a vaguely rectangular shape in the plasterboard at the base of the wall exactly opposite where I knew Binky sat, then used a screwdriver to pull and tear the hunk of drywall free. The commotion should have tipped Binky off, but since no amount of thumping had ever driven him from a hiding place, he remained still just long enough for me to make a grab at him. He was sitting too far forward, with just his hindquarters framed by the wallboard cut-out, and he wriggled from my grasp just as I tried darting a hand in front of his chest. He came out from behind the wall the way he had gone in and, before I could catch him, ran across the basement floor toward the stairs to the kitchen.

Binky's independence angered me, and the fact that he angered me angered me further. After almost two years in our house, he wasn't becoming any more domesticated. If anything, he seemed to be growing wilder by the day. I didn't like the feeling of chaos that Binky brought to our environment, the notion that I could be innocently reading the Lowell Ledger newspaper thinking all was well with the world when some portion of the house was being eaten away under our feet. I also took his disobedience as a conscious thumbing of his wiggly nose at my alleged authority.

I came to this conclusion after the most impressive of Binky's numerous escapes from the backyard pen that I had cobbled together for him. I had based his pen around the structure of a play area and sandbox that the previous owner of my house had built. I added metal fence posts between the existing four-by-four timbers and looped a roll of chicken-wire fencing around the whole thing. At first, escaping was simply a matter of Binky perfecting his hurdling skills to clear the three-foot-high fence I had foolishly assumed would keep him in. When I raised the height a couple of feet by adding another roll of fencing, he started probing my less-than-sterling workmanship. My fence posts protruded from the ground at widely varying angles like a bad set of teeth. Upon locating the post that leaned away from the pen at the greatest angle, Binky developed the fancy footwork needed to scramble up the steeply inclined fencing. Or he would run in circles around the pen until he'd built up sufficient speed for an impressive leap onto a board and enough residual momentum to launch himself over the fence. In the end, I had no choice but to add a third level of fencing, bringing the total height to an insurmountable six feet.

"That's one pen he won't get out of," I bragged to Linda, after depositing Binky in his newly refurbished stockade. Fifteen minutes later, I was upstairs trolling for African music on my shortwave radio when Linda called to me.

"Sweetie, I don't see Binky."

"Don't worry," I hollered down to her. "He's in there."

"I sure don't see him."

Surveying his pen from the upstairs window, I couldn't see him either. He was usually a blur of motion as he busied himself with an escape attempt, but the cage was calm and apparently quite empty.

Linda bolted out the front door in hopes of intercepting him before he hopped out into our busy street or lodged himself under one of our cars. I ran out the side door and nearly tripped over him as I went down the outside steps. He was sitting on the second step licking himself with unusual gusto, as triumphant as Houdini at the completion of a spectacular feat. "Running away isn't the object," Binky's presence at the door told me. "Escaping from your stupid pen is the point." How had he pulled it off? I'd never paid any attention to the numerous holes Binky had excavated while out in the yard. He would dig down a foot or so, then immediately abandon his burrow to start another one. But never before had he extended a hole into a bona fide tunnel.

"I wonder how long he was working on this?" Linda marveled, as we surveyed the exit hole that had popped up through the grass a couple of feet from the northeast corner of his pen. His ingenuity forced me to line the inside perimeter of his cage with rocks of a weight that would thwart any more escape hatches.

"This is our last rabbit," I subsequently told Linda. "They don't make good pets."

"There's nothing wrong with Binky."

"He belongs in the barn," I fumed.

"You shouldn't talk about Binky like that," Linda said. "He's crazy about you."

In fact, Binky had begun to exhibit one or two endearing characteristics. Often when I puttered around in my upstairs office, he would sit on the floor beside my chair and groom himself, happy as long as neither of us acknowledged the other's presence. Sometimes when I came home from work, I'd find him upstairs under my desk, apparently waiting for me. I experienced a small but unmistakable flinch of pleasure at seeing him, and if I approached him on hands and knees, pretending to be searching for a mechanical pencil that had jumped out of my pocket, he'd even tolerate a few light strokes of my fingers.

We marveled at his brashness with our cat, Penny, whom we had brought home as a companion for him. Though Penny did play a little roughly once she had outgrown the kitten stage, Binky could give as good as he got. Head bent low, he would grunt and launch a rhinoceros charge at her, forcing her to leap to the top of the couch for safety. They were especially rambunctious in the morning, waking us by bounding onto the bed in pursuit of one another. Even without Penny, Binky had begun greeting us by jumping on the bed, scampering across our legs, then immediately returning to the floor. From any other animal, these morning leaps would have served as mere footnotes—and leg notes. From Binky they were a veritable declaration of love.

As the first week of May rolled around, however, he failed to act as our alarm clock. He kept to himself in a corner, displaying unusual listlessness. His appetite was poor. When I would carry him back to his cage, he didn't fight me. We knew he had to be sick, but didn't realize that rabbits often show symptoms of illness only once it has advanced too far to easily treat. One morning his condition had obviously worsened. He barely moved at all. Linda hurried Binky to the veterinarian a half-mile up the street, but returned home less than ten minutes later with the extraordinary news that Binky had died before she could get him in to see the doctor.

"Not Binky," Linda wailed, sitting on the edge of the bed. "Not Binky," she repeated through her tears.

I put my arms around her. Well, that's that, I thought. Life will be much simpler now. Then, it was as if a stranger had stepped into my body and taken over. I found myself sobbing like a steam engine. We wrapped him in a blue bath towel and buried him on the edge of our property beyond our backyard fence. We left the house, driving north to Greenville and eating lunch at the local Big Boy— hoping, I suppose, that things would seem better by comparison with our lackluster lunch.

That night, though, I couldn't get to sleep. There was a full moon, and it seemed as if all the luminescence were concentrated in a spotlight that shone on Binky's grave.

"I can't stand the thought of him being all alone out there," I said to Linda. The sense of him buried in the ground was intolerable. I was connected to him by an invisible wire, and I wished he were alive to chew through it.

IN THE END, I memorialized Binky by building him an elaborate grave complex that would have impressed the pharaohs, crowning his grave with an inordinately large pile of rocks. One damp spring afternoon, after standing at his resting place, I brought the flat central rock into the basement workroom and with the dregs of a can of latex house paint, I inscribed a headstone: BINKY 1990–1992—FAREWELL TO OUR DEAR FRIEND.

"This I've got to see," my mother muttered when Linda told her about the monument. But I was far from finished. Using a grass whip, I cleared out all the weeds and brush between the boundary fence of our backyard and Binky's grave beneath a stand of maples. I laid out a straight path to the site, bordering it first with two-by-fours abandoned in our barn by the previous homeowner, then anchoring the boards on both sides with cabbage-size rocks. I filled the mourning path with a three-inch-deep layer of wood chips. Then, I created a second rock-and-board-bounded, woodchip-filled path that meandered from the mourning path down the hill beyond the burn barrel, turned west to wander roughly parallel with the backyard fence, then jogged north and joined the fence, which I lowered at that point to step-over height with a pair of bolt cutters. For a distance of thirty feet or so, I tore out the weeds and brambles, turned over the soil with a hoe, and planted an incompatible mixture of ground-level creeping myrtle and billowing purple vetch. The latter spread that summer like dandelions, burying the myrtle in balls of woody vegetation.

The next summer, only the barest traces of my paths remained, just rocks and boards to stub the toe of anyone foolish enough to fight their way through the virulent weeds, wild blackberry bushes, stinging nettles, purple thistle, mullein, and out-of-control vetch. The paint had long since flaked off Binky's marker. I had already touched up the inscription once, but finally let it go. I soon found I had little energy to pine for him. We had unwittingly taken in a new pet who was every ounce as belligerent as Binky.

CHAPTER 2

Ollie Takes Over

During the first year of our struggles with Binky, Linda bought me a yellow-and-black canary as a Christmas present. The addition of Chester to our household was as effortless as our glum bunny's was troublesome. He sang merrily at the slightest provocation. The rush of warm air through the kitchen register, the whine of the vacuum cleaner, or the tinny sound from the speaker of our portable TV triggered ecstatic passages of warbles and rolling trills from him. Unlike Binky, Chester had little craving for freedom. Whenever we opened the door to his cage, he would flutter worriedly around our dining room and occasionally settle onto a perch I had hung from the wall. But he didn't care for any interaction with us.

"Maybe we can tame him," I suggested with unfounded eagerness. When I had first moved into our house, I'd read Alfred G. Martin's book *Hand-Taming Wild Birds at the Feeder* about tempting chickadees and tufted titmice to take food from a human hand. But standing motionless in front of the bird feeder, arm outstretched, cupped palm spilling black- oil sunflower seeds while birds scolded me from a nearby pine tree lost its charm after a matter of minutes. Still, if wild birds could theoretically be coaxed into fellowship, I reasoned that a bird raised and kept by humans ought to be a pushover. I extended a wooden dowel identical to his wall-mounted perch toward Chester and urged him to land on it, but this activity quickly degenerated into my chasing Chester around the room with a stick. A better way to proceed, a pet-bird magazine informed me, was to begin by merely placing my hand into his cage until he became used to its presence. From there, I could gradually acclimate him to my finger. But when I introduced my thumb into his cage, Chester threw himself against the bars in fright, a poor foundation for building a bond of trust.

Remembering how Binky's independence had grown rather than diminished over his months with us, we decided that we'd give up trying to change Chester's personality and enjoy him for his effusive voice. The obvious solution was a second bird that would willingly perch upon our shoulders and enjoy our company.

Now, if out of ignorance I decided to stretch my right leg across a set of railroad tracks and a passing freight train clipped it off just above the knee, I'd think twice before putting my left leg on the rails. But after impulse-buying Binky, I still hadn't grasped the consequences of purchasing an animal merely because we liked its looks. No voice in our heads cautioned us to interview bird owners about which type of bird would make the least troublesome pet. Had we known anything of substance about caged birds, we would have proceeded with great caution before subjecting ourselves to a parrot. And had we known anything about parrots, we wouldn't have blithely brought home a breed that had justifiably fallen out of favor even among the most hardboiled hookbill enthusiasts.

Once imported in great numbers, brotogeris "pocket parrots" were sold at department stores throughout the 1960s along with goldfish, turtles, hermit crabs, budgies, and other low-maintenance critters. I remember seeing, in my high school years, these small parrots for sale under the relatively innocuous label "bee-bee parrots" (though later I'd learn that the B-B tag accurately describes the sting of a brotogeris bite). In the early 1990s, just before the 1992 Wild Bird Act banned the import of wild-caught birds for the pet trade, aviculturists across the country furiously stocked up on macaws, cockatoos, Amazon parrots, toucans, flamingoes, and anything else they could breed and unload on animal lovers. Few bothered with the pocket parrots, ostensibly because of their low selling price. I now think they probably let the brotogeris dwindle due to its temperament, which fluctuates between a lack of civility and demonic possession.

Our first choice for a bird was actually a cockatiel, based solely on the fact that we knew what a cockatiel looked like. One afternoon Linda rushed into the house waving a slip of paper. "Sweetie, look what I found! A lady at Food City had an ad on the bulletin board for two pet birds."

I took the paper from her. "I wouldn't trust anyone with handwriting like this. It looks demented."

"That's *my* handwriting. And it does not." She snatched back her note. "This lady has a cockatiel for sale with cage for a hundred dollars and a Quaker parakeet with cage for a hundred and fifty."

"A Quaker parakeet? We don't want one of those."

"What is it?"

"I don't know," I admitted. "But it probably only eats oatmeal."

The cockatiel deal sounded good. And by the time we drove across the Grand River to find a secluded house in the woods guarded by the only ferocious Saint Bernard on the planet—"Stay in the car until I get a chain on him," the husband recommended as the beast raked my windshield with its massive forepaws—the Quaker parakeet had already been taken off the market.

"Our son doesn't want us to sell his bird," said the wife, and sure enough, a pudgy-faced boy glowered at us as if we were set on shooting his dog in the bargain. Near him hunkered the Quaker, a pudgy-faced, robin-size, green bird that glowered at us as if we were set on packing up the boy.

In an effort to make sure we would prefer their cockatiel to the verboten Quaker, the husband had already trimmed her flight feathers for us. But he had badly botched the job by cutting them far too short. Whenever the addled creature flapped her wings, she spattered the eggshell-colored wall nearest her cage with cockatiel blood.

"I don't think she's bleeding anymore," the chagrined wife informed us as we backed out of their living room, our senses on alert for the return of the Volvo-size Saint Bernard. "We sprinkled flour on her feathers," she added, citing that well-known coagulating trick favored by ambulance drivers and emergency room physicians around the world.

Though the experience unnerved us, we still came away favoring a cockatiel, and I bought a cage in anticipation. Unfortunately, when we brought the cage to the Jonah's Ark, a local pet shop specializing in birds, it became clear that it was too small for a cockatiel. A cockatiel would have been able to sit in the cage but wouldn't have had the room to turn around without catching its tail between the bars. Plus, the cockatiels in the store struck us as disappointingly parakeet-like, as if someone had taken a common yellow budgie, added a crest and drawn-out tail, and applied a little orange rouge to the cheeks. But sensing that we were in purchasing mode, the clerk, Joyce, plucked a Quaker parakeet from a

Plexiglas display area and placed it on Linda's finger. In contrast to the other Quaker we had seen, this one was lively and handsome, causing my hand to migrate toward my checkbook. But the bird was about the same size as a cockatiel and wouldn't fit our cage. Joyce's admonition unnerved us, too.

"Don't let him get hold of your fingernail. He'll think it's a nut and try to crack it."

Duly warned, I buried my hands in my pockets as Linda and I walked up and down the aisles in search of an alternative to the cockatiel and the Quaker. In our flush to buy a bird, we didn't stop to question why the inventory was depleted. The first time we had visited Jonah's, the store was atwitter with all manner of birds. This time, however, most of the cages were empty except for a pair of menacing macaws that growled if we approached them, a sleepy-eyed cockatoo that barely noticed us, and a wild-caught, wild-eyed Senegal parrot that had mangled a clerk's forearm our last time in the store. In an isolated cage near the cash register, the prettiest of the few birds scaled to fit our cage hung upside-down from the bars. He was a stubby-tailed, parakeet-size, animated fellow endowed with every possible hue of green and wearing a brilliant patch of orange just beneath his beak.

"What kind of bird is he?" Linda asked the clerk.

"You can take him out of the cage," she replied brightly, bypassing the question. Then a cloud passed over her expression as if she had just remembered a troubling event from her childhood. "I'll get him for you," she offered, turning her back to block the cage-to-finger transaction from our view. Before passing the bird to Linda, she cautioned, "Now, he might use his beak to climb onto your hand, but don't worry, he's not trying to bite you. He's just keeping his balance."

True to Joyce's words, when the small green bird bent forward, he pinched the flesh of Linda's finger in his beak as he pulled himself up with his foot. Linda laughed in surprise. Responding to Linda's voice, the bird unleashed an amiable series of squeals and chirps. "You're a friendly little guy," said Linda, and the bird burbled back to her.

"Let me hold him!" I begged, extending a finger in friendship to the cheerful bird who cheerfully leaned over and bit me with great gusto.

"He's just being possessive," Joyce hastily explained, as I studied the neat pair of puncture marks below my knuckle. "He loves his people!" she assured us. "He loves his cage a lot, too," she decided, snatching the bird from us and returning him to his perch before he could inflict another incision. Having worked up a hearty appetite biting a gullible pair of newcomers, the bird turned his attention to his seed dish.

"So, what kind of bird did you say he is?" I asked, as I massaged my finger.

"Violet, the store owner, isn't here today," Joyce apologized. When we begged her for a hint, she finally acceded, "I think he's a peach face," but no further explanation followed. The $150 price tag on its cage was more than we had intended on spending, but it seemed a shame to miss out on the chance to bring home a friendly bird who had only bitten me due to extraordinary circumstances that would never occur again. That must have been my thinking. Either that, or all the blood had rushed from my brain to my throbbing finger, because otherwise I never would have even considered such a Jekyll and Hyde of a bird. As it turned out, the dual nature of the misnamed "peach face" was precisely why it was one of the few birds in the store. Violet was out of town at an aviary show, and with her had gone all the well-behaved parrots, parakeets, and lovebirds.

WE SHOULD HAVE KNOWN better than to trust the stock at Jonah's Ark. A month or so before cockatiel fever struck, we had flirted with the idea of the budgie parakeet as our dream bird, but only if we could locate one that had been hand-raised, socialized, and hypnotized to enjoy close interactions with people. Violet assured us she had exactly such a bird and apologized for the high price of eighty dollars versus around twenty dollars anywhere else.

"It takes a lot of work to bond a parakeet to humans," she had explained, as she plucked a small blue budgie off its perch, "and this one is really special." Almost at once, the bird squirmed from her grasp to lead the three of us on a floor-level chase around the store. If his wings hadn't been clipped, we never could have caught him. "He's just nervous," she told us, when we had finally surrounded him near a refrigerator bearing a sign that read, LIVE BAIT, suggesting that the bird business at Jonah's Ark wasn't all that it could be. Both Linda and I made an attempt to get the bird to sit on our index fingers, but he thrashed with fear whenever we approached him.

Our "peach face"—actually an orange-chin pocket parrot—responded to the car ride home with aplomb. Instantly taking to his cage, he hung from the bars while trying to dismantle his virgin birdie swing with a surgical application of his beak, ignoring the honking car horns and frequent stops and starts as we battled a spurt of rush hour traffic. We set him up in our living room, placing his cage on a plastic floor-standing pedestal whose base we had filled with twenty pounds of aquarium gravel to discourage our cat, Penny, from tipping over the stand. Within a couple hours of owning our parrot, Linda suggested the name, Ollie, which promptly stuck. At about the same time, I made a reluctant observation.

"Am I imagining things," I asked Linda, "Or does it seem like whenever we leave the room, Ollie starts chirping?"

"I noticed that, too."

We exchanged a look of dread, hoping this was merely a coincidence.

"Didn't Violet once tell us that birds eventually accept their owners as members of their flock?" Linda asked. "Or even as substitutes for mates?"

"Mates?" I experienced another pang of dread. "Ollie certainly wouldn't have bonded to us in such a short period of time."

But he had. As long as we stood at his cage talking to him or coddling him on our finger, he acted reasonably. But if we turned our attention away, he would immediately begin calling us with high-pitched, scolding chirps. His voice was inoffensive enough, as parrots go—certainly nothing like the scream of a cockatoo, which can cause your ears to bleed—but the chirps were unrelenting. He unleashed them in strings of tens, hundreds, and thousands, and nothing short of our surrender would abate the bad behavior. Warily, I would introduce my hand into his cage and hold my breath as he stepped onto my finger. His bright green body would wiggle from side to side, his black eyes gleaming as he alternated his beak, left foot, beak again, and right foot to scramble up my sleeve and settle triumphantly on my shoulder. He'd nuzzle my neck with affection as I walked around the house. Then, once he had decided that the scenery had grown stale, he would deliver a wire cutter–like bite to my face.

After three days, Ollie's tyranny had completely worn us down. With one ear constantly cocked in his direction, I had trouble concentrating on anything else. My shirt collars sported beak-holes. Linda's cries at yet another biting reverberated throughout the house. Dinner was the final straw. Linda had prepared a small dish of Purina Monkey Chow, the recommended food for an adolescent brotogeris, by soaking the pellets in warm water until soggy.

Trustingly, she placed the dish on top of his cage, and we took our places at the table.

"You've got to say one thing for him. He's got a healthy appetite," Linda pointed out.

"Too healthy," I complained, leaning forward in my chair as Ollie dipped his beak into the goo and slung it in all directions. "We might as well eat outside in the rain."

With the gleeful demeanor of an infant who has just discovered the law of gravity, he gave the dish a shove. It plummeted from his cage top, hitting the counter at exactly the proper angle to spatter monkey gruel all over our food. He squealed in happiness as our voices rose.

"Do we really want a pet like this?" I whined to Linda. We had erred by not returning Binky to Warren before his sullen presence around the house had seemed inevitable. We didn't want to make the same mistake with Ollie. We had to act at once. The next morning we were back at Jonah's Ark explaining the situation to an unsympathetic Violet. Our claim that we were unable to control the small orange-chin clearly struck her as ridiculous, given that a pterodactyl-size blue and gold macaw with a beak slightly larger than Ollie's entire body had been perched on her forearm when we slunk into the store.

"These pocket parrots are on sale now," she told us gruffly. "I can't give you what you paid for him, that's more than what I could sell him for. You're looking at around $120 maybe." Discerning that we were at a breaking point where we might actually pay her to take Ollie back, she made an even better deal for herself. She talked us into exchanging him for a different member of the brotogeris family that had a reputation for comparative gentleness. "She's a greycheek parakeet," said Violet, as she presented a meek bird on her finger and pulled a wing away from its body to show us the yellow underlying feathers. All of this the grey- cheek suffered without complaint. She was pretty enough, resembling an orange-chin whose forehead, cheeks, and chin had been dusted with a grey-green powder. But her colors, like her temperament, lacked Ollie's fire.

"Just keep in mind that she was wild-caught," Violet advised us, meaning that instead of having been hand raised and socialized to humans, the unfortunate bird had been stolen from her nest before the import ban on birds had taken effect. Having barely survived our encounter with a hand-raised bird, we eagerly took home the unexcitable wild-caught parakeet.

She bit me not a whit when I took her from her cage. She suffered being placed on my shoulder without aggression or complaint. Likewise, she exhibited no joy. I walked with her to the couch and sat. Ollie would have squealed into my ear when I spoke to him. The grey-cheek clambered down my shirt, descended the front of the couch, and toddled across the carpet. She climbed the aquarium pump tubing, briefly explored the top of the fish tank, located the electrical cord to the heater, and followed it back down to the floor. She was searching, I imagined, for her lush, lost birthplace in the branches of a rainforest. I put the quiet bird back in her cage.

"She's got a nice disposition," Linda pointed out.

"Especially compared to Ollie," I seconded.

"She'll get used to us."

"She'll be a very nice bird."

The following morning I blubbered into my slice of toast, "I miss Ollie," and soon had Linda weeping along with me at the loss of our ill-tempered pocket parrot. Like kidnap victims who had fallen under the spell of their captor, we were crushed at his absence. After only three days of Ollie's abuse, the house seemed empty and lifeless without his maniacal chirping.

Swallowing my pride, I made yet another visit to Jonah's Ark while Linda was still at work and asked Violet for the return of our tormentor. I had expected her to angrily refuse my request, but the bother of the exchange was nothing compared to the bother of hanging on to Ollie, and she agreed with ill-disguised satisfaction. We learned much later that we had been the second people to buy and return Ollie within a two-week period, but the only ones foolish enough to retrieve him.

"We need to give lessons to you people when you buy a bird," she told me, shooting a knowing look at a seasoned parrot-owner friend of hers. Without the slightest fear of injury, she whisked Ollie from his cage, turning him upside down so that his back rested in the palm of her left hand while his feet still clung to the two fingers of her right hand. Making a walking motion with those two fingers, she moved his feet back and forth while singing a chorus of "Row, Row, Row Your Boat." Ollie clucked in appreciation. Force of personality was obviously the key to dealing with him. I had no force of personality, but I did have Ollie back.

Hardly a day goes by that we haven't regretted his return.

We learned to handle him with greater ease, understanding that the more hesitant we acted, the more inclined he was to bite. That doesn't mean his temperament improved. From the moment the cover is removed from his cage in the morning to early evening when he's put to bed, Ollie clamors for attention. His behavior contradicts the expert opinion of Robbie Harris, author of *Grey-cheeked Parakeets and Other Brotogeris,* the only guide to the brotogeris family I've discovered so far. "Their chattering voices can be loud at times," the author understates, "but a bird kept singly as a pet is seldom noisy." I'm not sure how Harris might define "noisy," but on a summer day when the dining room windows are open, we've heard Ollie's chirps as far away as the riverbank some five hundred feet from the house—down the hill, across the swamp, and through thickets of trees and brush, as cars and trucks clattered past the house. Late mornings, just before leaving for a housecleaning job, Linda usually eats her lunch in the car rather than sitting in the kitchen and suffering through Ollie's shrill demands for a morsel of food.

Throwing a towel over Ollie's cage calms but does not quiet him, eliciting a toned-down chatter that has the semblance of an apology. Even when he seems genuinely happy, as when practicing his limited English vocabulary, he shoehorns the words into a stream of parrot invective. It's not surprising that "Do you hear me?" and "Now, listen!" are two of his most accomplished phrases. He's heard these often enough from us to work them to a fine polish.

"A great many people in Peru keep Brotogeris parakeets as pets," Harris writes, "because many are tame and sweet, learn to talk, and become quite attached to their owners." Attached by their mandibles, I might add to the author's generous description. Ollie literally bites the hand that feeds him. When Linda offers him a corner of a windmill cookie, he'll lunge at her and let the treat fall to the floor. He bites out of imperious impatience that the cookie wasn't his the instant he first glimpsed it in Linda's fingers. He bites in anger that access to his favorite cookie should ever have been denied him at all. He bites for the simple pleasure of biting human flesh. Many are the times that one of us foolishly forgets to carry his cage by the top handle, picking it up between our hands instead. The succulent folds of our palms protruding through the bars comprise too much of a temptation for Ollie to resist. He's smart enough to recognize a cookie while it's still in the package. He should be smart enough to understand that biting us while his cage is in transit threatens his personal safety. But the instinct to bite, like his urge to squawk, transcends mundane concepts of reason.

As loud as Ollie is, he's surprisingly sensitive to sounds. Removing a handful of kibbles from a bag of cat food invites a fusillade of offended squawks. So does scraping a knife against a plate, shaking a pill out of a bottle, running water in the sink, emptying or loading the dishwasher, rustling a plastic trash bag, cutting paper with scissors, pouring coffee beans into the coffee grinder, or dumping cornflakes into a bowl. He's a jackhammer complaining that a cricket is too loud.

If any instincts bind Ollie to the natural world, they are well concealed. We placed his cage near a window so he could watch the chickadees, nuthatches, woodpeckers, titmice, goldfinches, and other birds making the circuit to our feeder, but he expressed no recognition of them. He did seem to enjoy it when we'd hang his cage outdoors on sunny days, so we started taking him on walks. As we wandered the wooded trails of a county park a few miles from our house, he showed little interest in anything except the attention of the person who carried him. When he began biting Linda, Linda would pass him to her friend Deanne. When he began biting Deanne, Deanne would pass him to me. Whenever I carried him, the lovely hulking tree stumps, darting insects, splashes of wild asters, and incursions of creek meanders faded away as I was forced to shift my focus to Ollie.

"Isn't this nice?" I'd cajole him with a steady stream of encouragement, hoping to keep his beak at bay. "Pretty boy, Ollie. Oh, there's a good boy. We'll be back home soon."

Because Ollie's wings were clipped, we had not thought we were endangering him by letting him ride through the park on our shoulders. We were wrong. We read an article in *Bird Talk* magazine that described how a bird with trimmed flight feathers could still catch a gust of air just right and soar to the top of a tree. We kept him indoors exclusively from then on. But one afternoon he still managed to find his way outside and lose himself in the woods behind our house. While Linda was working in the living room and I napped obliviously upstairs, something scared Ollie off his cage top in the kitchen. It may have been Linda carrying newspapers past the kitchen door, or it could have been a breeze rustling the pages of a notepad on the table.

With the distinctive, rolling squawk he produces whenever he takes flight, Ollie abandoned his cage top and launched himself down the basement stairs. And then, because his hatred of the gloomy, low-ceilinged cellar trumped his ambivalence toward the great outdoors, he made a second wobbly flight around the oil furnace, through the workshop, and out the basement door, which either Linda or I had accidentally left open. Our backyard runs flat for about nine feet beyond our house, then in two dips it descends to meet the flood plain of the Grand River. As Ollie flapped across the yard at the level of the basement floor, the ground dropped beneath his feet. Snagging a spring breeze, he rose above the gully, floundering into the shoe-sucking swamp that separates us from the river.

Fortunately, Linda had been keeping tabs on Ollie from the living room. Finding the kitchen uncharacteristically quiet, she headed down to the basement and in disbelief traced the sound of his angry chirps outdoors, down the hill, and beyond the backyard fence. She ran back into the house and hollered up the stairs, "Ollie's out in the yard way in the top of a tree."

I thundered down the steps and followed her outside. Linda pointed and shouted, but I couldn't pick him out from the foliage. His emerald-colored body blended in perfectly with the newly emerged leaves. For once Ollie's incessant chirping served him well, and using his voice as a guide, I pinpointed him in a hackberry tree just on the other side of the fence, clinging to a branch about twenty feet off the ground. I was shocked at how small and vulnerable our avian dictator looked. Though escaped Quaker parakeets have taken root in environments as inhospitable as Chicago and New York City, there wasn't a chance Ollie would survive outdoors if we couldn't lay our hands on him. His bad attitude was nothing like street smarts. It was the pampered personality of a spoiled rich kid in feathered knickers who was tough only when it came to dominating his owners. Bluff and bluster would mean nothing to a hawk, and none of the trees on our property sprouted spaghetti or mashed potatoes at mealtime.

"Ollie, come down from there," Linda said, but she was talking to the wind. Under the best of circumstances, Ollie had never listened to us, and in this case he had determined that safety constituted the branch his toes were wrapped around. Our only chance was to try to reach him, which struck me as extremely unlikely. I don't climb trees, chop them down, or even plant them. A ladder was the obvious recourse, but the last time I had used one, it was to clear debris off the nearly flat roof above our dining room, and once there I had been too frightened to climb down again.

This time I had no option but to fight my fear of heights. I wrestled an aluminum stepladder over our wire backyard fence and with no small effort followed the ladder with my body. I managed to penetrate a clinging barrier of wild black raspberry bushes and was already panting by the time I reached the base of the tree. Ollie scolded me as I searched in vain for a semisolid patch of ground that would simultaneously support all four legs of the ladder. The front legs immediately sank as I made my ascent, knocking the ladder against the tree trunk and almost pitching me off.

As I began my shaky climb, I lost all sight of Ollie. "I don't see him anymore!" I shouted to Linda, who was helping to steady the ladder.

"He's right there," she called back, grazing my chest with the pointing finger at the end of her arm. From the way we were shouting at each other, you would have thought we were on opposite sides of the swamp instead of within backslapping distance. "On this one?" I exclaimed, my voice rising louder with hope as I indicated a shoulder-height branch at a level a scant two steps up the ladder.

"No, that one," Linda said, thrusting her finger toward a patch of sky split at a dizzying height by a thick grey line of bark. Blood hissed in my ears as I continued my ascent. After each successive step, I'd stop and raise my head from my thumping chest, hoping that the branch was suddenly closer than it had last appeared and our bird was miraculously within arm's reach. He seemed more distant than ever when I arrived at the last step. The edge of the top platform pressed sharply against my shin, stimulating various bad ideas whirling through my brain, including spraying him with a hose or wrapping the hose around the branch and pulling it down to where I could grab him. Any plan that involved a hose somehow seemed appealing.

Linda directed my attention to a long, thin branch that branched off Ollie's branch. "Can you get hold of that?" she asked me.

"I think I'm okay," I told her, then I realized it wasn't my safety that concerned her at the moment.

"To pull his branch down!" she shouted.

My legs oscillated as I climbed to the top platform of the ladder, which was emblazoned with an orange sticker depicting the teetering silhouette of a foolish man with an X stricken over his body, along with the warning DO NOT STAND ON TOP STEP. Wondering why it was called a top step if it wasn't a step at all, I hugged the tree trunk with one arm, stretching myself into an impossible geometric shape in order to snag the tip of the dangling tendril. "Got it," I told Linda with more confidence than I was feeling. The branch was a match for my own physique, far too weak and spindly to be of much help. It barely budged the parent branch when I gave it a healthy yank. By pulling it in a waltz rhythm, however, I managed to get the tree limb swaying a little. I gradually increased the momentum until, at the far end where Ollie sat, the swaying was converted to a crack-the-whip bounce that snapped him squawking into the air.

Awkwardly stretched between branch and ladder like a wishbone, I was unable to turn my head to follow Ollie's flight path without losing my footing and joining his descent. He was a green blur at the edge of my vision as he shot off the tree limb and began an arc toward the ground. Linda scrambled past me. I felt rather than saw her brief pursuit of him across the litter of last year's fallen leaves, then heard his indignant squawk as she scooped him up.

"I got him!" Linda told me.

"Is he okay?" I called out in a pinched voice, as I slowly reeled myself in.

Clutching Ollie in her hand, she thrust him under the open front of her jacket and rushed toward the house. "Are you okay?" she asked him. I realized that he was in perfect shape, none the worse for his brush with disaster, when I heard her cry out in pain. Happy and healthy, Ollie gave her a healthy bite.

He wasn't grateful, of course. He simply took it for granted that when he squawked, we would cater to his whim. It didn't matter if he was stranded on top of the highest oak or merely wanted another spaghetti noodle to nibble on, then fling at us. He gave the order, we obeyed—and were typically punished anyway. We must have been masochists to allow such an imperious creature into our house. Little did we know that his willfulness was all too typical of birds.

CHAPTER 3

Stanley Sue's Identity Crisis

By all logic, Ollie should have thoroughly discouraged us from ever owning another parrot. He had exactly the opposite effect. Whenever Linda and I went on vacation to dream destinations like Grindstone City, Michigan, or Wisconsin's House on the Rock, rather than inflicting Ollie on the housesitter who looked after our pets and princely possessions, we'd board him at Jonah's Ark. It was our way of getting back at the people who sold him to us. While dropping him off at Jonah's, which had inexplicably moved to the cramped back room of an office-supplies wholesaler, we found ourselves mesmerized by parrots that had appealing personalities. When we ventured into bird shows at local motels, dealers thrilled us with live birds that didn't bite.

We wanted one of these. Sadder, wiser, and beaten down by Ollie, I did actual research this time. After much thumbing through bird magazines and gawking at well-behaved pet shop hookbills, we came up with a checklist. Our wish was for a bird that was quiet, friendly, undemanding, could talk, wouldn't bite us, and wouldn't bite us. In other words, except for the talking part—if you count under-the-breath muttering as talking—we were looking for the polar opposite of Ollie.

Of all the breeds, the African grey seemed exactly what we were looking for, except for the problem of price. Betsy's Beasts, our local pet shop in Lowell, displayed a handsome fourteen-inch-tall Congo African grey named Oscar selling for a wallet-flattening $1,350—"but that's including the cage," owner Jerry assured us. We came close to considering an installment plan, but dallied so long that Jerry was forced to return Oscar to the breeder who had placed him at Betsy's on consignment. It didn't pay to try to make a living selling expensive birds in our small town. Shortly after returning Oscar, Jerry went out of business. His store was taken over by an oddball who refused to sell us a mirror for our canary —"It makes them mean," he insisted—and posted the confidence-building sign over his aquariums NO REFUND WITHOUT FISH CARCASS.

Despairing of our chances of latching on to an affordable grey, we drove to the nearby town of Coopersville, where a breeder who advertised in the *Grand Rapids Press* classifieds waved his arm at a pungent floor-standing cage full of meat-eating African hornbills. The owner suggested I keep my hands well away from the bars, lest these birds that resembled a charmless variation on the toucan mistake my fingers for chicken strips. Motioning Linda and me into another room, he introduced us to an Amazon parrot he admitted needed some work. "I wouldn't trust him," he confided. Extending one of the longest wooden perches I'd ever seen, he removed the attractive red and blue bird from its cage, making sure to keep it well away from any of our bodies. "This bird isn't for everyone," he warned in an intimate tone that implied we'd be special people in his book if we bought his problem bird. "I don't accept returns," he hastened to add. At least not without a carcass, I assumed.

Deciding against bringing home a larger, meaner, louder version of Ollie, we held out until the afternoon we were buying perches for Ollie at Pet Supplies "Plus." Linda breathlessly dragged me over to a bulletin board near the entrance.

"Sweetie, this lady's selling an African grey named Stanley. Her ad's even got a picture. Isn't he cute?" An overexposed photo stapled to the file card showed a parrot tearing apart a box of Sun-Maid raisins. The condition of the couch Stanley perched upon made me wonder what else the parrot enjoyed chewing. "He's only three hundred and fifty dollars including the cage," she squeaked.

"I'm sure he's already sold."

"I'm going to call her right now."

"You might as well wait until we get home. It's long distance."

"I've got a bunch of quarters in my purse."

"I wouldn't even bother," I sighed, laying a consoling hand on her shoulder. "Too bad we didn't see this a couple of days earlier."

I turned and headed for the car as Linda made a beeline for the pay phone. A few minutes later she delivered the news that the woman hadn't sold Stanley yet.

"Gee, it's kind of far to White Cloud," I complained. Anything spur-of-the-moment distressed me. I wanted to go home and brood about it for a while, but Linda's momentum nudged us northward instead.

Lynn was packing boxes when we arrived at her box of a house set in the middle of a neighborhood of miniature cottage-style homes from the 1950s. The houses on her block huddled closely together despite the vast wooded tracts and open fields that flowed out in all directions from the town. Across a compact front yard, Lynn's car was waiting with open hatchback for the armload of jackets and dresses that met us at the door.

"I won't be needing these," Lynn told us, as she stuffed the clothing into a carton, led us out to her car, then took us briskly through a side door into the kitchen where another box was waiting. As we scurried behind her, she explained that she was moving to California to become something known as a mobile nurse. I envisioned Lynn conducting medical treatment from a speeding vehicle while patients ran alongside trying to keep up with her. "I'll work in one city for a few months, and then get assigned a new hospital in another part of the state," she said. "So I have to get rid of all my birds. Stanley's the only one left. He's an African grey Timneh. I just sold the Congo African grey and used to have a cockatoo."

"What about your dog?" I asked. A Boston terrier scampered at her heels, toenails clicking on the hardwood floors. He backed off as we trailed Lynn into a cluttered living room, where a pigeon-size parrot clinging to the flap of an empty box flashed the terrier a look of warning. No fan of small, hyperactive dogs, I immediately admired Stanley. From his fluffed-up mantle of silver-tipped grey feathers to the sense I got of blazing intelligence behind each of his reptilian eyes, Stanley was clearly cut from a different cloth than our clownish orange chin parakeet. A patch of bare white skin encircled his eyes, but the skin of his feet was scaly grey, and the stubby tail feathers were tinged with the deepest maroon.

"Casey's coming along. He doesn't mind riding in a car. Stanley's another story. Aren't you, big boy? That's one of the phrases he knows. 'Big boy, Stanley.' Two people owned him before me, and he must have picked up the 'big boy' from the girl and the 'Stanley' from the guy. So he'll say 'big boy' in the woman's voice, then 'Stanley' in a deep voice," she chuckled, lowering her own voice an octave to emphasize the "Stanley."

"Is he bitey?" Linda asked.

"Stanley is very gentle. With people," she added, looking across the room at Casey. "I used to let my Congo and Stanley out together, but Stanley started jumping on her back. Casey's gotten nipped a number of times. But Stanley won't bite me." Stanley lowered his head and parted his beak ominously as Lynn extended her hand to the parrot, but there was no sign of Ollie-style belligerence. "I don't know if he'll take to you right away," she warned, as she brought Stanley toward us. But I was spared the decision of surrendering my flesh to a bird whose mandible strength was capable of crushing walnuts when a flutter of wings sent Stanley disappearing into another room.

"That's one thing I should tell you," Lynn added. "Stanley loves the bathroom. He'll sit all day on the towel rack, and he loves to take a shower with me. He's really low maintenance. He isn't fussy and only gets loud around dinner time."

As we murmured our appreciation for a bird that didn't squawk from dawn to dusk, Lynn grabbed a stack of *Bird Talk* magazines and Mattie Sue Athan's *Guide to a Well-Behaved Parrot* and packed them in a box for us. That would make our third copy of the book. I was too embarrassed to mention that my sister and a friend of ours had both presented us with the *Guide* in response to their not entirely satisfactory encounters with Ollie. As she assembled our care package, Lynn rattled off Stanley's preferences: apples, pizza crust, and Neil Young records. "When I come home at night from the hospital, I'll turn on the lights, put on *After the Goldrush,* and Stanley will wake right up and start bobbing his head to the beat."

I had a couple of Neil Young LPs and an old harmonica stashed away in a dresser drawer, so I felt confident as I traded Lynn a check for the music-loving parrot. The cage went in the back of Linda's Escort, and because a cage wasn't the safest traveling container for a bird, Lynn plopped Stanley in a carton with a plump towel under him and sealed the top with a roll of brown tape. Her movements were so fluid, I glanced behind us to make sure she hadn't inadvertently boxed up Casey, too.

"He sure seems like a nice bird," Linda told her consolingly, before closing the car door, expecting Lynn would want to bid Stanley a heartfelt farewell through the cardboard. But with a brisk wave to us, the mobile nurse was already headed back to the house, her mental gears engaged with the problem of what to pack away next.

While Ollie had spewed forth the full, unadulterated extent of his personality as soon as we had brought him home, Stanley would barely make eye contact with us at first. Sulking inside the cage with his back turned to us, he intermittently emitted a sharp whistle while ringing a hanging bell, a combination we later learned signified disapproval. Though wary of the new surroundings, he at least did not seem traumatized by the move. After giving Stanley a couple of hours to get used to the kitchen, we opened the cage door and Stanley climbed out with no hesitation to stand on top of the cage, facing away from us.

Unsure what welcoming step to take next, Linda and I retreated to the living room. I had just spread out the newspaper on the couch when Stanley surprised me by flying in and perching uneasily on a lampshade.

"Now what do we do?" I asked Linda.

"Pick him up, I guess."

I raised my hand, paused to study Stanley's wicked-looking beak, then turned to Linda, and asked her, "How?"

Linda strode past me and moved her hand toward Stanley, who lowered his head the better to reach her for a bite. "Maybe we'd better wait," she decided. "He'll probably fly right back to his cage."

But Stanley showed no sign of budging, preferring to nip at the top of the lampshade instead. Remembering what had happened to the raisin box in the photo, I unplugged the floor lamp and carried the whole thing, bird and all, back to Stanley's cage in the kitchen.

We wanted to keep close tabs on Stanley that first evening, but we were already committed to eating dinner with our friends Brad and Pam. They were remodeling their home, paying contractors for the kind of large-scale devastation of existing walls and flooring that Binky had provided us for free. Instead of dining in a cluttered kitchen that also served as their living room, bedroom, and walk-in closet, the MacMillans whisked us to a pleasant vegetarian restaurant in the middle of farming country. While Brad and Pam spoke excitedly about the renovation, I was shrouded in a fog of concern for Stanley. From the remoteness on Linda's face, I could tell her mind wasn't on double-pane insulated windows or ceiling joists either.

"We're after the effect of an Elizabethan-cottage style," Brad admitted. "Which means we'll probably end up painting the tongue-and-groove woodwork in the kitchen white to match the walls and ceiling in the rest of the house."

I nodded my wholehearted agreement and added, "If Stanley really hates it in the corner of the room, we can always move his cage closer to the windows."

That night I had trouble sleeping. From our ongoing battles with Ollie, I had expected that our biggest problem with a second parrot would be managing another boisterous personality. But Stanley was truly an unknown entity. I hadn't realized that parrots were sensitive enough to be stressed out by new living situations. I did recall boarding Ollie at Jonah's Ark while we were on vacation the previous year and a young clerk telling us when we reluctantly reclaimed him how fortunate we were to own such a sweet creature. She had reportedly kept the little terror on her shoulder while tending her duties at the pet shop. When Linda inquired how many times Ollie had bitten her over the course of the week, the girl looked as perplexed as she would've been if Linda had asked how frequently Ollie had beaten her at canasta.

In the same vein, Stanley's behavior in our home contradicted much of what Lynn had told us. Though far quieter than Ollie, Stanley vocalized throughout the day at various volume levels, with an impressive roster of whistles, chirps, and the occasional squawk. Dinnertime unleashed Stanley's miserly quartet of English-language words—"Big boy, Stanley" and "Hello"—along with an adamant rejection of his supposedly favorite foods. Pizza crust with or without tomato sauce was snubbed with a snap of the head. Apple slices were accepted into his beak only as a prelude to their being flung onto the floor. On the Neil Young front, not a single ditty from *After the Goldrush, Everybody Knows This Is Nowhere,* or a bootleg live LP roused a discernible tic of pleasure. Nor did the bathroom towel rack, shower, or leaky faucet.

True to Lynn's word, Stanley was gentle, though "gentle" barely scratched the surface of his almost neurotic timidity. Any unfamiliar object passing within a seven-foot radius made him jump and flap his wings. As a cage-warming gift, I bought him the kind of pressed-seed-and-fruit treat on a stick that Ollie would rip apart and devour the instant I hung it from the bars of his cage. But Stanley regarded the parrot paddle-pop as a threat, retreating to the far corner of his cage until I removed it. Toys brought an even more exaggerated reaction. Because he already had a bell in his cage, I thought Stanley might welcome other diversions. But merely showing him a second tiny bell or a knotted rawhide string ornamented with chewable wood beads was equivalent to strolling into the room with a hawk perched on my arm.

Stanley's nervousness made us nervous to approach him. Any encroachment of a hand into his personal space brought on the classic attack pose of lowered body, extended neck, and, if we persisted, bent head with open beak. But his demeanor markedly changed if we presented him with food. Unlike Ollie, who delighted in vigorously biting the hand that fed him, Stanley surprised us by accepting the smallest morsel of food with no attempt to nip us. I began with the largest double peanut I could find, nervously offering him the nut while grasping it by a withered root hair that dangled from the shell. Next I tried a single nut, then moved on to a series of progressively shrinking foodstuffs, from a purple grape, to a large lima bean, to a striped sunflower seed, and, finally, a couple of stuck-together cookie crumbs that Stanley had to brush his beak against my fingertips to extract. Had I been able to offer him a single molecule of a favored snack, I felt certain he would have claimed it with the same delicacy. Engaging in this safe form of physical contact with us was obviously as important to him as the food. Linda proved this the evening she softly called me into the kitchen while Stanley was slurping lukewarm herbal tea from a coffee mug.

"Sweetheart, look at this," she told me.

As an overture toward being held, Stanley had climbed onto the mug that Linda was holding. I held my breath as Linda curled her index finger around the rim of the cup. "Watch it," I whispered. Stanley leaned forward and softly encircled Linda's knuckle with his black lower beak and horn-colored upper mandible.

"He's just exploring," she told me, then held her breath as he nibbled her finger.

I managed the same trick with Stanley a little later. But attempts to dispense with the mug and present him with a naked hand resulted in a nip. Even though they were minor compared to the bites that Ollie doled out daily, we were intimidated by the potential trauma that we knew Stanley's powerful jaws could inflict.

"There's really no reason to be afraid of him," I explained loftily to Linda. "Most dogs or cats could kill their owners if they thought about it, but we trust them not to act like wild animals. So it's the same with parrots. Just because they could take our fingers off doesn't mean they will."

"But you wouldn't try to pet a wild dog, would you?"

She had me there. Stanley was a wild-caught bird. Stolen from his nest and forced to undergo a miserable journey to America, Stanley had every reason to despise people. He hadn't fared much better as a pet, enduring four different owners in just five years of life. How deeply these circumstances had affected him was clear from the eerie noise he produced each evening once we had covered his cage and switched out the lights.

"What is that?" I asked Linda, turning down the volume on *Wheel of Fortune*'s "Bonus Round" the first time I heard what sounded like a person sobbing in our kitchen.

The following day, our vet, Dr. Benedict, told me over the phone, "It's amazing the range of vocalizations these birds can emit. They can imitate anything and everything from your voice to a ringing telephone. But you have to remember that those sobbing sounds are just air passing through his throat when his muscles are in a state of relaxation."

"So he's not really crying?" I asked,

"The phenomenon has no meaning," he assured me in one of several potentially disastrous misdiagnoses of our pets. Though we trusted Dr. Benedict, we trusted our senses more. Stanley was clearly upset at having been thrust into yet another new environment with unfamiliar people. We did our best to put him at ease. Whenever one of us heard him sobbing, we would lift his cage cover and talk to him, reassuring him that he had finally found a home with easily manipulated humans who would cater to him for the rest of his life.

The crying was so persistent throughout the summer, we warned our pet-sitter Hannah about it before leaving on vacation to South Dakota, lest she think our home harbored a troubled ghost. Once we managed to breach the wall of Hannah's phone calls to her boyfriend, she confirmed that our bird was continuing his crying jags. But things turned around when we returned. Stanley was relieved to see us and immediately seemed more relaxed. As soon as we flung open his cage door, he climbed on top, fluffed his feathers, and preened contentedly, eyeing us with the same affectionate attentiveness he had heaped on Lynn. That first night back, he didn't cry. In fact, he never cried again. Instead of sobbing when he wanted his usual after-bed peanut, he summoned his servants by ringing his bell. Bell-clanging accompanied by squawks meant that the TV in the living room was too loud, or that we were otherwise disturbing his beauty sleep. If I retired him too early, his vocal with instrumental accompaniment flowed unabated, and I soon learned for all our sakes not to cover him up until he was good and ready.

Stanley began slowly warming to us, and slow was the operative word. Far more reticent than Binky or even Ollie, Stanley was the teacher who relentlessly hammered home the true meaning of patience. Where Stanley was concerned, changes unfurled at a glacial, geological pace in which progress was measured by microscopic increments rather than discernible movement. One day I noticed that his cage lacked a perch close to the door. Maneuvering to the cage front from the single perch required him to climb horizontally around the cage walls, which struck me as awkward and inconvenient.

Normally, I would have simply installed another perch. But the mere sight of a notched and smoothly sanded stick sent Stanley into a wing-flapping tizzy. Introducing this malevolent entity into his world required first positioning it nonchalantly on the chair beside his cage for a day or two. Once he had ceased his vigilance over the perch, I was able to slip it inside his cage and set it on the bottom grate, tucked up against the cage body, where it called the least amount of attention to itself. A few days later, I attached it to the bars at the level of the bottom grate. Over a week's period, I gradually raised the perch an inch or so at a time, until finally it stood triumphantly at the same height as his other perch. But Stanley made a mockery of my success by treating the new piece of cage furniture as if it simply did not exist. Not only did he refuse to step on the perch for months, but he also stretched and contorted himself to avoid any accidental contact with the interloper.

Two parrots were, we realized, exponentially more work than owning one, giving us our first taste of the multiple-pet complexity to come. Like Ollie, Stanley insisted on eating dinner with us. In other words, we shared our table food in order to avoid ear-splitting disturbances. African gray parrots are prone to vitamin deficiencies that can lead to health problems if the bird is restricted to a seed diet, so we were only too happy to provide the pasta, tofu, and Jell-O that a wild bird would have scavenged from the forest. But he didn't make it easy.

Ollie's small cage sat on the counter behind my chair at mealtime. Serving him involved depositing scraps into a small food dish tied securely to the top of his cage. Not counting the food morsels that occasionally rained upon my head and the frequent squawking fits, that was the extent of the fuss with him. Stanley, however, would not tolerate a dish of any description on his cage. He shrank from the seed containers, plastic jar lids, quarter-cup measuring cups, and pudding bowls we auditioned as if they were cleverly disguised pythons with their own dinner plans in mind. Yet he would happily take nourishment from an ordinary spoon—as long as the spoon remained in my hand. If I gradually lowered the spoon until it rested on the bars on top of his cage, ever so gently uncurled my fingers, and crept three paces back to my chair, before my fanny touched wood, the spoon would hit the floor, scattering food in all directions. Clamping the spoon to his cage bars with a clothespin only served to divert his attention from eating to prying open the clothespin and flinging down the spoon.

He was also unpredictable about what he might decide to eat. The corn he enjoyed one night was resoundingly snubbed the next. But it wasn't necessarily a matter of his liking or disliking for a particular vegetable or tuber, we learned. The key was serving them in the proper order, but the constantly changing preferred sequence was a secret so impenetrable it would have pleased cryptography experts at the CIA. Thus, the helping of peas Stanley disdained with dramatic throat puffs that mimicked gagging gained quick acceptance after he had made a few lunges at a spoonful of broccoli. Stanley's behavior transformed our dinner table into a merry-go-round that sent me bobbing up and down, in and out of my chair, rounding the table, then circling back again.

BIRD EXPERTS AGREE that the first step in gaining control over a parrot is convincing it to "step up" on your hand upon command. Bird experts are easily identified by their scarred hands, and I realized that the road to a better bond with Stanley wouldn't necessarily be painless. Hoping that Lynn might have taught him the appropriate verbals, I tried calling "Step up, Stanley," from across the room and waited vainly for a raised foot to wave at me. Repeating the experiment a few inches from him resulted in the expected lowered head and threat to bite. And bite he did when I slid my hand closer. After examining my flesh for punctures and finding only a minor indentation, I shelved my usual cowardice and braved a second attempt. Stanley nipped me again, but when I refused to withdraw he seemed to sigh with his whole body as he graciously stepped onto my hand. Lifting him to chest level, my exhilaration soured when I realized I had no idea what to do with him now. To make Stanley think my command had been part of a grand plan instead of mere grandstanding, I took him on a short tour of the living room, pointing out such landmarks as the couch, TV, and coat rack.

Once I became skilled at picking up our parrot, I needed something to do with him. The logical choice was taking him into the living room after dinner to share the entertainment spectacle of *Wheel of Fortune* with us. Amazingly, the antics of Pat and Vanna failed to divert him from making his usual "put me back" peeps. I determined that he might be happier if he could move around a little. Wishing to preserve our heirloom burlap-fabric couch, Linda suggested setting Stanley on a broken birdcage that had been languishing in the basement. The microwave-size cage stood at seat level when I placed it on the floor, and to my great surprise Stanley had no hesitation about perching on it next to the couch. To occupy his time while the magical wheel was spinning, he readily chewed on magazine reply cards, which I transformed into irresistible objects through a series of accordion folds. He loved shredding these as much for the mastication as for the joy of watching us clean up the mess he had made on the floor.

Though I was delighted with the progress Stanley had made, I had to admit a basic feeling of disappointment as our first year with him ground on. African greys are potentially the best talkers in the bird world, able not only to remember complex phrases, but also to deliver them in tape-recorder-perfect, embarrassing imitations of their owners' voices. Researchers have even wangled grants to investigate whether greys can use language deliberately. Animal behavioralist Dr. Irene Pepperberg taught her Congo African grey, Alex, to identify objects by describing their color, shape, texture, and numbers up to three. Presented with a trio of lime-colored, velveteen-flocked wooden blocks nicely arranged on a tea tray, Alex might tell Dr. Pepperberg, "Three square green fuzzy," which is as good as I talk most days. Anecdotes made claims about grey speech that went way beyond those of Alex's professorial responses. *Pet Bird Report,* a magazine published by bird behavioralist Sally Blanchard, carried reports of parrots requesting foods and beverages by name, or critiquing the city lights from a Bay Area high-rise window.

So I had hopes that Stanley would be a kind of homunculus with whom I could converse, joke, collaborate on crossword puzzles, and conspire against Linda. But his phrase book began and ended with "Big boy, Stanley" and "Hello," which barely opened the door to banter, much less discussions of particle physics. Even worse, the more comfortable he grew with us, the less exercise he gave these four words, apparently deciding that they were superfluous psychic baggage from his former life with Lynn. Instead, he sharpened his mimicry skills on household sounds, including door squeaks and oven-timer beeps. Whenever Linda was foolish enough to kiss me in his presence, he made kissing noises back at us. I learned that this was mockery when the same editorializing greeted any nice words that I lavished on Ollie or our cat Penny. He's made an impressive mental leap from imitation to recognition of the larger context of smooching, but I had expected that intelligence to manifest itself more in his striving to develop desirable human traits like mine. Vaguely and hollowly, I longed for more from Stanley.

"Look what I've been reduced to," I complained to Linda in the living room, while a *Wheel* contestant from Bangor was busy buying a vowel. Perched per his usual routine on the couch-side cage top, Stanley lowered his head and presented the nape of his neck to me. His pupils contracted with bliss as I rubbed the skin beneath the shafts of his feathers with a crooked index finger.

"Stanley loves you," Linda shot back.

"Then why doesn't he rub *my* neck once in a while? Everything is give, give, give. It's the same thing every night," I sighed, little realizing that I would soon have cause to long for uncomplicated tedium.

The following evening, when I bent down to pick up Stanley, he refused to cooperate, backing away and flashing me a wary look. "Step up, Stanley," I insisted.

"Step on Poppy's hand," offered Linda from her perennial kitchen-sweeping posture.

"What did you just call me?"

"You're their poppy."

"I'm not anybody's poppy," I grumbled, thrusting my hand at Stanley a second time. He reluctantly got on board. But once I began carrying him toward the living room, he unleashed a harried yelp and flew back to his cage. Deciding that some benign inanimate object such as Linda's broom had scared him, I tried again. This time the squawk was louder, and he bit the back of my hand, drawing blood. "What's gotten into you?" I demanded, retreating to the bathroom to douse the tiny wound in torrents of cold tap water. But I knew better than to press a disaffected parrot.

The issue of his behavior grew more serious over the next few days. Sensing I was agitated over this new development, Stanley considerately didn't bite. But he refused to stay on my hand, crying out and fluttering desperately across the room each time I tried to lift him. When he emitted the same painful squawk while scaling the bars of his cage, I scheduled an appointment with Dr. Benedict.

I'd always been impressed by the liberties that the quiet and diminutive Dr. Benedict managed to take with an unfamiliar bird. Shortly after we acquired Stanley, I took him in for a checkup, and our vet had handled him with aplomb at a stage when Stanley would barely glance at me, much less climb upon my coffee mug. This time neither of us succeeded in picking him up, forcing us to corner Stanley on the floor and throw a towel over his head as if we were parrot-nappers. Carefully wrapping the whimpering bird to protect himself from the beak, Dr. Benedict wiggled the bird's toes with his fingers, gave him a lightning-quick nail trim, then probed the length of his legs. "Here's the difficulty," he murmured. In the area the doctor called Stanley's groin, and which Linda referred to as "Stanley's armpits," where each of the bird's legs met his rounded abdomen, our vet showed me an angry lima-bean-size patch of featherless, abraded skin. He couldn't say what caused the painful condition, though he added, "Except in the case of certain rashes, symmetrical lesions are extremely rare."

"So you think this is a rash?" I asked, once we had returned Stanley to his carrier.

"It would be worth checking the literature," he told me with a smile, implying he was leaving to do just that, as he popped out the examining room door. He reappeared minutes later accompanied by a stern young woman who towered over him in a telltale veterinarian's smock. "This is my new colleague, Dr. Stallings," he told me. "I've asked her to consult with me." Having already performed the glamorous part of the job, Dr. Benedict was turning Stanley's treatment over to an associate, apparently freeing himself to trim more nails and check the literature on other problematic cases. Since brusqueness often passes for efficiency, I was impressed by the speed with which Dr. Stallings produced a squeeze bottle of ointment from the lab, complete with a perfectly centered, pasted-on instruction label and a baggie full of cotton swabs as a sidekick.

"Apply this to the injured area twice a day," she informed me. Detecting my hesitation, she said, "You can handle your bird, can't you?"

"Certainly," I nodded, envisioning Linda taking on the job.

We managed to bushwhack and towel-wrap Stanley that evening in the manner taught to me by Dr. Benedict. He chewed at the folded material as we swabbed his twin groins with a Q-Tip, but he didn't make a serious effort to pay us back with a bite. His gentleness impressed me even as his condition worsened. Within forty-eight hours, his droppings had become watery, and soon we were changing the newspapers on the bottom of his cage three times a day. A phone call to Dr. Stallings elicited the bland response, "That's a typical side effect of the medicine. If it continues," she said, "it may mean your bird has suffered liver damage, and we would have to investigate possible treatment protocols for that condition."

Numbness radiated through my body. "And this is all because of the drug you gave me?" I asked.

"It happens occasionally."

"Why didn't you tell me that?" I demanded. "Why wouldn't you warn me about the side effects of a drug before prescribing it?"

"It's your responsibility as a pet owner to ask about side effects before administering any medicine," she insisted. "If we were to get bogged down with the question of side effects, we couldn't even prescribe aspirin."

Sickened and depressed, I basted my worries with the glum certainty that I had somehow harmed my bird through negligence, failing Lynn, failing Stanley's previous two owners, and reneging on a promise whispered through a cage cover to spoil our bird, not ruin him. I managed to squeak a request to Linda to make an appointment for Stanley with the dependable Dr. Hedley.

Dr. Hedley divided his time between his private clinic and consultations with zoos in several cities. Though neither massive nor obviously muscular, he projected a sense of strength that made it easy to envision him wrestling an ostrich to the ground to administer an antibiotic injection or placing his head in a lion's mouth to check its molars. If anyone could help Stanley, I figured it would be a man who dealt regularly with rhesus monkeys and Maribou storks, and Dr. Hedley didn't disappoint me. He told me he'd been busy at his northern Wisconsin cottage excavating hollows in dead trees at fifty-foot elevations to serve as housing for pileated woodpeckers.

"Doesn't the height bother you?" I asked.

"If it doesn't bother the woodpeckers, now why should it bother me?" he laughed. "Actually, your bird looks pretty good. We've got a couple of leathery scabs developing where the injuries were, and they make a natural bandage better than anything I could prescribe."

When I showed him the medication Dr. Stallings had prescribed, he assured me Stanley's watery droppings were nothing more serious than a short-term side effect. "But I would never use a cortisone-based medicine for a bird," he admonished. "The problem is that birds won't leave an injured area alone. They lick it, and any topical ointment gets into their systems through their tongues. Our best bet is to let Stanley continue to heal without any intervention."

Eager to prevent another parrot owner from going through a similar experience, I naively called Dr. Benedict that same day and told him what Dr. Hedley had advised me regarding Dr. Stallings's prescription. Dr. Benedict had been our vet of choice in dealing with the difficult Ollie, and we enjoyed such a good rapport, Linda had more than once considered inviting him over for dinner. After hearing me out, he was silent for a moment.

"So you've been badmouthing our practice," he said.

"I haven't been badmouthing anyone," I replied, as my delight at sharing a clinical insight evaporated. "I didn't mention any names,"

I insisted, failing to mention that Dr. Stallings's name was clearly visible on the perfectly centered squeeze-bottle label. "I simply told Dr. Hedley what another vet had instructed us to do and the effect it had on Stanley, who seems to be doing a little better," I added brightly. But Dr. Benedict would not be lured into discussing Stanley's health.

He made me explain in detail how we had administered the ointment to our bird, then quizzed me on minute aspects of the procedure like a prosecuting attorney probing for the weakness in a robbery suspect's alibi.

"Dr. Stallings's instructions call for the application of a thin layer of the ointment. How did you determine whether you were applying a thin layer or not?" he asked with great satisfaction.

After several minutes of cross-examination, I managed to hang up the phone.

Following Dr. Hedley's orders, we ignored Stanley's abrasions, and he healed, to enjoy once again a half-hour of television after dinner. But I soon learned to avoid nature programs, since the appearance of a hawk in flight prompted him to emit an ear-piercing alarm call. A year later, his mysterious condition recurred, though it was far milder the second time around. Dr. Hedley was in Illinois treating a wildebeest, forcing us to try yet another vet. The lanky and affable Dr. Fuller told us that Stanley's problems were behavioral. When I asked for a translation, he told me, "He's chewing on himself." He reminded me that parrots occasionally engage in feather-plucking and other self-mutilating behavior when they become agitated over a prolonged period of time. "You told me this occurred the first time almost exactly a year ago. Is there anything that happens this time of year which might be causing your bird anxiety?"

"Nothing that I can think of," I answered. "This is the time of year we always go on vacation."

"That could well be the cause," he said. "Especially if your bird has a tendency toward nervousness." Just to be on the safe side that nothing microbial was amiss, Dr. Fuller took a blood test, then asked if I'd like a drop of Stanley's blood reserved for determining his gender through a new DNA test. I agreed to the procedure without giving it much thought. But a week later I was shocked to receive a laboratory report in the mail that stated:

> Subject's name: Stanley
> Type of bird: African grey Timneh parrot
> Gender: Female

"I knew it," Linda moaned. "You never should have gotten him tested."

"We had to know," I insisted. "I really should have figured it out a long time ago, anyway. She's way too much of a pest to be a male."

Nevertheless, I didn't want to start over with a brand-new name. Stanley had been through enough trauma in her short life, and suddenly calling her Guinevere or Edwina could send her over the top. Recalling that bird behavioralist Sally Blanchard had rechristened her African grey Bongo as Bongo Marie once she had learned the parrot's true gender, I promptly adopted Stanley Sue as the full legal name for our pet.

"Oh, no you don't," Linda complained. "That's my middle name."

"You took my name when we got married. You were Linda Bush. Now you're Linda Tarte. So you can share one of your many names with Stanley. Fair is fair."

As it turned out, Stanley's self-inflicted injury did not amount to much the second time around, though she was fussy about hopping onto my hand for about a month. Dr. Fuller opined that Stanley was learning to trust us. My thinking was that finally calling her a name that more or less suited her gender had deflated a latent sexual identity problem. Or something along those lines. But so much had happened over the last twelve months that Stanley's gender switcheroo was a minor adjustment. Our animal population had suddenly exploded. Somehow, when my attention had apparently been vaguely directed elsewhere, we had taken on a rabbit, a ring-neck dove, and three parakeets, a combination that dramatically complicated our lives.

CHAPTER 4

Howard the Clumsy Romeo

N o more animals," I told Linda.

"We hardly have any."

"A cat, two parrots, and a canary. That's more animals than I've ever seen together at one time. And they all live in our house."

"Well," she shrugged, "I told you we should get some animals for outdoors. I can't understand why anyone fortunate to own a barn like ours wouldn't want a couple of cows or a donkey."

Linda had always lived out in the country, and that was a big difference between us. Her past included subsistence living with a pig and several chickens in the Michigan north woods, while I had merely lived with Catholics in suburbia.

Antirural sentiments ran deep in the Blessed Sacrament Parish neighborhood of my youth, where no one would admit to watching *The Andy Griffith Show, The Beverly Hillbillies,* or *Petticoat Junction,* though with shades drawn, such activities undoubtedly took place. During the five-hour trip from Grand Rapids to my mom's hometown of Port Huron in the ancient pre-interstate era, whenever we got stuck behind a poky driver on the sense-dulling cornfield-lined roads along the way, my good-natured father would inevitably grumble about "another damn farmer." Branding a person a farmer was one of the choicest insults you could level at any hapless soul. In high school, we drew a line between the suburban high-steppers and the downtrodden yokels from outside the city limits. Even during the rebellious 1960s, however much I disdained the middle-class pursuit of manicured lawns bounded by smooth, rolling sidewalks, I considered life in the country a fearful remnant of Dark Ages chaos.

By the time I bought our 1907-vintage farmhouse in 1989, my attitude had shifted to the degree that I esteemed rural life as an escape from a series of apartments in crime-spattered downtown Grand Rapids. In a single year, thieves had broken into my battered Toyota so often that I installed old stove knobs on the in-dash cassette deck to demonstrate its worthlessness and left the doors unlocked at night to spare myself the cost of yet another broken window. Even so, some crack-crazed kid snatched the eighty-nine-cent notebook I used for jotting down business mileage, along with the stick-on digital clock my dad had gotten as a freebie with his subscription to *Time*.

Linda, who had been living in an ailing trailer with no phones, lights, or plumbing in northern Michigan, immediately loved the house on the outskirts of Lowell. And it answered my need for a yard where I could walk around without people looking out their windows and seeing that I was walking around a yard.

The first time I drove my parents out to see the house, their reaction to our little slab of rustic Shangri-La wasn't particularly positive. When I proudly showed off the two acres of swampy thicket behind the back fence, my mother asked, "How are you going to get a lawnmower in there?" She gestured toward the rear door of the barn. "You'd better keep that closed," she advised me, "Otherwise an animal is liable to get in." I should have listened to her.

To this day, the barn remains something of a puzzler. Earlier owners of our property must have found something to grow and harvest somewhere, unless the vast storage capacity of the double-decker barn was sheer whimsy. Steep, nonfarmable hills shoot up just across the road. What I suspect was formerly arable land out back has since become a swamp. I blame a century of industrial tinkering with the Grand River for the biannual flooding that forces our neighbor to resort to rowboat trips to reach his truck each spring and fall. Initially used as a lumber waterway, the Grand River was later exploited as a source of fill-dirt for the cities on its route, though it also conveyed the clam harvesters pursuing cheap mother-of-pearl shell substitutes for a button factory in Lowell. The clammers camped on the shores of our property in the years before World War I, announcing their presence with the hearty smell of bivalves boiling in great cauldrons and, no doubt, the shouted melodies of traditional clamming songs.

More recently, the folks who sold us our house had spent decades grazing cows in the cowslip and kept porkers that were wont to stray upon the porch. After I moved in, and as my lifelong immunity to animals shifted to susceptibility, I came to suspect that an *Amityville Horror*–like entity was drawing beasts to our house, and I was merely the spirit's latest vehicle for pet acquisitiveness.

Certainly I seemed fated to house a procession of rabbits whether I sought them out or not. Bertha came to us unbidden. Linda rushed in one afternoon from a housecleaning job and told me, "You'll never guess what I saw at Joyce Howell's underneath her bird feeder."

"A bird."

"A little charcoal grey bunny with brown and silver highlights."

"I thought wild rabbits were solid brown."

Her eyes widened. "This was someone's pet. Joyce said the poor thing has been eating sunflower seeds all winter. I opened the patio door and tried to feed him. He came pretty close before he ran away. He's one of those tiny Netherland dwarf bunnies we looked at when we bought Binky. Joyce's husband is going to catch him."

"And do what with him?" Linda's glee had aroused my suspicions.

"He's been eating the lower branches of their shrubs, and they just want to catch it, that's all."

But I knew there was more to come. A couple of days later, George Howell caught the rabbit in a basketball hoop–size trout net and zipped it over to us. Someone had conveyed the idea to George that we would welcome a new rabbit, and that someone called me downstairs from my upstairs hideout to meet our new resident.

Wearing thick leather gloves capable of repelling eagle talons, George engulfed the tiny animal with his hands, extracted it from a cat carrier, and hurriedly plopped it in Binky's old cage, which someone had carried from the basement to its familiar place in our dining room. "I hope he doesn't bite you," George enthusiastically warned us. "That guy's been taking out branches thicker than my thumb. I think he's part beaver."

"Wonderful," I said, giving Linda the evil eye.

"He looks just like a Beatrix Potter bunny," Linda bubbled. "Can we let him out?"

"Wait till I get out of here," said George, who was clearly anticipating bloodletting and rampant destruction once we uncaged the beast. Before George was back in his car, Linda was petting the rabbit she'd initially named Bertie after P. G. Wodehouse's pampered and clueless protagonist. But we turned out to be the clueless ones, along with our new veterinarian, when Bertie pulled a gender switch similar to Stanley Sue's. Examining our bunny, whom we learned was the escaped pet of an unconcerned neighbor of Joyce and George's, Dr. Colby initially sustained our guess that our rabbit was a male and suggested a second appointment to have him neutered. An intact male rabbit can earn its disproportionate title of "buck" through aggressive behavior toward people, furnishings, and female "does," including occasionally spraying anything that moves or stands still. Having been hosed by Binky a couple of times, I was anxious to get Bertie snipped. But the day we dropped him off for surgery, Linda casually asked Dr. Colby just before leaving the examination room, "Are you sure he's a male?"

The effrontery to veterinary science embarrassed me. "Dr. Colby already told us that he was," I growled. Graciously our vet agreed to humor Linda by giving Bertie's nether regions a second look. With some chagrin she pronounced Bertie to be the female we renamed Bertha.

Not long after, Linda came home from work with another sad animal story. "You know that lady, Terri, with the teenagers who just bought the tropical fish? They've got a really sweet parakeet, and no one pays any attention to him now. He's all alone in a dark room, and his mate died a little while ago. He used to lecture the girl bird all the time, but now he just sits there and doesn't chirp or hop around the cage."

"That is a shame," I told her, foolishly assuming that a show of sympathy would cost me nothing.

"I'm trying to talk Terri into giving him to us," Linda concluded, as if we had already flung open the door to parakeet ownership.

Naturally, I was opposed to taking on another pet, but Linda convinced me that no less troublesome animal than the parakeet existed anywhere in nature, microscopic life included. I surrendered to the argument that an older bird wouldn't even want to come out of his cage. Fortunately this turned out to be true with the blue-and-yellow Farley, whom Linda named after the Canadian nature writer Farley Mowat. On the sole occasion that Linda urged our parakeet out, he flapped around the dining room in such a state of disorientation, we consequently left him contentedly behind bars.

Caring for Farley was easy indeed. But I hadn't figured on the companionship aspect.

"He misses Lilly," Linda told me. "Lilly was the mate who died. He needs a little friend."

"You're fairly little," I pointed out.

"Oh, look how sad he is. It's not right that he should spend the rest of his days all by himself."

"I don't know. I sort of envy him." But I had a feeling this discussion would recur until I finally gave in.

THE GREEN-AND-YELLOW budgie Linda picked out was so tame, she sat on Linda's shoulder on the car ride home from Betsy's Beasts. I illogically named her Rossy after a pop group from Madagascar. Within a couple of days, Farley's personality did a 180-degree flip-flop. The old guy went back to the happy chattering of his peak parakeet years, and like an elderly bachelor who marries a young thing, he died a month later of sheer bliss.

"Rossy isn't used to being by herself," Linda reported a day after Farley's demise.

"She can look at Stanley Sue," I countered uselessly. "Or she can latch on to Ollie. Ollie's her size, and he's just a cage away. They can forge a strong platonic bond."

"She needs a little friend."

Powerless, I gave in to a chipper blue-and-white male Linda named Reggie, because she liked the way the name went with Rossy.

But those two didn't go together at all, avoiding one another in the cage with the steely deliberateness of Stanley Sue ignoring a new perch. A third parakeet, the yellow Sophie, added balance to the batch with her retiring personality. Before I had a quasi-say in the matter, these most unobtrusive of all possible pets were flying around the dining room and kitchen, chewing on the upper-level woodwork, and sampling morsels from our plates. I worried that Ollie would make mincemeat of the effervescent budgies, but they were fast enough to tease him and steal food from his dish, too. Ollie and I could only watch and squawk. Rossy, who continued to spurn Reggie's affections, followed my suggestion of developing a crush on Ollie. She enjoyed sharing his cage top at mealtime just out of reach of his beak.

"We can't take in any more of these hard-luck cases," I groused during a particularly beleaguering dinner. Stanley was refusing one food after another via the fling method. Ollie was exercising his vocal tract. Penny, our usually well-mannered cat, kept sneaking into the dining room to get within pouncing range of the parakeets, who buzzed my head like deerflies. Bertha had somehow wormed her way into the inner springs of a small couch and was dulling her teeth on the wooden frame. "It would be one thing if there was a limit to them, but every single person you work for has an animal they're thrilled to foist on us."

It's difficult explaining why I hadn't mustered more resistance to the new arrivals, much less to any of the animals. If Linda had put the question to me, "Sweetie, should we get a rabbit, canary, cat, two parrots, and three parakeets?" and my answer would have had a meaningful effect on the consequences, I can't imagine replying yes, and I would never have taken the initiative to acquire any of these pets on my own—with the possible exception of a cat. I was essentially just going along for the ride, as I had with most everything in my life.

Back in my early college years, I'd been abstractly enthusiastic about saltwater aquarium fish, because my girlfriend, Mary, enthusiastically bought them for me. I loved the bright colors and fluidity of the clownfish and other reef fish, the strangeness of the anemones and other invertebrates, and the exclusivity of a hobby that required safaris to neighboring towns.

I didn't love my fish, but I loved the idea of having them. They were a logical extension to pawing copies of *National Geographic* and naively mooning over exotic alternatives to life in a bland suburban neighborhood that was more in line with *Reader's Digest*. To my parents' horror, my bedroom hobby expanded to fill several tanks, including a fifty-five-gallon aquarium whose water, salt, substrate, rocks, filters, pumps, and lights weighed over six hundred pounds and eventually cracked the ceiling plaster of the living room below.

Down the hall from my oceanarium was a second-story walkout porch my family called the airing deck. My parents had replaced the original tar-paper surface with a flooring of loose, crushed white stone. Because this material reminded me of the bottom of my tanks, or because I was addled by a mixture of hormones and self-absorption, I decided that the porch made a convenient dumping ground for dirty aquarium gravel and the expended contents of aquarium filters. Leaves, seedpods, twigs, and sparrow droppings fallen from the huge maple that overhung the airing deck disguised my lazy landfill for several months. By the time my crime came to light, the organic medium had nurtured the growth of a tenacious layer of moss that no amount of bleach or careful harvesting could remove.

"Did I tell you about the Taylors' French lop bunny, Bea?" Linda asked, as I chopped up a brussels sprout with my fork and tried to get Stanley to accept a bite.

"Whatever her problem is, we can't take her," I proclaimed, fully realizing that the firm line I was drawing could easily be erased. I was far more comfortable falling guilelessly into events rather than making decisions. I would endlessly second-guess my decisions if things went well, or blame myself if things went wrong. Letting circumstances wash over me was the way I navigated through life. It was how I had acquired a steady freelance writing job, how I had blundered into co-owning a typesetting business a decade earlier, and how I had acquired a column in a national music magazine. I was lucky that nothing dark and sinister had ever presented itself to me with each nut and bolt perfectly aligned to the mushy contours of my weak will, or I might have absorbed a felony just as I had absorbed reef fish, invertebrates, rabbits, a canary, a cat, two parrots, and three parakeets.

Linda must have recognized my attempted resolve by the quaver in my voice, because no rabbit named Bea or any other orphans directly followed. There were better ways of slipping animals into the house.

ON OUR THIRD wedding anniversary, Linda presented me with a large package whose festive, hole-punched wrapping paper concealed a cage.

"Oh, my gosh, another bird!" I said with a big smile on my face.

"It's a dove," Linda told me.

"Aw, you shouldn't have," I insisted, my smile still frozen in place. "I mean it, you really shouldn't have." But even I wasn't enough of a curmudgeon to object to a gift that my wife had carefully framed as an expression of love. Howard, for his part, refused to toe the line as a symbol of peace, opting instead to perpetuate interspecies incompatibility.

Most commonly called a ring-neck dove (but also referred to as a barbary dove, collared dove, or turtle dove), Howard was a fawn-colored, mourning dove–size bird with a thin black ring around the back of his neck. An apricot-colored eye with a large black iris gave him a demeanor of perpetual surprise. His straight yellow toothpick of a beak originated just in front of his eye, suggesting an artist's drunken slip of the hand while painting the upper mandible. Though he was handsome enough while standing still, the darting of his tiny head while the bulk of his body remained motionless gave Howard the air of a clown. His feet seemed borrowed from another species. In contrast to the velvety surface of his feathers, which often drew our finger pads to his back, Howard's legs and toes were a scaly earthworm red indented with concentric circles.

The first time we opened the door to his cage, Howard stayed rooted to his perch for several moments, as if he couldn't believe such magic were possible. With a hop he plopped both feet onto a lower perch, hesitated, turned his body toward the beckoning exit, then jumped onto the open door extending from his cage. A few steps across the bars took him to the door's edge, where he waited like an Olympic diver mustering concentration for a difficult combination. Finally he flung himself across the dining room, wings flapping heavily as he settled on a chair back facing the parakeets' cage. A maniac's laugh, *hoo-hoo-hoo-hoo*, erupted from his chest. Bowing rhythmically, he launched into a lusty series of hoots timed to the dipping of his body, raising one foot at the completion of each bow. His chest swelled as he hooted, but his beak remained clamped shut. As we soon learned, this series of hard-wired actions, instigated by the presence of other birds, was a fixed ritual for Howard. Whenever we freed him from his cage, he followed the same routine, from his initial look of disbelief to his concluding strutting-in-place recital.

The parakeets were unimpressed with Howard's unvarying song and dance, and after a couple of days, I had to throw in with them. Our dove was a bit of a dud in the companionship department. Though he'd contentedly sit on a wooden perch for hours, once out of his cage he refused to wrap his toes around a human finger, cling to a wrist, or rest upon a forearm. He didn't seem to be so much afraid of contact with us as he was completely disinterested in the concept. While Ollie cocked his head and chattered at the sound of our voices, and Stanley Sue at least cocked her head, Howard paid no more attention to my "Oh, what a pretty, pretty bird" soliloquies than rabbits Binky or Bertha had ever paid to the shouted command "No!" Howard struck me as a bird particularly ill suited to sharing space with people and their possessions, no more at home in a house than a rooster, and the cramped quarters of the dining room diminished whatever natural grace he possessed. Only when he abandoned those four walls and sailed into the living room to land on the handlebars of our exercise bike did a small hint of the beauty of his long-distance flight unfurl. Truly he belonged in the open sky or, at the very least, in a large aviary packed with palm trees, bromeliads, and docents.

My 1984 edition of *Simon & Schuster's Guide to Pet Birds* described Howard's ilk as "friendly birds, even toward small finches and such." But not, apparently, toward any birds we owned. Our initial fear was that the mischievous parakeets might pick on Howard the same way they got the best of Ollie. Instead, Howard delighted in chasing the three budgies and Chester the canary around our dining room. His flight was clumsy compared to theirs; he was a bomber outmaneuvered by looping stunt planes. But as long as he could scatter the competition and subsequently crow from the top of the refrigerator, he was satisfied with his work.

"I hope he doesn't hurt the other birds," I grumbled to Linda, less because I thought he could actually do any harm and more because I hoped to make her feel guilty for inflicting this rabble-rouser on us.

"What are you talking about?"

"He's harassing the parakeets."

"No he's not. Howard's a romantic. He's courting them. What do you think the bowing's all about?"

That made sense. He never hooted at his rival, Ollie. Instead, he'd plop down next to Ollie and make a cudgel of his wing, attempting to knock him off his cage. For the moment, Howard stayed well clear of Stanley Sue. But his attention toward the budgies did indeed smack of ardor. Rossy, who had her small black eyes set on Ollie, cold-shouldered Howard's come-ons. Sophie, who hadn't decided whether or not she cared for Reggie, never considered a liaison with a dove. But Reggie, the spurned blue bon vivant of the parakeet set, had ideas of his own. Once Howard had exhausted his erotic repertoire and settled on the countertop or chair back to survey his uncooperative harem, Reggie swooped in behind him. Landing in the middle of Howard's back, far removed from the business end, he would chatter excitedly while rubbing his loins against Howard's wings in a miniature frenzy of delight. Howard basked in the attention. Craning his neck, he'd twist his head backward and with a series of short pecks diddle Reggie's beak. Once his eyes had cleared of passion, Howard would snap to his senses and abruptly fly off, carrying Reggie on his back for a couple of wing strokes.

"Where's your camcorder, sweetheart? They'd pay us $10,000 for that," Linda urged me, referring to a television program that aired painful "home movies" from viewers each week.

"That's a family show," I quipped, little realizing that our boy-bird pals could actually make a grown adult blush.

One warm summer day, we received an unexpected visit from

Jeanne Trost and her niece, Susan. Jeanne was a member of the Mecosta County church that Linda had attended during her carefree, electricity-free life up north before marrying electricity-free me.

"Jeanne! What are you doing down here? Is this your little niece?" Linda exclaimed. Shepherding them into the dining room, Linda immediately kicked over the oscillating fan that sat on a small footstool just inside the doorway. Stanley Sue, who was pacing Bertha's cage top in search of a way of biting the bunny through the bars, jumped and flapped her wings at the noise. "That thing again," Linda complained, as I righted the much abused fan. It barely survived a four-hour span before getting its face pressed against blue linoleum. Its grille was bashed in within a molecule's breadth of the blades, resulting in intermittent ticking that numbered its days in our employ.

"Look at all these cages," marveled Jeanne in a tone of voice I had lately begun to recognize as meaning, "Are you people out of your minds?" Reaching behind the refrigerator, Linda grabbed the end of an ugly plywood board and let it crash to the floor within inches of my stockinged foot, forming a two-foot-high, partially effective rabbit-proof barrier between the dining room and the rest of the house.

"I'll let the bunny out in a minute," Linda explained.

"I thought Susan might enjoy visiting the 4-H fair," offered Jeanne, whose pinched mouth indicated that she wondered whether the fairgrounds would be less chaotic than our house. "This is my favorite niece in all the world."

"Jeanne, have you met my husband, Bob?"

"You got pigtails," said the little girl.

"I wish my hair was as pretty as yours," Linda answered.

"Aunt Jeanne, I'm your *only* niece."

By this time, I had safely squeezed behind Stanley Sue's cage and table, retreating to the far end of the room to pry an ornery Ollie off his perch. Chester was obligingly trilling an aria that earned him a more puzzled than appreciative glance from Linda's friend, who hadn't moved from her entry point beside the peninsular counter that separated the dining room from the kitchen. Stanley Sue, handsome as a small hawk and bristling with intelligence, got a brief moment of glory when she delicately plucked a peanut from Susan's fingers. "Isn't she a good girl? Stanley's a very good girl," Linda observed. I brought Ollie over to show the pair, dangling him upside down from my finger. Cradling his back in the palm of my hand, I spread a wing to show off his secret yellow feathers, receiving a painful bite for my trouble and a polite mumble from Jeanne.

The seven-year-old rewarded me by voicing my least favorite question in the world. "Does he talk?" she asked. I considered the question a cliché on the same order of asking a dog owner if his black Lab could speak. Of course, we always made the same inquiry of other parrot owners, but as bird people we were exempt from such taboos. I was spared the need to answer when the aunt's and niece's eyes simultaneously locked on Howard.

"Look at the beautiful pigeon, Aunt Jeanne," cried the seven-year-old.

"He doesn't talk," I said a little hotly, bitter that the ringneck had once again trumped every other animal in the room by magnetically generating interest all out of proportion to his attributes. Our ownership of Ollie and Stanley Sue was hard won, and it bothered me that trouble-free Howard grabbed the glory. It happened so frequently, I had formulated a theory. People expected to see parrots as pets. Few North Americans had ever encountered them in any other context. But nobody anticipated seeing a dove in an indoor cage. Insofar as the attention reflected back on me, I was happy to nestle Howard in my hands, presenting him first to Susan, who squealed at my suggestion that she stroke his silky back, and to Jeanne, who was obviously experiencing her first contact with a winged pet. Her finger brushed his feathers, then jerked back as the dove craned his neck backward and flicked his beak against my palm. I released him, and he flew hooting to the top of his cage.

"Want to come out, 'keets?" Linda opened the parakeets' door before busying herself in front of the refrigerator assembling four glasses of what she referred to as "fizzy water": carbonated water topped off with an inch of cranberry juice. Jeanne ducked slightly as the parakeets first hit the air, then stood with a hand covering her hair until she felt foolish enough to remove it. I was about to snag my beverage and leave Linda to her guests when I heard Susan exclaim, "He's riding piggyback!"

Not only had Reggie alighted on Howard, but he was also engaging in the most lurid display of interspecies affection that I had witnessed to date. Squawking in a high-pitched buzz, the blue parakeet curled his extended wings around Howard's sides in passionate embrace, the better to throw his whole body weight behind the grinding of his lower abdomen against his unlikely mate. In metronome fashion, his blue and black ribbon of a tail chugged back and forth against Howard's stout tail feathers. Equally enraptured, Howard wobbled his head back to give Reggie the avian equivalent of a kiss, beak rapidly rubbing against beak, his pupils dilated, his quivering carriage slanted forward in a submissive stoop.

"What are they doing?" Susan asked in wonder.

Because children raised in the country learn the facts of life in animal terms almost as soon as they can crawl around the sex-crazed barnyard, Linda laughed and told her visitors, "Reggie's trying to mate with Howard. He's a little bit mixed up."

I waved a stained dish towel in the birds' direction, once, twice, three times, and like adulterers in the parking lot of the Red Roof Inn, they parted without a glance. Jeanne's face, however, was anything but nonchalant. "That was a funny game, wasn't it?" asked Jeanne, shooting Linda a pained looked indicating that the sordid scene wasn't suitable for discussion in front of a youngster. "I wonder what kind of games they'll have at the fair? You like Whack the Mole the best, don't you Susan?"

"I like watching the animals play."

"You can see all the animals from way on top of the Ferris wheel," concluded Jeanne, who was obviously fearing a worst-case scenario of lusty pigs and goat satyrs.

I slunk upstairs to let Linda mediate, returning just a few minutes later to bid aunt and niece good-bye. At the door, Jeanne leaned her head into Linda's and told her with a smile, "We enjoyed our visit. But I don't think I'll bring Susan back until she's a little older." That marked the first time anyone had branded our house an adult establishment.

HOWARD SOON DEMONSTRATED a talent for thievery. Later that week, as I reviewed an album by a South African chorale group for my column, a song caught my attention on Black Umfolosi's *Festival Umdlalo*. It was an a cappella ditty called "Inobembela Njiba." Since my Kalanga language skills weren't up to snuff, I relied on the liner notes to learn that the song was about "a dove that steals from granaries and is then bewitched, resulting in it wandering around aimlessly in a confused state." I didn't know whether Howard had been bewitched, but his confused state was inarguable. The stealing reference was right on target, too. When not falling prey to Reggie's charms, Howard's favorite pastime was preying on our other birds' food.

Howard was energetic in his thievery. He had to be in order to squeeze his handbag of a body through the wallet-size door of the parakeets' cage only to revel in the exact same food he received in his own seed cup every day. Eating was secondary to the relentless search for some obscure fantasy delicacy that loomed large in his peanut brain. Using his beak as a rake, he dug deep into the dish to scatter impressive quantities of seeds admirable distances across the dining room. Compared to Howard, messy Ollie at mealtime was Miss Manners. Not even Stanley Sue discarded food with the dedication of our dove. I took to winding adding-machine tape around the invaded cage, threading it in and out of the bars as a backstop, which left heaps of otherwise untouched parakeet seed on the cage bottom. For all the industry of his mining operation, Howard retrieved few nuggets to his liking. He swallowed them whole with a total disregard for taste, leaving me to wonder if he weren't an aesthete whose love of food was driven by the pursuit of textural perfection.

As Stanley Sue became more relaxed in our household, she spent less of her free time on top of her cage, devoting her exercise hours to harassing Bertha, opening and banging shut floor-level cupboard doors, and energetically gouging our baseboards. While Howard ignored Stanley Sue, he considered her dish fair game. The varied shapes and sizes of the parrot seed mixture proved so irresistible, he was willing to risk the larger bird's wrath. Every week or so, I'd walk into the room to find a tattletale faun-colored tail feather on the floor of Stanley Sue's cage, while Howard nursed his wounded ego on a chair back across the room. Because Stanley Sue had never shown aggressiveness toward anyone but the bunny, and even that was mostly bluff, we hadn't realized we were putting Howard's life in danger.

I learned about Stanley Sue's temper the day I arrived home after a grueling five hours at the office and was going through my usual afternoon's routine in anticipation of my nap. I took Bertha outside and plopped her in her backyard pen. Indoors, I popped the latch on Chester's cage, liberated the parakeets, and then opened Howard's door. I could see him ruminating on how best to take advantage of this unexpected stroke of fortune. I said hello to Stanley Sue, fruitlessly repeating the desired answer, "Hi, Bob, hi, Bob," in hopes she would start talking again. Swinging open the door to her cage, I trundled off to the bedroom, where I upset a snoozing Penny by turning back the bedspread. Oh, what a strength-sapping half-day I'd had writing training materials for office-seating dealers. I closed the shades, shut my eyes, and slid into blissful unawareness.

Though I'm so light a sleeper, a falling dewdrop could disturb me, I heard no indication that anything was out of sorts. The only bird who might have alerted me to Stanley Sue's attack on Howard was Howard himself, and his vocabulary was inadequate for the task. While the parrots, parakeets, and even the canary had peeps, chirps, and squawks with which to signify a broad emotional spectrum, Howard was capable of emitting only a surprised laugh that indicated he was on the make and a boastful hooting that asserted his magnificent presence. I know of no other bird in nature limited to just two sounds, and marvel that two are sufficient for social interactions among doves. Maybe other ringnecks can glean vast quantities of information from these unvarying calls. If so, I wish an in-the-know dove had pecked me on the forehead and led me into the dining room before Howard ended up on the bottom of Stanley Sue's cage, his back torn open and smeared with blood.

"Oh, baby, baby, what's happened to you?" I moaned, certain he was dead or on the verge of death. Shouting for Linda, who had just walked in the door. I gingerly picked up Howard and carried him into the bathroom. His eyes were open but cloudy. He barely moved as I held him. "Stanley got him," I managed to say. "I think she must have cornered him in her cage."

Linda uncapped a mixture of hydrogen peroxide and antibacterial Betadine, which we kept on hand for emergencies. I could hardly watch as she daubed the wound with a cotton ball. "I don't think it's as bad as it first looked," she reassured me, as she cleaned him up. "It doesn't seem to be too deep." Still the silver dollar–size abrasion between his tail and wings was bad enough. If the pain was too great or if the wound became infected, he wouldn't last the night.

Linda rushed Howard to Dr. Carlotti, a country vet who ran a small practice from his farm a few miles from us. I stayed home, trying not to strangle Stanley Sue. Instead, I inflicted on her the worst punishment I could think of. I put her in her cage and took away her bell, the bell that functioned as her proxy voice. It was the bell she rang whenever she wanted out of her cage, whenever she wanted some attention, whenever she wanted something to eat, whenever something in the house disturbed her, or whenever she was just plain moody. Taking her bell was as serious as slapping a prisoner in solitary confinement. In the three years we had owned Stanley, I had only taken her bell away twice: once when she had bitten me for no apparent reason, and once when she had bitten Linda without asking my permission.

Within an hour I relented. "Here's your bell back," I sighed, realizing that Stanley hadn't been at fault for attacking a rival who had invaded her territory and stolen her food. She had simply followed her wild nature. I was to blame for Howard's injury. I had seen the signs of trouble but naively assumed nothing worse would happen than plucked tail feathers, because that wouldn't be nice, and Stanley Sue was a nice bird.

Stepping back from anthropomorphizing our pets while still

feeling close to them was always difficult. It took me years to accept the fact that animals don't act according to human standards of generosity and forgiveness—which I seldom followed, either. We could teach them certain behaviors we considered appropriate, but we couldn't override the instincts that had allowed their species to survive for thousands of years. When mixing potentially incompatible pets, the best we could do was provide an environment that kept the chances for serious conflict near zero. For every lovey-dovey Howard-and-Reggie relationship, there could just as easily be a Howard and Stanley Sue.

Linda returned from the vet, and I could tell from her mood that Howard's injury wasn't life threatening. She even smiled as she showed me the celluloid "Elizabethan collar" that Dr. Carlotti had fashioned for him. "The doctor gave him a shot of Baytril and said Howard would probably be okay if we can keep him from picking at himself. But he doesn't like that thing on his neck at all." No longer in shock, Howard twisted his head in one direction then the other, unable to believe he was encumbered with the plastic cone contraption.

"We could put a ruffle on it. Make him look more like a clown," I said.

"The trick will be getting him to eat. I don't know if he can eat from his dish with the collar on, and we can't take it off him for two weeks."

During the first days of his recovery, Howard was glum. He sat motionless on his perch, legs folded beneath him to allow his abdomen to help support his weight. For much of the time, he kept his eyes closed, as if putting himself into a yogic healing trance, never uttering a sound, not even a single "om." Linda performed the hard work of keeping his wound clean, though I took over some of the care once the injury became less evil looking. My role primarily consisted of hovering over Howard's cage and making encouraging noises, then clucking accusingly at Stanley Sue. I cajoled him to eat by wiggling homemade bread under his beak until he pecked at it purely out of exasperation. After a few days, he graduated to spray millet, a cluster of dried seeds that I attached to his bars with a wooden clothespin. Once he'd had his fill of such lackluster fare, he mastered balancing the weight of his collar well enough to lower his head and root through his dish. By the end of the first week, he was once again shoveling seeds in all directions and had recovered his appetite for hooting.

Dr. Carlotti had told Linda that the patch on Howard's back might never grow feathers again, or that feathers might only pop up here and there after his next molt. "Reggie won't like that," I complained. "It won't give him anything to grab on to." But within ten days, we could no longer see the rapidly healing wound through the feather shafts that sprouted up thicker than tattoos on a teenager's shoulder. As Howard's health improved, he grew restless in his cage. Collar or no collar, we decided to let him exercise. Owing to the peculiar aerodynamic qualities of the plastic cone, however, when he flapped his wings in an attempt to fly forward, he sailed backward across the room, startling the parakeets, who had never experienced so serious a violation of avian flight bylaws.

Linda and I had assumed that as long as we kept Stanley Sue's door closed when Howard was at large, we could eliminate future fights. But once our ringneck had returned to full fettle with a luxuriously feathered back, he immediately tried to stage a rematch, armed with no more impressive weapon than his own foolishness. Having two birds that needed separate out-of-cage time added to the complexity of pet-keeping. It was also a harbinger. Within a year, we would find ourselves juggling three rabbits who couldn't share a single room without engaging in fur-shredding melees. More complexity meant more scheduling, which meant more of my free time flew out the window.

As early as I can remember, I have always nursed a special contempt for people who make surrogate children of their pets. They're the people who dress their animals in small plaid suits, bring them along on dinner dates, and spend sleepless nights worrying that an isolated cough is the first sign of a dreaded virus. Though I hadn't done any of these, I knew that as soon as I had uttered the word "baby" when finding Howard hurt in Stanley Sue's cage, I had unwittingly crossed an emotional threshold.

But at least my affection was no longer unrequited. Along with his grudge against Stanley Sue, Howard had emerged from his disaster with a new appreciation for us. His heart still belonged to Reggie. But when he wasn't chasing the parakeets around the dining room, stealing seed from their dishes, or dreaming of vengeance against Stanley Sue, he might unexpectedly land upon my shoulder, bow and hoot in my direction, and tenderly chatter his beak against my cheek. The fact that this invariably happened during dinner, when I had a piece of bread in hand, I chalked up to mere coincidence.

CHAPTER 5

The Real Trouble Begins

Even with helping tend a cat, seven birds, and a rabbit, I was able to call most of the day my own. Breakfast was admittedly intense. Ollie and Stanley Sue insisted we hand-feed them portions of whatever Linda and I were eating. Penny, Bertha, Howard, the parakeets, and the canary each required individual servings rather than graciously sharing a communal bowl of cornflakes. They also each demanded a change of water and, once again, they wanted it in separate bowls. In the afternoon, juggling various out-of-cage times for the birds and the bunny, Bertha, nibbled away at more of our time. And Ollie still launched occasional wall-penetrating fits of attention-seeking throughout the day, though the companionship of the parakeets had blunted his vigor.

Dinner meant a repeat of parrot food-flinging antics followed by floor and ceiling cleaning. After dinner, once the parakeets and canaries had been cajoled into returning to their cages via handclaps and verbal threats, Stanley Sue demanded a half-hour of coddling with head scratches and exaggerated praises. Bertha then got her own romp through the house and a hide-and-seek-style roundup later. Finally, all six animal cages required covering at staggered beddy-bye times, and Stanley required peanuts at frequent intervals to curtail bouts of bell-ringing. Despite all this, and even though the day really wasn't my own after all, I still maintained the fiction that the animals were merely peripheral to my life. Needless to say, this fiction was soon to dry up and blow away.

Howard's injury had spurred us into a flurry of home-nursing, but our efforts were meager compared to the long struggle we soon faced with Bertha the rabbit. After surviving a harsh winter stripping evergreen foliage from the Howell's treasured shrubs, she adjusted nicely to the cushy conditions inside our house. Even though she retained a wild streak from her months on her own outdoors, her independence manifested itself as impishness rather than insolence, the quality Binky had taken as his trademark. She hid from us but never resented being found. Her guinea pig size made her an expert at wriggling into the most hopelessly obscure portions of our house geography, including a crack between the living room couch and wall so narrow it might thwart a chubby mouse. To keep her more visibly entertained, I found a long, narrow box that once held a Try and Put Me Together–brand CD rack and filled it with crumpled newspapers. Bertha could structure an entire evening around shooting in and out of the box to rearrange the papers or eject them with her back feet according to her whim.

A doglike good-naturedness was her strongest point. Here was a rabbit who would not only sit upon our laps and enjoy petting but would also lick us to show appreciation—and not so obsessively as to suggest mindlessness. But her mood could abruptly change once we plopped her outside in her pen. A female John Henry, she dug and tunneled furiously in the sand, though without obvious escape attempts in the works. Her ability to tear around the pen in furious circles put Binky's circumnavigation to shame, and I often kept an eye on the troposphere directly above our house for fear that she might generate a deadly funnel cloud. This ferocity was safely channeled as long as I left her to herself. But if I tried curtailing her fun too early, she might fling herself at my legs, snapping her teeth in crazed toy terrier fashion. I'd be forced to retreat to the house empty-handed, convinced that George Howell's thick leather gloves weren't such a bad idea.

"She misses running wild," Linda insisted. "Can't we just let her run loose in the backyard? The yard's fenced in."

"It's considered fenced in for anything larger than a beagle," I told her. "But Bertha would be out of there in a second. She could slip through the wires anywhere without even mussing a whisker."

"Couldn't you reinforce the fence somehow? Put in chicken wire along the bottom?"

"All around the yard?" I gasped. Our backyard was a healthy fifty feet deep and eighty feet wide. "Do you have any idea how much work that would be? That's absolutely not going to happen," I told her, ignorant that the chuckling gods had already ordained exactly this to happen.

The third week of spring, just three months after George had brought Bertha to our door, her appetite suddenly took a dive. As Linda and I sat at the breakfast table wondering what the problem was, we watched Bertha groom herself in front of the refrigerator. Each time she tried to rise on her haunches with her front legs off the floor, she lost her balance and nearly toppled over. We whisked Bertha to see Dr. Colby the next day. Dr. Colby determined that during her life outdoors in the Howell's neighborhood, Bertha had picked up a nasty parasite that was blooming in her bloodstream and making her too sick to eat. He gave her a shot of parasite killer plus a vitamin injection to perk her up. Within a few days she seemed back to her old self.

A month later, however, she stopped eating again. Her balance problems worsened. During dinner, Linda liked to reach down from her chair with a piece of the ubiquitous bread-machine toast that all of our animals loved except the cat. Bertha would stand on her tiptoes to reach a piece. Trying to rekindle her appetite, Linda tempted Bertha to her side with the morsel, but any attempts to reach the toast sent the rabbit crashing over backward. At the vet's the following day, Dr. Colby told us that the parasite had a thirty-day breeding cycle. A second injection should eradicate the little buggers for good. But she passed along the bad news that the accompanying digestive problems had allowed a buildup of toxins in Bertha's body, causing irreversible nerve damage.

"Rabbits' digestive systems are extremely sensitive," she explained. "If you make a sudden change in a rabbit's diet, or if a rabbit goes too long without eating, toxins that are normally expelled with the feces get into their systems." She told us it was imperative that, if anything like this ever happened to Bertha again, we should keep her eating by whatever means possible.

We saw Dr. Colby again the following month when Bertha's symptoms recurred. A month later when another bout made her even weaker, she told us that nothing further could be done. She had researched Bertha's condition. She had even consulted with experts at the Michigan State University School of Veterinary Medicine, and they had offered no solution.

We took her at her word and resigned ourselves to keeping Bertha as happy as possible no matter what the outcome. I combed our yard for tender dandelion leaves every afternoon and evening and coaxed her into eating these. Because she was occasionally too weak to chew the pelleted food she needed, we soaked her rabbit Purina in water or pineapple juice until it attained an oatmealish consistency. Shoving this under her nose several times a day, we erupted in delighted cries of encouragement whenever she took a mouthful. I don't know much about the alien psyche of rabbits, but I'm convinced that she ate the mush for our sake as much as hers.

By the end of the summer, she had lost so much strength that we were feeding her from a syringe. Even then, she seemed to enjoy life too much for us to take it away from her, stretching out in the sunlight in her pen and rolling delightedly on the ground. When I'd pick her up to carry her back into the house, she would give my hand a grateful lick instead of fighting me as before. A new round of nerve damage left her listing to one side like a cargo ship that had made too many transatlantic passages. Because she was no longer able to travel in a straight line and couldn't slip away through the backyard fence, we finally gave her the chance to run free. As soon as I set her down in the warm grass, she took off in a long, smooth curve that eventually brought her right back to our feet. "We should change her name to Boomerang," I joked.

One Saturday morning, when Linda was out of town and Bertha could barely sit up anymore, I took her to a vet down the road and had her put to sleep as I held her. Back at home I carried her around the yard until I found a pleasant spot beneath a large pine tree to bury her. A number of times in the ensuing weeks, I was sure I saw her ghost cantering through our living room or sitting on the upstairs steps.

I can think of no other circumstances where we develop such closeness with our animals as when we see them through serious illness. Linda's attentiveness always put mine to shame. Each time Bertha had experienced a setback, I'd be so demoralized, I could hardly bear to be in the same room with the bunny. But Linda plugged away with a resolute cheeriness that helped me keep going. After Bertha died, my initial sense of relief shifted to a thick gloom. As sorry as I was about losing the bunny, I was sorrier for myself. I grew expert at sitting stonily on the edge of the bed in half-darkness or lying sprawled on the couch with an arm cocked over my eyes. Motivating myself to simply move my brooding to another room required the gathering up of vast internal forces. Strangely, I was in pretty fair spirits at the office. The environment was different, the tasks were clearly defined, and attendance was imperative in order to keep the paychecks flowing. That meant I wasn't as far gone as I acted at home, but still bad enough that I woke up shaking most mornings.

We were having dinner at our friend Claudia's house one evening. Linda was praising the baked vegetables while I slumped in my chair next to the vegetable tureen. Claudia convinced me to make an appointment with a psychiatrist to try Zoloft, which she had just begun taking with good results. "It will make an enormous change in your life," she insisted. "I heard about this old guy at a nursing home, he was one of these downtrodden guys people love to run over, and Zoloft worked wonders for that little man." I considered this all the endorsement I needed.

DR. GLASER CAME close to proving the old saw that psychiatrists have more neuroses than the neurotics they treat. Tall, stiff with unease at being human, and wearing the demeanor of a fussy choral-group leader, along with a mustard-colored suit, he drifted into the waiting room and introduced himself. When I offered him my hand, he took it as reluctantly as if I had presented him with a halibut. Inside a charmless office that might have belonged to a loan officer, I gave him a detailed description of my bedspread concealment during Stanley's sickness, prolonged sadness at Bertha's passing, bouts of chair-gripping nervousness at breakfast, and panic attacks dating back to the Ford administration. "I just finished reading *Listening to Prozac*," I said, "and it sounds like I'm living in what the author calls 'the penumbra of depression.' I would like to try an antianxiety drug and see if it helps."

"A parrot?" he inquired, after my outpouring had ended. "Was it a real parrot?" he asked in a tone of voice usually reserved for dealing with dangerous individuals. Immediately I understood the folly of choosing a mental health professional from the Yellow Pages based solely on proximity to home.

"Yes, it was a real parrot. An African grey parrot." I answered. "Named Stanley Sue," I heedlessly added, though he ignored this last ripe piece of Freudian fruit.

"Which antianxiety medication would you like to try?"

"I've heard good things about Zoloft," I ventured, amazed that getting brain chemistry–altering prescription drugs should be this effortless. I had anticipated the kind of resistance my physician had mustered when I had asked him about serotonin drugs. Instead of writing me a prescription, he had suggested I take up racquetball instead.

"Zoloft is an antianxiety drug," Dr. Glaser agreed, "and the side effects are minimal. What dosage would you like to try?"

"What would you recommend?" I asked, uncertain how my advice on this point could matter.

"The lowest clinical dosage is fifty milligrams. Would you like to start out on one hundred milligrams?" His faint smile conveyed a measure of genuine pleasure.

"You're the doctor," I rejoined weakly.

"I'll have to ask you a few questions first." He paused before cracking open his laptop. "Will the computer bother you? Some people don't like the computer."

"The computer doesn't bother me."

"If you're sure." On the Formica-topped desk behind him sat a second computer with a full-size monitor displaying the screen saver Johnny Castaway. The cartoon depicted the misadventures of a luckless soul marooned on a desert island, which struck me as a bad choice for a psychiatrist's office. Reading from a file on his laptop, Dr. Glaser took me through a series of questions concerning my medical history, upbringing, education, and propensity for suicide. At the conclusion of each question, he looked me squarely in the middle of my forehead. I was unsure whether he had a vision problem or was as adverse to ocular intimacy with his patients as he was to shaking hands. Lowering his head as if embarrassed by this aspect of his profession, he delivered the last queries in a monotone. "Do people follow you? Do you hear voices? Do people plot against you?" He spoke so quietly, he might have been talking to himself. I wanted to truthfully answer "sometimes" to each of these poorly worded questions in order to score semantic points, but decided it was better to tell him no and make a fast escape from the island.

Four days later, I experienced my first Zoloft jolt. Poised on the living room couch with a half-hour to go until *Wheel of Fortune,* I was enveloped by an energized calm. The world and my outlook on the world became suffused with light. "It's as if I've had this cotton in my head for all these years, and now it's fallen out," I explained to Linda, who smiled warily in response. Anxious to share my newly acquired Buddha nature, I strode upstairs and petted Penny. Neither of us exchanged a word, but as I stared at her, I received a revelation. I suddenly saw her as a being. Not as a pet or an underling, but as a complex personality. On the one hand, her face and eyes revealed the same trapped intensity as a human soul stuck in a physical body, but on the other hand her depth far exceeded any anthropomorphizing I might throw at her. She was limitless and unknowable, and I was honored to have her as my friend. Then I changed her litter and floated back downstairs.

The next day, my mood was even brighter. Under a spell of unusual ambitiousness, I devoted my Saturday to long neglected tasks around the house rather than glumly avoiding work per my usual weekend schedule. I carted animal cages outdoors and washed them to a shine with a high-pressure hose nozzle. I revved up the gasoline-powered trimmer and decimated an army of weeds between the side yard and the barn. The evergreen tree under which we'd buried Bertha had succumbed to an unknown blight, and Linda had repeatedly encouraged me to hire a man to chop it down. Now, wielding my chain saw for only the sixth time since I had purchased it and somehow mastering my timidity at its ability to maim, I lopped down the tree, cut the trunk and branches into matchsticks, and scattered them to the winds beyond our fence. Toppling the evergreen revealed a three-foot-high redbud tree standing almost on top of Bertha's grave. Neither of us had ever seen the tree before.

"It's a gift from God," said Linda.

The Zoloft, as it turned out, was not. As the day progressed, I burned too intensely with energy that was not my own, a 110-volt bulb spliced into a 220-volt line. By Sunday, my nerves were acting up. By Monday, I was a blubbering wreck barely able to quiver into the office. En route to an out-of-town relative's house the following Saturday, I vaulted out of the car and collapsed wailing on the grass next to a freeway mileage marker. A call to my psychiatrist brought a surprisingly lighthearted response. "You might want to play with your dosage a little bit. Try cutting it in half."

The half dosage turned out to be just the half ticket I needed to feel half human again. Events like eating an egg at breakfast felt substantially less threatening, and I could actually make it through an entire morning sitting at my desk at work for periods of up fifteen minutes at a continuous stretch. While I couldn't claim to have achieved the meditative state of mind I had hoped pharmaceuticals might bestow upon me, neither was I any longer a teakettle on rolling boil. I happily made due with simmer.

Things could have been a lot worse. I could have been a duck. A phone call from my sister, Joan, brought the news that her husband, Jack, had rescued a Muscovy duck from the parking lot of the automotive-parts business where he maintained the inventory database. The escaped domestic animal had blundered onto the property to search beneath a Dumpster for tidbits from employee lunches. Jack's coworkers welcomed the hungry visitor with a mirthful stone-throwing contest until Jack eased the competition to a halt. Flinging a jacket over the bird, he caught her easily, stashing her in his truck until quitting time.

Stretching our kitchen phone cord to the limit, Linda relayed Joan's description on a sentence-by-sentence basis of how they had managed to obtain the duck, while I sat in the bedroom, eyes foolishly brushing the same two sentences of a mystery novel. "Now they don't know what to do with the poor thing," Linda reported. "They would love to keep the duck, but they don't have anywhere to put her," she relayed. "She wants to know if we could possibly take her." She pointed the handset at me from the doorway to the living room. "Here, talk to your sister."

I waved off the phone in surrender. "Okay."

"Don't we have room for a duck?" Linda urged, certain she had misunderstood my answer. She tightened the phone cord even more to move a step into the bedroom, giving new meaning to the concept of a telephone extension.

"I'm perfectly happy to take the duck," I assured her. At that moment, a lifetime with a duck seemed a small price to pay for avoiding her otherwise inescapable argument that a duck wouldn't be any trouble at all. Having heard that line of reasoning speciously applied to a rabbit and a parrot, I never wanted to hear it again. Anyway, two factors stood in the duck's corner. First, we owned a barn large enough to house a family of duck-billed dinosaurs. And the barn was situated far enough from the house that with luck I would have little involvement in the duck's upbringing, maintenance, and walks at the end of a leash. Second, we had visited a farmer who extolled the quiet voices of his female Muscovies. According to him, they made a gentle rasping sound inaudible at fifty feet.

"We can take her?" asked Linda delightedly, when she understood that I had caved in. "He said we can take her," Linda told my sister. "Oh, I've always wanted to have a duck." Averting her face from the phone, she passed along the news to me. "I've always wanted a duck."

It had been just after dinner when Joan called, but in the inky recesses of the barn it seemed closer to midnight. Instead of expecting a duck to settle into such gloomy accommodations, we cordoned off the workroom from the rest of the basement with a plastic kitchen gate that Binky had once chewed through, establishing an equally gloomy area for the Muscovy that was at least inside the house. Linda spread two weeks' worth of newspapers on the floor while I studied a wall bristling with six hand tools that had so far seen employment only in pen- and fence-building projects. I had hoped I'd never have to pick them up again, but I now experienced a twinge of foreboding.

Wearing a buckskin fringed jacket, Joan swept in with a beer in one hand and a large pet carrier in the other—a much larger pet carrier than I had anticipated.

"Didn't you say, 'a poor little duck?'" I asked her. She dismissed me with the joyful laugh of an older sister not only relieving herself of a burden, but also putting that burden onto her brother.

"Let's see her!" Linda cried.

"Come on out, duck," commanded Joan, setting the carrier on the workroom floor and stepping back behind us to enjoy the fun.

"I think the duck needs room," I explained as an excuse to step behind Joan. A serpentlike neck capped with a salt-and-pepper head emerged from the open door. As the Muscovy regarded us, a crest of sparse feathers atop her skull shot up like a quiver of arrows. As I regarded the Muscovy, I was morbidly transfixed by a fleshy red mask that extended from the base of her upper beak to encircle both wild eyes. She drew herself out of the carrier, raising her head to its normal height, doubling her dimensions to my expectations. This was a formidable duck. Populations of escaped Muscovies have established themselves in parks across America and in the Falcon Dam region of Texas, prompting an entry in *Peterson's Field Guide to Eastern Birds*, which calls the species, "a clumsy, black, goose-like duck." The *National Geographic Field Guide to the Birds of North America* describes the Muscovy as "bulky." Our duck was twice as large as a female Mallard and far more massive from her chest to the flat, wide tail that wiggled nervously as her head tilted and swiveled to appraise us from various directions.

"Hah!" laughed my sister. "That's one grateful-looking duck."

"She looks annoyed to me," I answered, calculating the height of the plastic gate behind me in relation to the angle of my tensed body.

If the staff at *National Geographic* was correct about the "bulky" epithet, Roger Tory Peterson was even more on the mark with the "clumsy." Fearlessly approaching the duck, Linda set out a ceramic soup bowl of water. Then, in charming innocence, I watched her scoop out and into another bowl a mixture of cracked corn and grains—known as scratch feed—from the first bag of hundreds and hundreds of bags I was destined to eventually lug into the basement. She set the bowl on the floor next to the water. Rather than scarf up the food as expected, the duck ran underneath the wooden workbench, turned around, ran through the bowls of food and water, knocking them over, and hid in an especially dark area beneath the aluminum workbench. Linda dutifully cleaned up the scattered grain, spread another week's worth of newspapers on top of the spilled water, and replaced the cereal bowls with more substantial, less unstable plastic buckets.

Before bedtime, the two of us crept downstairs to dowse the lights, only to find the Muscovy dunking her head in the water, splashing the room and ruining a second helping of scratch feed.

"We'll have to buy a pool for the barn," Linda announced.

"A pool?"

"A plastic wading pool. I saw some up at the dime store."

"They've got them at the hardware store, too. Half price. End of summer sale."

Linda shook her head. "Those are with the stupid Ninja Turtle patterns. I don't like the way they look."

THE NEXT MORNING, I volunteered to carry the Muscovy, which Linda had named Daphne, to the barn while Linda cleaned up the disaster area that had formerly been our workroom.

"Be careful," she cautioned me, when I bent over to pick up the duck.

"Do you think she'll bite?"

"It's her wings you need to be careful of," she warned, relating the story of how a goose had almost knocked her out with a pinion to the jaw years ago.

I encircled the duck with both arms, clutching her tightly to my chest, but aside from managing a couple of energy bursts that gave me an indication of her strength, she didn't put up a struggle. Once

I was inside the barn, the thought struck me that I was actually using the building for its intended purpose. Previously I had viewed the barn the same way a visitor to Italy might view the ruins of Pompeii—as a relic of a lost way of life. Surveying the architecture of cow stanchions and smaller pens had never failed to fill me with a grateful superiority to the agrarian beings who had come before me. Now I was one of them.

When I followed Linda back to the barn later that afternoon, we were surprised to find Daphne perched on top of a wooden stanchion four feet off the ground. "My chickens used to roost in trees every night," Linda told me, adding to my storehouse of information I could never use. As she spun the plastic pool into the duck's part of the barn, I attached a hose to an all-season hydrant that had waited its entire life near the middle door of the barn for this very moment. The duck watched with disinterest as we filled the blandly blue non–Ninja Turtle pool, then flapped heavily to the cement floor when I wandered over to check the progress of the water. Linda's gleeful smile faded as the moments ticked by without the portable pond attracting Daphne. Linda opened the waist-high gate to urge the duck to take to water, but almost instantly this act evolved into Linda's chasing the duck around the pen and in and out of the pool. Of the gallons of water displaced by Daphne's plunges, the majority was absorbed by Linda's aqua dress.

"At least she knows where the pool is now," I pointed out.

A couple of hours later, we checked on the duck again. The floor was dry, the pool unused, her food uneaten. "She's not happy in here," Linda decided. "She needs an outdoor pen."

I didn't like the way this was going at all. "We'll let her run around the backyard during the day and put her in the barn at night."

"Who's going to catch her and carry her back and forth?" That gave me pause. "And what if a dog got in our yard during the day? A large dog like a German shepherd dog could jump right over our fence and kill her."

Other than the dogless family that lived behind us on the river, our nearest neighbor was almost a mile away. "And where might this German shepherd dog come from?"

"We can use Binky's old pen. We'll hire a handyman to fix it up. Unless you want to do it yourself," she added.

"A handyman," I sputtered in thickening despair, envisioning an otherwise unemployable eccentric with a prison record and hair sprouting from his ears.

In the main, my fears seemed to ring true. After Linda placed an ad in the local shopping newspaper, we were deluged with disconcerting phone calls. A gravelly voiced man wanted to know the name of our business and what kind of benefits we offered. A fellow who was friendly with the bottle wondered if we could offer him night work. Three people were confused as to why they had called our number, two were abusive when I explained we wanted a duck pen, and another phoned to hone his English-language skills. Anyone remotely qualified wouldn't touch a job so small. "Let me see that ad," I demanded, convinced that Linda must have written a wildly misleading description of a Mackinaw Bridge–scale project, but her prose was on the nose. Just as we were giving up, a chipper and plain-spoken fellow named Dell asked to come over and look at the job, surprised us by showing up, and then shocked us by quoting a reasonable price.

I learned fast to stay out of Dell's way. It wasn't that his attitude was unfriendly. He spoke to me with a pleasant singsong delivery I accepted as his natural voice until I heard him engaged in clipped dialogue with his son. An ex-missionary in his early sixties who had spent years among the Yanomami people in Venezuela, Dell had seen a little of everything in life, but nothing as ridiculous as this fish-out-of-water city boy and his duck-pampering wife. "Sure, we can fix it so that the snow won't pile up on top of the pen and cause it to collapse," he responded exuberantly. "Of course, we wouldn't expect too much snow to accumulate on top of a wire-mesh roof, now would we, Bob?" His excessively affable tone suggested that he was talking to an idiot for whom everything had to be clearly laid out in the most positive terms possible. "Can we put a latch on the door?" he exclaimed so forcefully on another occasion, mocking a question I had asked, that I took a startled step backward, nearly knocking down the fencing he had tentatively tacked in place. "Sure, we'll put a latch on her. You bet we'll do that, Bob. But how about if we wait until we put the door up first?"

Once the door was hung, in a mistaken attempt to ingratiate myself, I complimented him on how well it fit. "That's fantastic," I simpered. "You can hardly see a sliver of daylight between the door and the frame when the door is closed."

"Cut it out, Bob," he growled, with only a trace of a smile.

Though Dell and I stood on opposite sides of the personality fence, he got along famously with Linda, apparently recognizing a fellow generous-hearted soul who was forced to put up with me. He complimented her on the morning glories climbing the side of our house in the brisk fall weather. He talked effusively about his family, joked about retiring to a warmer climate, and told stories about his missionary days in South America. Even after his tools were neatly put away and his son waited silently in the truck, Dell stood chatting with Linda in front of our open basement door, never once answering a question with a quip like, "Where does this kind of wood come from? I don't know, Bob. I think it comes from a tree."

Some of Linda's success with Dell came from a natural-born

ability to talk that she had honed to a fine sheen through unflagging exercise. She would talk to anyone anywhere, as I learned early in our relationship. On a trip through Michigan's "thumb region," we visited the Lake Huron town of Grindstone City, which in the early 1900s had been a bustling millstone-manufacturing center. A friend of mine had enticed me there with a surreal photograph of a beach littered with massive defective grindstones dumped at the last minute while being loaded on a ship. "The whole town is like that," he had insisted. "You'll see grindstones everywhere," but we saw none at all. Nonplussed, Linda marched to the door of the first house she saw. Five minutes later we were sitting on a porch swing poring over a Grindstone City scrapbook with an elderly woman as loquacious as my wife.

But that was merely a warm-up. Years later on a bird-watching jaunt to Ontario's Point Pelee National Park, we overnighted in the tomato-producing town of Leamington. Deciding to take a walk after dinner, we trundled down a one-block street in back of our motel. The outing was uneventful until Linda noticed a woman tending a garden. A full half hour later, we broke free of her backyard pond and ceramic frog collection only to encounter another woman with a hose and a patch of flowers. Two doors down and twenty minutes later, a young couple en route to their house from their station wagon was waylaid by my wife. Finally, with most of the block still stretching before us, I told Linda, "I'm sure several families have called the police by now to tell them about the suspicious characters casing their neighborhood." Though our Canadian vacation had included visits to spectacular waterfalls, charming zoos, a historic basilica, and a whale-watching cruise, Linda would refer to the Leamington walk as "almost the best part of the trip."

Three days after starting the job, Dell closed his toolbox for the last time, and I shamed myself by studying Daphne's new home. I had originally based Binky's pen around the leftover structure of a rectangular play area and sandbox. To transform the cozy rabbit pen into a raccoon-proof villa for Daphne, Dell had merely planted a few posts in the ground to extend the walls toward our back fence, covered the sides and top with wire, and added a wooden door. Even with my nonexistent construction skills, I should have been able to do the same. Little did I realize that our duck population was destined to outgrow the pen.

Once we transferred her from the gloomy interior of the barn to the fresh air and hazy sunshine of her pen, Daphne was a changed duck. She showed her appreciation by consuming great quantities of the scratch feed she had previously ignored. But the swimming pool went untouched. Neophytes to waterfowl, we didn't know that Muscovies shared neither water pool nor gene pool with American domestic ducks that trace their roots to the common mallard. Unlike the Mallard derivatives, whose lives revolve around the pond, the tropical-born, marsh-dwelling Muscovies have comparatively underdeveloped oil glands and aren't very waterproof. Consequently, they are poorly adapted to swimming. Because we were ignorant of these facts, Daphne's failure to take advantage of the local pool facilities struck Linda as a wrong that demanded righting, a failure of nurturing whose blame we had inherited.

"She needs a little friend to show her how to swim," Linda told me.

"You showed her pretty well a couple of days ago."

"Ducks are very social. They aren't happy by themselves."

"Then," I heard myself tell my wife as if through another person's ears, "we'd better get her another duck." In truth, I couldn't think of a single reason not to. Having already bought the proposition that one duck was no trouble at all to keep, no trouble times two still equaled zero bother. How could it be otherwise? The ducks would live outdoors rather than gnaw at our woodwork, eat when stirred by hunger rather than dominate our meals, and wander our yard unsupervised rather than require complicated, coordinated periods of freedom.

With ruthless efficiency, Linda located a source for a companion duck in the person of a farmer a few miles north with the remarkable name of Rupert Murdoch. On the evidence, I decided that he probably wasn't the infamous media mogul. Though his house was in no worse shape than ours and of similar vintage, the matchstick barn barely hung together, and the denuded yard of hard-packed mud boasted indescribable clutter. Duck pens claimed the area, but these were nothing like the roomy, open-air living quarters that delighted Daphne. The two dozen or so wooden-sided, side-by-side, four-by-six-foot pens each contained a flock of ducks or a gaggle of geese of heretofore undreamed of breeds. "That's a black and white Cayuga," the elderly Rupert Murdoch drawled, elongating the word "Cayuga" into poetry at odds with the squalor. "That one's a Blue Swede," though it appeared neither blue nor Swedish.

If the varieties of waterfowl were bewildering, the range of chickens wandering free-range or cooped up in the disconcertingly backward-leaning barn truly boggled the mind. We witnessed chickens whose feathers curled up like chrysanthemum petals, chickens with pom-poms on their feet, chickens with bald heads and necks, mouse-size chickens, mastiff-size chickens, and chickens whose complex color patterns turned them into optical illusions with beaks. A flock of what he termed "fancy pigeons" with feathered britches in place of naked legs scattered as he took us to the back of the barn to show us an inch-long, vitamin capsule–shaped white object. "Do you know what some fellows call these?" he asked us.

"I wouldn't know what to call it," I admitted.

"Some fellows call them rooster eggs. But they've never seen a rooster lay one."

"What is it?"

"It's an egg. But roosters don't lay any kinds of eggs," he explained with a wise grin.

After viewing various turkeys, pheasants, guinea fowl, grouse, and goats, and after stooping to pet a couple of barn cats and an old dog in a bandana, we followed Rupert Murdoch back to the duck ghetto. While Linda decided which duck to take home, I mentally recounted the plot of every episode of *Hogan's Heroes* I could remember and was almost through the series run of *The Prisoner* when she finally picked out a female black and white Cayuga. "She's a show duck," the farmer warned us. "Costs a little more than your White Pekins or Khaki Campbells."

"She would have to," I agreed, unsure what either of those animals were but bracing for a bite to the wallet. The cheapest parrot, after all, wore a two-hundred-dollar price tag, cockatiels flew as high as one hundred dollars, and hand-raised parakeets at Jonah's Ark commanded eighty dollars.

"Have to charge you ten dollars," he insisted.

Using a long-handled net from a catfish farm, Rupert Murdoch dipped into the Cayuga pen, cornered the female, and with a twist of an arm, scooped her up. "You don't want her flying nowhere," he stated. When we nodded our agreement, he deftly plucked five primary flight feathers from her right wing. The duck never even flinched. "That will keep her on the ground." As I helped him put the Cayuga in a cardboard box and tape it—this seemed to be the preferred method of transporting birds of every ilk—Linda shouted to me, "Sweetheart, come quick and see a little white bathtub duck."

"That's what you call a call duck," Rupert told us.

"Another of your show ducks?" I asked.

He nodded. "It's all the bigger they get." I felt the pressure of

Linda's eyes. I shrugged. I nodded. The farmer netted a fourteen-inch-tall pure white duck with an orange beak and orange feet, and popped her in another box. If I knew how to whistle, I might have. No anxiety gnawed at me. We had a spacious pen capable of easily absorbing all three birds. We had a large fenced-in yard. We had a big bag of scratch feed. I had finally adjusted to my Zoloft dosage. Calmer and less crabby than I had been for years, I had nary a care in the world. Everything seemed, well . . . everything seemed just ducky.

CHAPTER 6

A Wild Duck Chase

A ren't your ducks supposed to be in the yard?" Shirley piped up, as Linda slid falafel patties onto our plates.

"They're probably behind the spirea bush sticking their beaks in decayed leaves," I said, attempting to infuse even these odd words with a sense of welcoming.

A bowl bisected by an oversize spoon crashed into a crock of mashed potatoes. "This is a cucumber dressing," Linda explained.

"Should we avert our eyes?"

Shirley stopped squinting out the windows and slid back into her chair. Her light skin and short curled hair were almost exactly the same shade of beige, and I kept losing track of her eyebrows as she talked. "You wouldn't believe the people that come into my flower shop and have no idea how much work goes into flowers," she was telling Linda.

"They must think they grow on trees," I quipped.

"They expect to get them for free."

"For free?" Linda shouted. "They want them for free?"

She didn't really own a flower shop. It was actually a flower re-frigerator, and the refrigerator didn't even belong to her. The owner of a produce store in Hubbs had subcontracted Shirley to keep a cooler in his store stocked with cut flowers in an attempt to win some customers. The business wasn't doing well, but no new busi-ness did well in our area. If a restaurant or store managed to hang on for a couple of years through sheer force of will, the locals might begin trickling in. Our own front-porch pottery shop, designated by a sign in the front yard as Pink Pig Pottery, attracted about six visitors a month, and most of these balked at the eight-dollar price tag on our hand-thrown, one-of-a-kind, never-to-be-duplicated coffee mugs and off-center bowls.

"Those are some of your flowers in a vase Bob made."

Sharing centerpiece duties with a heaped dish of rice, a vaguely bottle-shaped vessel surprisingly thick and heavy for its size sup-ported a graceful trio of lavender Peruvian lilies. Linda had bought the flowers from Shirley partly as a means of getting acquainted. She was drawn to Shirley's enthusiasm for gardening along with her professed love of "talking about the Lord." Excited that she had finally made her first Lowell friend, Linda had asked the flower-refrigerator lady over for lunch. But Shirley, we learned, wasn't a lo-cal at all. She commuted forty-five miles from a village near Lansing, where her husband worked in a butter factory. And rather than be-ing a source of joy, as Linda's Christian zeal was, Shirley's religious faith was bitter solace for a spouse whom she suspected was cheat-ing on her, a daughter who belonged to a New Age cult, a trailer that suffered from mice in the walls, and people who didn't appre-ciate the value of her flowers.

"One of these days, I'm going into their yards and start helping myself to their roses, and if they say anything, I'll just go, 'Well, you told me in the store they're not really worth anything.'"

"Oh, my gosh," exclaimed Linda. "You really wouldn't do that, would you? You really wouldn't pick someone else's flowers."

Shirley swiveled to face the parrot's cage. "Stanley wouldn't act like that," she declared in a little girl voice. "Stanley's too nice a boy to pick on me."

"Careful," I admonished, as her fingers strayed perilously close to the bars of Stanley Sue's cage. "She's not what you'd call a people bird. She will definitely bite you if she gets the chance." I emphasized Stanley Sue's correct gender along with the warning.

"Not a nice boy like Stanley. He wouldn't do a thing like that."

"She would."

Shirley began expounding on her family problems, and my mind naturally migrated to my own misfortunes.

A bad winter even by Michigan measure had tossed cold water on our assumptions that keeping ducks would be a cinch. Daily chores kicked off each morning with our bundling up from head to toe, trudging across an arctic landscape, and struggling to get inside the duck pen. Since the frozen outdoor spigot on the back of the house was unusable, we were forced to drag a long hose down the hill from the leaky laundry sink inside the basement. By midwinter, the backyard snowpack had compacted to a treacherous glaze, and we took to strapping metal cleats designed for ice fisherman onto our boots. Snow and slush from the previous day delighted in hardening overnight and blocking the pen's wooden door. Tired of chipping at the ground with a shovel, I twice raised the bottom of the door by hacking off the planks, but I still had to shovel, sweep, and chip to free it most days. Once inside the pen, changing the water in the plastic wading pool involved first breaking up the half-inch-thick surface ice and sloshing out the chunks with a push broom. Liberating the largest icebergs meant plung-

ing our hands in the pool and wresting them out, ending up with
soaked arms and with bodies chilled to the nubbins.

I hated the exertion. The frigid temperatures depleted my tiny
energy reserves, but they didn't daunt the ducks, who merrily took
to the pool even when the television weatherman gloated that the
thermometer had bottomed out below zero. In the throes of a
howling blizzard, as Linda and I stood shivering, wrapped in blankets as the furnace labored to keep up, we would peer outside
through the blowing snow to find all three ducks trolling in the water. Taking to a pool in icicle weather baffled me until I realized that
the coldest water was still tens of degrees warmer than the ground
and air temperatures. The swimming pool was a kind of low-grade
sauna. Even the hydrophobic Daphne splashed around with enthusiasm. But because of her underpowered oil gland, her belly
feathers accumulated ice crystals that could grow to Christmas tree
ornament size by night. "Do you know where the blow-dryer
went?" Linda would ask me. "I have to defrost Daphne again."

Spring came as a great relief, but not immediately. Throughout
winter, we had scattered straw on the pen floor to insulate the
ducks from the ground. When the straw-and-ice sandwich melted,
the accumulated droppings and spilled food grew redolent in the
sun. I had never regarded straw in any quantity as a material of
consequence. Even a bale the size of a file cabinet was easy to lug
one-handed across the yard. But an armload of this soggy, com-
pressed, waste-laden mulch was staggeringly cumbersome for the
weak of frame such as myself. Transforming the smelly pen-floor
burden from a biohazard to potential compost necessitated my
wading deep into the pit of rural life by wielding an actual pitch-
fork. Added to this was the indignity of donning rubber work
gloves and hitching myself to the back end of a wheelbarrow that

I had always sniffily regarded as a useless curio. I carted countless loads from the pen to the back fence, holding my breath as I pitched the fetid debris into our field. Afterward, I lay panting as Linda effortlessly brought the ducks a brand-new layer of light and airy fresh straw bedding.

Simple drudgery followed, as the season matured. Although I avoided duck duties weekday mornings by dint of a freelance job away from home, when I returned in the afternoon, I couldn't escape Phoebe's continual clamor to be let out of the pen. Muscovy Daphne emitted little noise. Tiny white call duck Peggy quacked an agreeable whispery purr. But black and white Cayuga Phoebe unleashed an atmosphere-cleaving series of complaints. Like Ollie, she was unrelenting. We began to give the trio the run of the yard as soon as either Linda or I pulled into the driveway. We would leave them out for hours, rarely glancing in their direction, reasoning that farmers like Rupert Murdoch gave their ducks, geese, chickens, goats, and pigs free run from morning to dusk. And we had the advantage of having a fence around our yard that would keep our ducks from straying.

"Aren't those your ducks just beyond the fence?" Shirley asked, once Linda had finished a lengthy grace that blessed our food, each of our animals, and the majority of our living relatives by name.

I was out the side door on Linda's heels before my napkin could hit the linoleum. At the bottom of the hill, Daphne paced back and forth on the correct side of our fence only because she was too fat to wriggle through and join the two escapees. Peggy and Phoebe flickered in and out of sight amid a tangle of wild black raspberry bushes. As I flopped over the fence, Linda galloped across the grass and yanked open a crude metal gate on the far side of the yard. "Try to herd them this way, I'll shoo them back in," she hollered. At the

top of the cement steps one stride outside the kitchen, Shirley towered with her arms crossed high on her chest. She was chewing and
held a fork in her fist.

Shielding my face, I plunged through stubborn foliage that mustered the full strength of its xylem and phloem to resist my passage.
Flashes of white and black feathers ahead of me indicated that the
ducks were racing forward alongside the fence. I took this as a
hopeful indication that they were searching for a passage back inside the yard, preferring their plastic pool to the seasonal pond that
glittered in a greening vista between our backyard and the river.
Urging the ducks eastward as plant life stung my skin, I fought to
keep my feet in view to avoid a tumble down the boulder-strewn
slope. Unhampered by height, the ducks moved nimbly through
narrow openings at ground level below a maddening thicket of
whips and razor wire masquerading as branches.

I broke through the bushes, catching sight of Linda seconds after the ducks had noticed her. She had hoped to get below them on
the hill and turn them toward the open gate, but wife and waterfowl intersected at the edge of the woods just beyond our property.
Linda made a leap for Phoebe, barely missing her. I chased the
ducks through the trees, unable to catch up until Phoebe changed
direction and headed due south for the water.

Born of virile late-spring rains, the pond was no less than fifty
feet wide and seductive in its sheltered calm. Its length stretched
an unknowable distance east through tracts of trees that guarded
a boundary of leg-enveloping muck. If the ducks reached the water, we would have no chance whatsoever of retrieving them. Fortunately, the truants paused long enough to contemplate the
majesty of the pond for me to stumble down the slope and cut
them off. Wildly waving my arms, I sent them zigzagging back toward Linda. This time a flying tackle successfully nabbed Peggy.

"Put her back in the pen," Linda panted, thrusting the football-size duck into my hands. "I'll get Phoebe." I saw great wisdom in this. My fear of self-injury put me in an altogether different class than my self-sacrificing spouse. Plus, my long hours sitting in chairs were poor preparation for tearing willy-nilly through the scrub, and I was quickly running out of steam.

At the open gate I met Daphne, poised to start her own wilderness excursion. She ambled back to the duck house a few steps ahead of me. I dumped a complaining Peggy in the straw, latched the pen door, and walked toward the gate, expecting Linda with Phoebe. Instead, I heard a call whose plaintiveness rivaled the horn of a distant freight train.

"Phoebe! Phoebe!"

I joined my wife in the woods. She had come within an arm's length of the escapee when a log had intervened. The nearly flightless duck had sailed over the obstruction, which halted Linda with a blow to her shin.

For the next half hour, we combed the woods, swale, and swamp, snapping our heads toward a suggestive ripple of sunlight in the weeds, an empty Jay's potato chip bag trapped by deadfall, a white Styrofoam cup, the scrabbling of a squirrel, a red-bellied woodpecker spiraling up a tree, a headless doll, and the flutter of chickadees unhappy with our intrusion. We wandered as far as an unfordable stream splicing the Grand River to our pond. Changing direction, we trudged back a half mile until the pond petered out at the neighbor's raised dirt driveway. Flip-flopping, we fanned eastward again. We shouted pointlessly for Phoebe, singing out the name of a duck who had never responded to anything but food, the wading pool, and the company of other ducks. "She's always wanted a husband," Linda announced, as we broke through to the busy road in front of our property and the billboard promising MCDONALD'S—2 SMILES AHEAD. We turned toward the house. "She wants to have babies," Linda amplified.

"Maybe she'll come home when she's hungry."

I never even considered what poor luncheon hosts we had been until I followed Linda into the kitchen to find Shirley sitting at the table. Several thicknesses of paper towel covered her index finger. A blush of blood stained the surface. "Stanley bit me," she said. "I was just trying to make friends with him."

Waving off our apologies, Shirley politely resumed her meal with us, stayed for coffee, joked about her injury as she tarried on our porch, and never visited us again. We saw nothing further of Phoebe, whose clipped wing prevented her from flying away. Linda swore she glimpsed a black and white duck on the pond two mornings in a row, but the sightings were too distant and fleeting to confirm. Since only mallards and wood ducks included us on their travel itineraries, the visitor might indeed have been Phoebe. Unless she was very lucky, our earthbound duck had little chance of surviving among the raccoons, owls, and foxes that lived in the woods, nor could she easily feed herself. But we liked to imagine she had waddled down to the river and floated with the current toward Lake Michigan, joining welcoming flocks of ducks along the way.

Our sadness at losing Phoebe hit me especially hard. It obliged me to reinforce our backyard fence to prevent continued escapes. That meant spending several hours on my knees fastening a two-foot-high length of chicken wire along the bottom of the fence for its full length. An unskilled male or female could have finished the job in a single afternoon, but my unique approach spanned days. Unrolling a bail of fencing the proper length a few yards ahead of my progress and balancing the bail just right consumed a distressing amount of time. If I didn't unroll the bail far enough, it loved snapping back at me like a spring, or toppling over and jerking the wire from my hands. If I unrolled too much chicken wire, it tangled itself in the wild black raspberries and other revenge-hungry bushes that poked branches at me through the fence. I twisted finger-piercing stubs of bailing wire to the fencing every nine inches or so, staggering them from the top to the bottom of the chicken wire. Not until I was two-thirds finished with the project and my hands were misshapen into bleeding claws did I conceive of wearing work gloves and using pliers to twist the wire.

"Peggy and Daphne are lonely," Linda informed me the Saturday afternoon I had finished the fencing upgrade. I had planned on spending the rest of the day unbending my back, but a car trip loomed instead. "They miss Phoebe. They need a little friend."

We found Rupert Murdoch busily preparing for the first of countless county fairs that spanned the summer around our portion of the state. He waved when he saw us, but his grin wasn't as sustained as on our last visit. "My wife says she's tired of me spending so much time with my animals," he lamented. "She's making me cut back on how many I show this year."

"How many are you taking to the fair?" I asked.

"Way less than normal," he told us sheepishly. "Not more than two hundred chickens and ducks, all tolled."

As Rupert gave Linda an updated tour of his duck pens, and Linda agonized over choosing a new duck, I wrestled with the fact that a septuagenarian with a limp easily outclassed me in terms of strength, energy, and ambition. Judging from his glacial movements, I figured it would take him an entire day to cage two hundred birds and load them on his truck. But at least he would get the whole job done. If working slowly was the key to accomplishing more, I wanted no part of that system. I gauged a successful day not by how many tasks I had finished, but by how much leisure time remained following a minimal show of effort.

"They call that one a Blue Swede," he explained to Linda, when she had picked out a bluish-gray duck with a black hood and white trim. Extending his long-handled net into the small enclosure reserved for Swedes, he chased a half dozen or so birds back and forth until he had cornered the designated duck. Linda told him she wanted the fatter one near the feed trough instead, and he began the culling all over again. The process reminded me of goldfish-buying, when my wife would point out a particular individual in a tank of perhaps a hundred essentially identical carp, and the clerk would risk inserting his upper body in the water in pursuit of exactly the right fish.

As Rupert regrouped, I cast my mental net upon what I later learned was an Indian Runner Duck, an improbably tall and thin bird that resembled a wine bottle with wings. Bustling about its pen with a nervous pitch and stiff vertical posture, one of these, in fact, was nearly my identical twin. I fantasized herding myself around our yard and wondered if, like the salamander in Julio Cortázar's short story "Axolotl," I might identify so closely with the bird that we would exchange psyches. Before I could explain the possibilities to Linda, she had nixed the runner duck on appearance issues.

"Every time I looked at him, I would just feel sorry for him."

"But you married me anyway."

"What are you talking about?"

Rupert lifted up the Blue Swede for Linda's approval. "Now she's what you term a show duck," he warned us, as he popped the bird in the requisite cardboard box. "They come a little more expensive than your White Pekins or Rouens." The fee was exactly what we had paid for the black and white Cayuga, an affordable ten dollars, though the nuisance value of a duck was infinitely greater, of course.

Linda named our putative Scandinavian Martha, "because she looks like a Martha," she said. The Swede got along fine with Daphne and Peggy right out of the box—once the usual formalities of pinning down the newcomer and showing her who was boss were dispensed with. Her temperament pleased us. She was less wild than Phoebe, more accustomed to people, and also every bit as noisy, which spared me the trauma of having to adjust to a quiet environment.

Though Martha was Daphne's equal in terms of size, neither of the two matched Peggy in the feistiness department. The fearless little duck took charge of the flock without so much as submitting to a popular vote. Whenever we let them out of their pen, Peggy invariably took the lead. When it was time to shoo them back inside, she brought up the rear, herding them a few steps in front of me. She was first at the feed trough, eating unmolested while the others indulged their queen. She was first in the pool, too, clouding the freshly changed water by rinsing a small beak that held an impressive cache of backyard mud. While she generously allowed the others to swim alongside her, she might launch a peck at a wing or feathered back as a reminder of her authority. But Peggy didn't merely boss her subjects. She seemed bent on protecting them. If I trespassed into the pen to check their food or change their water, she would insert herself between her flock and me. Then, as I was closing the door behind me, she would dart forward, quacking a hoarse stream of duck invectives as if to prove to Martha and Daphne that she had chased me out. "You're lucky I'm letting you leave in one piece," she seemed to boast.

We were crazy about Peggy, as were most people who laid eyes on her. "How's that little white duck with the bright orange feet?" my sister, Joan, would ask me when we ran into one another at my mom and dad's house. "I've got to see Peggy," Linda's friend Deanne would insist when she came by for a visit.

"One of these days, I'm going to pick you up," I'd warn Peggy, though I never assaulted her pride by carrying out the threat.

"Let's get a baby call duck and raise it to like being held," Linda suggested.

Rupert Murdoch told us such things were possible. "The more you fool with them, the tamer they get," he counseled Linda on the phone. But he didn't have any call duck ducklings. Or bush baby babies, presumably. Applying herself to the quest with her usual intensity, Linda located a matched pair of them at a business called Dorflinger's, a few miles north of Rupert's farm, between Rockford and Cedar Springs.

"Dorflinger's?" I demanded. "That's a nursery. Not a poultry nursery. It's a greenhouse, isn't it?"

"I stopped in to look at their perennials and got to telling Mrs. Dorflinger we were trying to find a baby call duck, and she said they had a couple in the back."

"Wait, wait. Why would you tell Mrs. Dorflinger we wanted a call duck?"

She regarded me with amazement bordering on pity. "I always talk to people in stores, and that's what we talked about." And it was true. Linda measured the success of any commercial transaction less by whether she received fair goods at a fair price than by the length of time the store personnel spent chatting with her. She discussed the stickier aspects of Paul's Epistle to the Galatians with Eddie, the clerk at the Lowell Blimpie sandwich shop. She knew intimate medical details about most of the cashiers at the Food City supermarket and shared a stack of our Quebec vacation photos with Salvador of Salvador's Pizza. Not long ago, I had been praising a fast-food joint whose gooey cinnamon rolls particularly appealed to me. "I won't even go in there," Linda huffed. "They're not friendly at all. I was telling this one girl about how my windshield wiper fell off when I was driving. It was a very funny story that anyone else would have enjoyed hearing, but she just gave me a mean look like she couldn't be bothered and asked me if I wanted to order anything."

As it turned out, in addition to its advertised business selling flowers and shrubs, Dorflinger's conducted a speakeasy-style side trade in ducks, chickens, and pygmy goats, but only if you were in-the-know enough to ask to see the pens behind the store.

"Come out to the car, sweetie. I've got the two call duck babies in the backseat."

"You bought two of them?"

"Of course, I bought them both. You wouldn't want them to get lonely, would you? And this way, there's one for each of us to fool with."

DECIDING THE DUCKLINGS would benefit from maximum contact with us, we installed them on our enclosed front porch in Bertha-Simon-Binky's old rabbit cage. This arrangement didn't please the fuzzy yellow fussbudgets. Despite a mere six days' experience in the world and ignorance about the essentials of life, they had already formed an unyielding dislike of people in general and duckling-fancying people in particular. Every time a human shadow fell upon them, the pair exploded in a flurry of feathers and peeps, scattering food and water in all directions in a miniature yet intensified version of our initial experience with Daphne.

"They just need to get used to being held," Linda suggested.

"That's what you said about Binky," I reminded her.

Linda was sure that the duck hostility would melt once our loving intentions toward them became clear. We gave it our best shot. Twice a day, we cradled them in our hands and petted them, crooning, "Oh, what nice little ducks you are." Squirming and squeaking when we first plucked them up, the ducklings would gradually ratchet their attitudes down to those of simmering displeasure. They tolerated our stroking their heads and necks, mainly because they were still too young to have mastered biting us. By the end of the first week, we fooled ourselves into thinking that we were making progress. But each time we approached them in their cage, they acted as if they had never seen such travesties of creation before, throwing themselves into their food and water dishes with compact fury. By the end of the first week, the mixture of duck droppings and spoiled food splattered on the walls and floor made our porch an olfactorally memorable spot.

One furnace and plumbing technician, Greg, paid us a service call the afternoon our well pump stopped working. Our well apparatus was the bulky old-fashioned type; below our bathroom window crouched an apparent doghouse containing a well pump that could have come from the boiler room of the RMS *Lusitania*. To access the machinery, Greg had to unbolt one wall of the pump house, poke his legs inside, and drop down four feet to an earthen-floor well pit. After the customary fifteen-minute minimum-billing wait, I sidled outdoors and stuck my head through the opening to ask if he had located the problem.

"Some critter has made himself at home inside your well," he told me, with barely suppressed amusement. He stuck a shovel in the pile of dirt he had already excavated. "He buried your pump and it overheated." Here and there a flanged mesmer valve or grommeted phlogiston regulator emerged from the heaped earth like a Chichen Itzan artifact, but the body of the antique pump remained hidden.

"An animal," I groaned. With so many domestic creatures causing us grief, it didn't seem fair that we should suffer from the whims of wild animals, too.

"Probably a woodchuck. He dug so far underground, I can't even find the entrance to his hole."

"Have you run into this kind of thing before?" I inquired, hoping that woodchuck vandalism was commonplace in our area.

"Let's just say, I'll put this in my memoirs."

By the time Greg had emerged from digging out our pump and

replacing the burned-out points in the motor, his clothes were stained with soil and sweat. It was all part of a day's work in a profession that plunged him into the dankest recesses of his customers' domestic lives. He climbed into dusty attics that had never seen the light of an alternating-current lamp, thrust himself under kitchen sinks whose cupboard enclosures bred undiscovered species of mildew, probed sewage-pipe entrances, and squeezed his frame through crawl spaces where filth frolicked unfettered. Our house was no exception. The previous winter, he had scooped buckets of soot from our chimney and pulled a fried bat from the oil furnace burner. He suffered these jobs without complaint. But as he stood on our front porch drinking a glass of ice water while I wrote him a check, he sniffed the air, aimed his nose at the agitated ducklings, and winced, "Are they always this smelly?"

That's when Linda and I abandoned our roles as surrogate hen and drake and surrendered the ducklings to their peers. While Linda was still disinfecting the porch, we heard Martha's clamorous quacking and the beat of wings against the plastic swimming pool. Instead of adopting the ducklings, the three adults pursued them without pause. Peggy led the attack against her own kind with vigor. By the time I reached them, their yellow down feathers were damp and flecked with mud, but they preferred a beating to the safety of my arms. We put the pair inside the bunny cage, but the adults still managed to get to them. Peggy poked her beak through the wire from the front while Martha harassed them from the back. Before we could intervene, they had bloodied the smaller duckling's wing. Grabbing a length of chicken wire fence, I made a double-thickness ring around the babies. That finally ended the assaults.

"You'd think we had some endangered species out here," I complained to Linda. "We've got the ducklings inside a cage, inside a fence, inside a pen, inside a fenced-in yard. The last passenger pigeon in America was never this well protected."

As the call ducks grew, we put aside the bunny pen while enlarging and reinforcing the ring of fencing. Whenever we let the adults out of the pen, we put the ring out in the yard around them, thereby allowing the youngsters to peck at the grass unmolested. The attacks had taken their toll, however. The female developed a condition known as slipped wing, in which the tips of both wings jutted outward rather than hugging her body, caused by a combination of stress and poor nutrition. Mrs. Dorflinger had told Linda to feed the babies the same food as the adults, but we learned too late from the folks at the Lowell feed mill that ducklings need a special vitamin-and-mineral supplement. At least the visual clue allowed us to tell the female, Wing Ding, apart from her brother, Blabby.

The siblings didn't forget the treatment they had received from Daphne, Martha, and Peggy. Once they grew to adult size by the middle of the summer, we released them with the others in the yard, hoping they could finally defend themselves. Defense wasn't the issue. Within seconds the young call ducks had begun chasing the other ducks, snapping at their tails and wings and forcing us to return them to the chicken-wire jail. Repeatedly we tried peacefully integrating them with the established flock, but the newcomers were incorrigible hellions.

We couldn't in good conscience keep the pair imprisoned in a small enclosure any longer, and we couldn't release them into the duck community on their own recognizance. The solution was to find them another home.

When Linda called Dorflinger's to ask if they might take the youngsters back, Mrs. Dorflinger replied that she already had enough call ducks, and would Linda like to buy a couple more?

Rupert Murdoch, however, agreed to take them off our hands even after Linda stipulated that he couldn't sell them.

"That's how I got the last batch of call ducks," he told. "Some people gave them to me because they wouldn't leave their great big Embden geese alone. I think you ended up with one of them." That, of course, was Peggy, whose virtues soon became apparent as our duck population shifted again.

CHAPTER 7

Raccoon Rustlers

P rior to the day that the duck pen door was left unlatched, the potential danger to our ducks had been
purely anecdotal. "We've heard that raccoons eat ducks," Linda ventured, during a visit to Rupert Murdoch's farm.

"They don't bother me," Rupert declared as a procession of his
geese marched by.

"Raccoons don't eat ducks?" I asked.

"Not when you keep a dog around to scare off the raccoons. Get
out of there!" he shouted to a goat that had joined the parade and
was worrying the tail feathers of the last goose in line. "Some of
your dogs will chase down a duck, and if they don't learn, you've
got to get rid of the dog. Especially if it's a hound."

"So you haven't lost any ducks to raccoons?" I tried again.

"We've had problems with owls. There's nothing an owl likes
better than a duckling. An owl can smell a duckling from miles
away, and you've got to keep them inside your barn until they're
too big for an owl. Even that won't necessarily stop the owl. We had
an owl come around and eat just the heads off a few of our full-grown

ducks. He didn't touch the rest of the duck, he just ate off the head."

"Aye-yi-yi!" exclaimed Linda. "What did you do?"

"I waited outside in the yard all night, and when the owl came down, I shot him."

"But you haven't had trouble with raccoons," I prompted.

"If I ever do, I'll shoot them."

Clearly, the placid world of the plastic duck pond possessed a violent flip side that we knew nothing about. Not until the morning we woke up to hear Peggy's rasping voice just below our bedroom window. "The ducks are out!" Linda cried. She was outside in the half-darkness rounding them up before I was even out of bed, and she was back inside before I had a chance to throw on my clothes. She was as upset as I had ever seen her. "Something got Martha," she sobbed. The shades were still drawn. Light filtered in from the living room along with the sound of fluttering wings from one of the caged birds in the dining room. "It's all my fault. I should have checked the pen when I put them back yesterday."

A familiar numbness passed through me, a prickling sensation like the nearness of heat, a disembodying calm that often carried me past the first stages of a bad event. "It's not your fault," I told her, as I worked the buttons of a shirt. "We're both responsible for checking the pen. These things sometimes happen."

"It's my fault." She stood stiff and shivering. "Part of her is down by the fence. Another part of her is on the back deck."

"I'll take care of it," I told her. But I couldn't think of a worse way to start the morning.

At the bottom of the hill, I found a hollow thing with feathers, a thing I didn't recognize as having once been our duck. Its black and grey plumage was more like a crude charcoal sketch of Martha than any aspect of Martha herself. It wasn't simply that the life had been taken from her. What was left of her was literally hollow. On the worn rectangle of cement just outside the basement door, I found an internal organ that looked too large to ever fit inside the hollow thing. I put my eyes on it just long enough to scoop it up onto the flat blade of a snow shovel and carry it down the hill for reunification with the feathered part. I sobbed as I buried both pieces, but the sobs felt forced as the abruptness of the incident and the dregs of sleep drearily circled one another. I hadn't been close to Martha. The ducks were cozy with one other, not with us. But I had failed the most basic responsibility of keeping an animal safe, and the mistake had no remedy.

Linda squeezed a prayer through her tears. "Dear Lord, please tell Martha that we're sorry. Tell her that we miss her. And we hope she's with Simon and Binky in a wonderful place with lots of other ducks. Tell her that we love her, and please protect our other pets."

"If she's with Binky," I told Linda, clutching her hand, "I wouldn't necessarily call it a wonderful place."

Linda thought that a dog had taken Martha, but I disagreed. Since Martha had apparently been killed for food, a raccoon was the likelier suspect. The only dogs within a mile of us were fat and happy individuals that might have killed a duck for sport, but not for food. And a dog that killed for sport probably would not have stopped at attacking a single flightless duck. It would have gone after our entire flock. There were certainly enough resident raccoons to do the deed, but in spite of my suspicions, I continued leaving table scraps near the bird feeder for our nocturnal visitors. Especially after losing Martha, I saw logic in keeping their stomachs filled. I also refused to believe that the bird feeder raccoons would bite the duck that belonged to the hand that fed them. The killer had to be an outsider, I surmised, a rogue raccoon that didn't benefit from our largesse. After all, by eating our food, the bird feeder raccoons had entered into a social contract with us that prohibited them from attacking our pets. I imagined they had the intelligence to understand our tacit deal, and the stories I had heard about raccoons supported my belief.

SIX YEARS BEFORE we met, Linda had briefly lived in a rough-hewn rental house near the northern Michigan town of Pierson. One November evening while she was washing dishes, she heard a scuffling against the outside wall and decided to investigate. The door felt heavy when she opened it, almost as if she were pushing against a mound of snow, and the latch was difficult to turn. As the door swung open, she confronted a full-grown female raccoon hanging from the doorknob by both arms. Taking little notice of Linda, the animal dropped to the floor and sauntered through the kitchen into the living room where Linda's eleven-year-old son, Erin, sat on a throw rug, engrossed in *The Dukes of Hazzard*. As Linda watched in horror, the raccoon reached for Erin's head, but only to begin carefully grooming the boy's blond hair.

Early the next morning, Linda called her landlady to report the strange behavior of the raccoon and ask her what she might know about it. "I was afraid the raccoon was going to hurt Erin, so I threw a blanket over her and put her outside, but she kept getting back into the house somehow," Linda told Mrs. Handleman. "I must have put her out three times before I figured out how she was doing it. You know that hole in the bathroom floor? She was getting in through there. I had to block it off with an old board I found in the garage and stick a rock on top of it that we've been using to prop up the woodstove pipe. After that, she left us alone."

The older woman chuckled. "Oh, you must have had a visit from Jackie."

"Jackie? Who's Jackie?"

"Jackie was one of our favorite houseguests," Mrs. Handleman explained. "She must have dropped by to say hello. She was probably looking for my husband."

Jackie's saga began years earlier, when the Handlemans had been enjoying a country breakfast of freshly laid eggs and store-bought bread. As he was spreading margarine on his toast, Mr. Handleman experienced the unnerving sensation that someone was watching him. It wasn't the children, who were too involved in an argument over whose turn it was to chop the firewood to give their beleaguered father more than a glance. Unable to shrug off the spied-upon feeling, he glanced up at the ceiling to find a raccoon peering down at the breakfast table through a baseball-size hole in the plaster and lath. Rather than shoo the animal away, Mr. Handleman stood up and handed it his toast. From then on, Jackie was fed at every meal. Jackie repaid the favor by emerging through the bathroom-floor hole to introduce the Handleman family to the family she had been raising between the walls. Her cubs grew so tame that a young male adopted the Handleman beagle as his protégé, leading Mickey on daylong adventures in the woods that left the dog wet and panting by dinnertime but unmolested by raccoon tooth or claw.

As impressive as this account was all by its lonesome, I had even more evidence that raccoons were inherently civilized sorts. When my brother-in-law, Jack, was a child, his family had taken in an orphaned raccoon named Raffles who sat on the couch with the kids and plucked popcorn from a bowl. A cousin of mine in Houston kept a dish of canned cat food on the kitchen floor for a raccoon that slipped in through the kitty door each night, ate his fill, and left without a single breach of etiquette. A Canadian TV program profiled a Toronto woman who opened the patio sliders to her living room each night to ply a full dozen well-behaved raccoons with treats. Because raccoons easily form close relationships with people, and because they have cute faces and handlike paws, I romanticized these semimysterious nighttime visitors as the next best thing to elves. Once they had been properly habituated to humans, the most mischievous and unschooled raccoons were no more threatening to our ducks than overweight squirrels.

After losing Martha, Peggy and Daphne needed another little friend, according to Linda. Thus I found myself in Rupert Murdoch's backyard watching Linda orbit his double row of duck pens like the electron of a waterfowl atom. Though Rupert had as many ducks as ever, she immediately disqualified the majority from consideration. Linda didn't want to bring home a rerun of the breeds we had already owned, which eliminated call ducks, black and white Cayugas, Muscovies, and Blue Swedes, nor would she consider the Indian Runner duck that had captured my soul. Male ducks were also out of the question, since we didn't trust Daphne and Peggy's ability to remain celibate. That narrowed the choices to either a Bali duck, which resembled an Indian Runner duck with a feather pompom on its head, or a drab brown Khaki Campbell female that undoubtedly compensated for her plainness with a great personality and wonderful sense of humor. After caroming from pen to pen to make sure no potential alternatives concealed themselves behind a feed dish, Linda finally gave a Khaki the nod.

"The Khaki Campbell is considered a show duck, you know," Rupert apologized, as he transferred the female to a plastic cat carrier we had brought with us in place of the usual cardboard box. "I'll have to charge you ten dollars for her."

After a modest fashion, the Khaki female was attractive. The soft nobility of her face was complemented by eyes set high up on a narrow skull, giving her an air of royal inbreeding, while a close examination of the feathers on her back revealed unexpected flecks of golden brown. Nevertheless, by no stretch of the imagination could this plain brown wrapper of a waterfowl be gilded with the label of show duck, and I told Rupert Murdoch so. "I don't think ten dollars is too much to spend on a duck, but I sure don't see anything showy about her," I said.

"The females are nothing special," Rupert admitted, as if he were breaking the first law of duck husbandry by owning up to this obvious fact. "The drakes are the show pieces. Handsomest things you ever saw. I'm just sorry I don't have any here to prove it. But you get yourself a Khaki Campbell drake as a mate, and this little hen will produce a male you could show in any fair." On the way back home with our new duck, I prayed that I'd be spared such a fate.

Chloe, as we named the newcomer, won quick acceptance from Daphne and Peggy. Watching her splash around the plastic swimming pool, probe the mud in a freshly watered flower garden with enthusiastic stabs of her beak, or race across the yard flapping her wings in mindless joy reminded me why I subjected myself to the bother of keeping ducks. My worst moods seldom survived watching the trio tool through the grass like wind-up toys as they pursued some obscure goal that apparently evaporated just as they reached it with a disappointed breaking of ranks. None of our rabbits had impressed me with its cerebral intensity, but the lowliest of them was a savant compared to the brightest quacker. A fence was too abstract an object for a duck to comprehend with any degree of reliability. When agitated, she might suddenly disregard the solidity of wire mesh inches from her breast and try to strain her plump body through the holes. But I had to admire our ducks' powers of observation. They would freeze en masse in the middle of the yard, cocking an eye toward the heavens. Looking up, I wouldn't be able to see anything at first, but if I strained my eyes to vein-bursting extremes, I could just make out the dust speck of a bird of prey soaring hundreds of feet above the ground.

Despite a voice as boisterous as Martha's, bland brown Chloe was the demure female of the trio. As far as any duck could be said to be delicate, mild-mannered Chloe carried off the feat by balancing her waddle with an airy sense of poise. Much to my dismay, she would also later prove to be a diligent if unwed mother when we added abstinence-disdaining male Khakis to the flock.

The Internet had just gone mainstream, and I was upstairs engaged in important on-line activities, when I heard Linda calling from the yard.

"Something's wrong with Chloe," she told me, as I joined her in the pen. "She can't walk. She can't even stand up." It was a rare June day in Michigan; the sun was shining unobstructed by slabs of clouds, and gusty breezes swept deliciously through waggling trees. Unfortunately, on such fine days we hadn't yet learned to put a rock in front of the duck-pen door to prevent it from slamming upon an entering or exiting duck, which was what apparently had happened to poor Chloe. We waited until the next morning, hoping for improvement. When none was evident, I took her to Dr. Hedley, the robust veterinarian who had correctly treated Stanley's groin injury with a no-nonsense regimen of intensive nontreatment. After examining Chloe's leg and then x-raying the bone, he prescribed around-the-clock nontreatment for her, too.

"The femur is broken," he said and frowned, setting down the kitty carrier that was fast becoming our duck transport of choice. The tip of an olive-colored bill poked through the carrier-door grate. Chloe was calm. I was the ruffled one. "The break occurred at the top of the bone about as close to her abdomen as you could possibly get. That would make the bone very difficult to pin, since there's almost nothing to pin it." He deftly pantomimed a broken femur and an ineffectual pin with his thumb and index fingers as he spoke. "We could anesthetize her and try exploratory surgery to see if something else could be done, but I wouldn't recommend it. Number one, ducks don't do well with anesthesia. Number two, they can be slow recovering from surgery."

"What's the alternative?" I asked, feeling about as useful as the pin.

"Do nothing. Let nature take its course. Give the bone a chance to heal on its own."

"Does she need a splint or something?"

"I thought of taping her leg. But because of where the break is situated, I would have to wrap the tape all the way around her body underneath her wings, and that would make a great big mess. There's a much better solution if you have a small cage at home. It needs to be large enough so that she could stand up if she's able to, but small enough to confine her movements and keep her from thrashing around."

I remembered the rabbit cage that had most recently housed the demon ducklings and nodded. From somewhere down the hall, a parrot's squawk complained about whatever indignity it was undergoing. Chloe shifted around a little in her carrier, but otherwise didn't make a peep. This was fortunate. The parrot was loud enough, but if Chloe had let loose her braying quack inside the examination room, Dr. Hedley and I would have both been forced to communicate with the world by note pad for the next couple of days.

"If we can keep her relatively still for about three weeks, there's a ninety-percent chance that the broken bone pieces will knit back together. Now, they may not knit together in the right alignment, and she could end up pigeon-toed." His outstretched hands demonstrated this consequence. "But unless the misalignment is serious, it shouldn't be a problem for the bird. We had a similar case with a Maribou stork that got a foot tangled in a rope, and we caged him and let him heal on his own. He hobbles a little when he walks, but he regained full use of the broken leg."

I understood that Dr. Hedley was referring to his consultation at a zoo. He never made direct reference to the zoo. It was always a "we had to sandpaper the teeth of a Komodo dragon last week" sort of mention that took it for granted I knew about his specialized patients. If this was a form of bragging, it never bothered me.

"Put her cage out with the other ducks so that her environment is familiar and she isn't unnecessarily stressed. After three weeks you can try letting her out. If her leg is going to heal, it will have healed by that point. If not, we'll take it from there." Then, instead of rushing off to see another client, he answered my questions about the pileated woodpecker houses he was still building up north, described the various visitors to his backyard bird feeder, and just generally made me happy that Chloe and I had such an exuberant personification of animal well-being in our corner.

As we transferred Chloe to the bunny cage, Linda reminded me of how Daphne and Peggy had managed to peck the call duck ducklings through the bars. Birds just could not resist ferreting out weakness in their flock and trying to drive off underlings, presumably to ensure the survival of the group. Dominance was another issue that led to bullying. Howard and Stanley continued to jockey for power in our dining room, no matter how close an eye we kept on them. We talked about encircling Chloe's cage with the ring of fencing that had protected the ducklings, but the fence proved unnecessary. As soon as I placed the cage in a corner of the duck pen, Peggy plunked herself in front of it and would not let Daphne get anywhere close. She did her best to menace us, too, forcing us to shoo her away whenever we wanted to give Chloe food or water.

Altruism in animals is unusual. I've read books about extra-ordinary pets like Philip Gonzalez's *The Dog Who Rescues Cats: The True Story of Ginny*, which chronicles a pooch whose goal in life is finding injured or abandoned cats and convincing her big-hearted owner to take them home. But you expect a certain degree of hero-ism in dogs that you don't expect in other pets. Otherwise, Saint Bernard might be the name for a gargantuan breed of helpful rab-bit, fire stations could use a speckled goose as mascot, and Lassie might signal danger by meowing strenuously. Talk to anyone who spends hours a day around animals, from farmers to zookeepers to misguided individuals like myself. They'll probably express admi-ration for their charges. They probably won't ever describe them as motivated by selflessness. But Peggy was an exception.

Peggy always relished her periods of freedom from the pen, when she could search the yard for worms, exotic varieties of mud, and other delicacies too refined for human tastes. During the weeks that Chloe was confined to her cage, Peggy barely budged from sentry duty. Once in a while, succumbing to Daphne's forlorn squeaks or the call of a luscious puddle after a heavy rain, she might briefly join the Muscovy for a jaunt across the lawn. But these outings were rare. Her place was at the convalescing patient's bedside, where her raspy voice offered occasional quiet mutterings of encouragement. "How's that drumstick today?" she might quack, in an attempt to cheer up the brown duck. "Your food looks good, but the grub's much better in the garden."

When three weeks passed and we could finally release an in-creasingly restless Chloe, Peggy seemed to anticipate the moment of liberation as much as we did. She darted around my feet as Linda kneeled down on the dampish straw of the duck pen, reached through the door of the bunny cage, and gently placed Chloe on the floor beside her. Chloe didn't keep us in suspense. Her chubby body immediately popped up on a pair of working legs that propelled her out into the yard. Wobbling significantly but still maintaining her balance, she moved with surprising speed toward an alluring patch of weeds, followed closely by Peggy, who, for perhaps the only time in her life, let Chloe take the lead.

I was still thrilled at Chloe's recovery when I held her in my arms at Dr. Hedley's office a couple of days later. He shared my joy, but his face grew tight as his fingers probed the length of her leg, carefully working her limb in every direction like a video-game joystick. Chloe's face, in contrast, was unperturbed, wearing the same look of mild forbearance that a duck acquires almost as soon as it lurches out of the egg.

"Do you mind if I take another X ray?" he asked. "I won't charge you for it. I just want to satisfy my own curiosity."

He was visibly more relaxed when he returned with Chloe, though my stomach clenched when he explained that the bone hadn't actually knitted back together at all. "The femur is still broken, just as I had thought. But she'll still do fine."

"If the leg is broken, how can she possibly walk?"

"The muscles in her leg are supporting the broken bone. Ducks are incredibly lightweight for their size, and their muscles are quite strong, as you would know if you ever tried to handle a large bird that wasn't this cooperative."

I grimaced. "Won't that hurt her to have the loose bone end spearing her muscle?"

"The muscles grip a large enough section of the bone to act as kind of a shock absorber," he explained, capping the fingers of his left hand with his cupped right hand in another of his dexterous broken-bone pantomimes. " I don't think she's experiencing too much discomfort, or she simply wouldn't walk at all. A few years ago we had a condition similar to this with another kind of bird—"

"A flamingo," I suggested, anticipating an anecdote about a zoo.

"Oh, good heavens, no," he chuckled. "Where on earth would I get my hands on a flamingo? No, it was a Magellanic penguin, the kind you see swimming off the South African coast. We never thought this little guy would ever walk again, but despite a break not unlike your duck's, he did very well for himself."

Dr. Hedley turned out to be right about Chloe. Her leg supported her throughout the summer, and when winter came she kept vertical as successfully as any South African penguin, Magellanic or otherwise. Thanks to her wide feet—the same clumsy boats I had laughed at during temperate months—the ice that sent me sprawling headlong down the hill barely troubled her at all, nor did the six inches of snow that fell one night shortly after Christmas. Buoyed by the fluff, all three ducks half-walked, half-swam away from their pen, kicking their legs to toboggan across the yard, leaving tattletale trenches behind them. But with no seasonal treats to forage for except varied flavors of slush, they only sledded as far as the closest patch of sun, basking contentedly while I wrestled miserably with the usual pushbroom, hose, and shovel.

WHEN SPRING FINALLY wormed its way loose from the beak of a fierce Michigan winter, a familiar visitor made his first appearance. While other raccoons played the part of stylish partygoers by waiting for darkness before dropping by, a young male favored us with his presence in the late afternoon. As early as five o'clock, we would find him on the flat roof of the milk house just outside our dining room window eating seeds I had flung up there for juncos, cardinals, and jays that would not use the hanging feeder. As we ate dinner, he scrounged whatever the birds had left behind. Soon he was joining us for breakfast, too, showing up at a sunlit hour when other self-respecting nocturnal creatures had long since retreated to their hidey-holes or closed the lids of their coffins.

Under normal conditions, I simply ignored the raccoon population, but this was anything but a normal spring. Raccoons and possums usually poked around our feeder as a lazy alternative to scavenging natural foods. But an uncharacteristically dry April and May evaporated a swamp that should have squirted out mosquitoes by the millions. The lack of rain also squelched other insects and early-blooming weeds that in past years our animal residents had plucked from nature's big buffet. Conditions were so desperate that bug- and berry-loving Baltimore orioles were reduced to eating our sunflower seeds. We had never seen that before. Linda split an orange in half and skewered it on the end of the bird feeder support pole. A male and female oriole pecked the fruit down to the pulp within hours. Soon she began putting out two orange halves each day. Since the raccoon's survival prospects seemed dire, I decided to share leftovers of Linda's tortilla-chip-crumb-and-potato-water casserole ("I never made that," she claims), skillet-fried tofu shapes, faux-tuna Tuno burgers, and failed bread-machine experiments.

While I trusted a human-habituated raccoon to steer clear of our ducks, we still took the precaution of keeping the girls inside their pen until the sun was high in the sky. Early mornings and late afternoons were off-limits, no matter how loudly Chloe quacked for freedom. We also double-checked the pen door latches at night to avoid a repeat of the attack on Martha. We were vigilant. We just weren't vigilant enough.

I was at work when I received an anguished call from Linda. She had waited until midmorning to let the ducks out, heard a commotion twenty minutes later, and found a frightened Daphne and Chloe wandering more aimlessly than usual. Peggy was missing. A trail of small white feathers leading to the back fence told a tale with a terrible ending.

Too upset to do anything else, I drove home from work and spent several pointless minutes calling for a duck we knew couldn't possibly come home. We didn't even find anything we could bury, though I stopped short of searching beyond the black raspberry bushes for the kind of grisly remains that Martha had left behind. I didn't want to remember Peggy like that. I wanted to remember her brimming with an intensity of life far out of proportion to her size, a lioness inhabiting the body of a twelve-inch-tall duck. There was no question in either of our minds that our daylight raccoon had extended his usual visiting hours for a meal on the wing. And Linda had no doubt that slow-moving Chloe was his intended target and that Peggy had intervened to save her life.

"I can just see Peggy protecting Chloe," Linda told me, after we had calmed down a bit. "She probably tried to chase him off while Chloe and Daphne ran away. She wasn't afraid of anything. That's exactly what she would do."

I missed Peggy more than I ever expected to miss a duck and turned my sorrow into rage against the raccoon. Whenever I saw him on top of the milk house, I tore outside and chased him off with a broom. Whacking the handle against the side of the roof from ground level, I scared him into jumping down, then ran to the back of the shed and threatened to pummel him with the broom head as he made a beeline for the back fence. His agility and my essential cowardice saved us both from harm. After a few of these chases, upon hearing the angry slam of the basement door, he would climb out of broom range up the hackberry tree overhanging the milk house. I peppered him with a hail of pebbles as he clung forlornly to the trunk. I sprayed him with jets of water from the backyard hose. I hollered at him until my throat hurt, "Kill my favorite duck, will you?" and "You're not welcome here anymore!" The raccoon just wouldn't take the hint. Staring down at me with a slightly perplexed air, he bided his time until I stalked back into the house, then resumed his usual seat at out rooftop cafe. Nothing I did had any effect.

"I'm just glad I don't own a gun," I said to Linda. Otherwise, of course, I might have shot myself in the foot.

I had trouble sleeping, sick about losing Peggy and obsessed with ridding our property of every last marauding raccoon. The following Saturday, on my weekly visit to the feed store, I asked the owner, Ted, if he sold live traps large enough to catch a raccoon. He had exactly the model I needed. The cardboard box even featured fanciful artwork of a captured raccoon whose wide eyes indicated he was anxious to make a fresh start at a remote location.

"You won't go wrong with this one," Ted said. "I use one of them myself."

"Is it tricky letting them go?" I asked. "I've read about people getting their leg chewed on by an animal they've just released."

"I don't release them," he said with an insinuating squint. "I take care of them."

The irony of using live traps to lure animals to their doom not only was lost on Ted, but it also escaped the trap manufacturer. Bait-and-capture instructions were provided, but not a word from the Humane Live Animal Trap, Inc., literature mentioned how to spring the raccoon. In fact, the pictured list of features referred to the Quick-Release Rear Hatch with Easy Slide-Out Bolt under the heading of Bait Insertion Door, though the door was clearly designed for the animal's escape. The whole procedure seemed so ominous from the raccoon's perspective, I shook the empty cardboard box to make sure I hadn't overlooked an included Humane Gutting Knife.

Once I had mastered the art of prying open the spring-loaded door and securing it to a hook that set the trigger without the door snapping shut and breaking my fingers, the trap was easy to use. Just before the raccoon's usual afternoon arrival, I positioned the primed and ready contraption underneath our bird feeder. Tipping open the rear escape hatch, I inserted pungent bait—week-old tofu stir fry plus a dollop of canned cat food—then slid in the Easy Slide-out Bolt. I barely made it back indoors before the raccoon sauntered into the neighborhood's newest miniature diner and found himself clapped behind bars.

I hated to make him spend a couple of hours in the trap, but I wanted to wait for nightfall to release the raccoon, not wanting to be seen releasing a raccoon. Stealth definitely required a trade-off. Darkness put me at a disadvantage with a nocturnal creature accustomed to biting and clawing in inky blackness, so I compensated by packing a flashlight and protecting my hands with leather gloves so thick and stiff I couldn't operate the flashlight. I swaddled my torso in a knee-length down jacket, stuck my feet into hiking boots the size of file-cabinet drawers, and pulled on a stocking cap to guard against a desperate lunge for my hair. After I was fully suited up, the full scope of the heat-generating ability of the human body hit me. I wasn't especially mobile inside my portable sauna, but at least my captive wouldn't be grabbing free samples of my flesh.

The caged raccoon's huddled posture and offended look tempted me to let him go on the spot. I stiffened my resolve. "Sorry, but you've got to find a new place to live," I explained, picking up the carrier. "Don't worry, you're all right." The centrally located handle put trap and trap carrier wildly off balance as the animal scuttled from one end to the other. I wrestled the oscillating apparatus into the trunk of my Camry, tuned the radio to a suitably dramatic piece of classical music, and took a back road into Lowell.

My first choice for release on the Grand River was nixed by necking teens in a station wagon certain to be unnerved by the Michelin Man. I crossed the river and chose an access road alongside the railroad tracks. Nervous and cooking inside my protective suit, I set the trap on the ground, aimed it toward a shallow woods on the riverbank, whisked the bolt from the escape hatch, and flopped back into the driver's seat, slamming the door behind me.

The raccoon did not budge.

Breathing hard, I cautiously left the car again and lifted the escape hatch with a screwdriver to demonstrate that nothing but a hinge impeded his departure. "You're free," I urged him. "You can go now. Go on!" He hid his head. The third time I raised the hatch, this animal—that I had never seen move faster than a lumbering trot—issued a menacing snort that sent me flailing backward and streaked into the trees faster than my eye could imprint.

Over the next two weeks, I trapped four more raccoons and released them at the same spot on the river. I congratulated myself, until I stepped outside the basement door one night just before bedtime to call our cat and saw another three raccoons beneath the feeder. I caught these as well, but more still came. They were as plentiful as mice. In fact, the snarl of successive raccoon shifts punching in throughout the night woke me up over the course of the summer.

The following August, Linda's friend Deanne was having dinner with us when a fat raccoon in search of a canapé wandered into the trap. The sun wouldn't set for another couple of hours, but Deanne was eager to witness the animal's joyous moment of freedom. I had never let a raccoon go in daylight. It just seemed to go against the catch-and-release lifestyle. But because my release spot was sheltered from prying human eyes, I agreed to show off my wildlife skills for our guest. Despite a voracious mosquito population near the river and a feisty raccoon that growled at me with uncharacteristic savagery, the liberation went off without a hitch. But just before we drove away, Deanne pointed to a break in the wall of trees that stood between the railroad tracks and the river and asked me, "Isn't that someone's driveway? I'm sure I see a house back there."

"Oh, no, nobody lives out here," I insisted. "We're in the middle of nowhere."

Linda pressed her head against the glass. "I see someone's house. It's yellow. And there's a red car in the driveway."

"There can't be," I whined, turning around on the access road as quickly and quietly as possible. "I would have noticed someone living here."

"We'd better get out of here," Linda urged. "Someone might come out with a gun. They're probably looking for you."

Her warning was surely excessive. Or maybe it wasn't. In the fifteen months since Peggy had died, I had dropped off at least thirteen raccoons on those people's doorstep. That's thirteen raccoons added to the local raccoon population—thirteen raccoons bitter about having been caught in a trap.

The realization of what I had done filled me with terrible guilt. It also increased my paranoia. Now, after dark, whenever a car grinds to a halt on the shoulder in front of our house, I no longer assume it's an innocent passerby stopping to check a map. Instead, I'm certain that some sneak with an animal problem is dumping raccoons on our property. And come to think of it, that's probably how we got so many of them in the first place.

CHAPTER 8

Enslaved by Ducks

J acob Lestermeyer was going on and on about the pharisee next door as he led us from one farm building to
another in search of the mystery duck. We started in a sprawling
barn with a baffling maze of pens and cubbyholes. We rooted
through squads of protesting hens, eyeballed nervous ducks resting on ancient straw bedding as hard-packed as driveway dirt,
combed a food-storage room cluttered with spilled feed sacks, and
slowed to admire dozens of day-old pheasant chicks trickling in
and out of the heat circle cast by a brood lamp. Out the back door,
we dodged a pygmy goat with a taste for shirt buttons in an otherwise deserted chicken coop, craned our necks behind a two-tiered
wall of rabbit cages, stuck our heads into a shed so gloomy, Bigfoot
could have lurked inside unnoticed, and collectively lifted one end
of an overturned wooden cart that hadn't rolled anywhere on its
spoked wheels since long before our host's beard had gone grey.

"The last time I saw her, she was under here."

Lestermeyer grunted from the exertion of twisting his thick
body into the proper angle to peer beneath the cart while still help-

ing to hold it up. "No, excuse me, that's our ducklings." Balls of yellow fluff flowed toward the shadows. An outburst of peeps was muffled as we eased the upended vehicle back to the ground.

"What kind of babies are they?" Linda beamed.

"I hope the pharisee didn't get his hands on her," he muttered.

"So, why do you call him the pharisee, again?" I asked, uncertain if I had missed the explanation.

He stopped and straightened a pair of glasses that somehow fit around a globular nose. "Because he can quote the letter of the law as fine as the Devil can quote scripture. Had the cops over here twice last week."

"The cops?" asked Linda. He was too angry to answer at once. As we followed him up a rise in back of the barn, a raw ditch of a miniature lake snapped into view, a great gouge of earth resembling the scar a meteor might have left behind. An excited stream of water from an angled pipe fed the long and narrow, apparently bottomless pit. Blazing reflected sunlight all but hid the score of ducks that paddled far out in the middle.

"Our geese make too much noise," he snarled. "They wake him in the morning. I told the cops I've lived here thirty years. You don't put up a house beside a petting zoo if you want to live the life of Riley. You see the sign out front that says 'Lestermeyer's Petting Zoo'? You can see it clean from the intersection. It wasn't any surprise."

"It's the only way we found our way here," I told him. "The house numbers don't make any sense. They go up for a while, then they go down for a while, then they go up again."

He nodded happily. "'Lestermeyer's Petting Zoo.' The pharisee erects his temple next door then complains that Noah got here first. There's your duck, out there."

We shielded out eyes but couldn't see a thing. "What does she look like?" Linda asked. "If she's a Khaki Campbell, or call duck, or black and white Cayuga, or Blue Swede, or Muscovy, we don't want one. We could have gotten one from Mr. Murdoch, but we didn't want to let him know some of the other ducks he sold us are dead."

"Raccoons," I added.

"We don't want an Indian Runner duck, either," Linda said.

"We couldn't get her out of there, anyway," Lestermeyer told us, waving an arm toward the pond. "Not until they go back to the barn on their own about the time it gets dark."

"Hours from now," I explained.

"Mr. Murdoch doesn't have anything we want right now. We like his ducks, but we want something different."

"Raccoons," pondered Lestermeyer. "We get skunks after our chicken eggs."

"Let's look around," I urged Linda. "There must be another duck here you'd like."

"How about a Rouen," he suggested. "A Rouen," he repeated in response to our blank expressions. "The drakes have got green heads exactly like your mallards."

"A Rouen is a domestic mallard."

"We can't have boys," Linda lamented. "My husband doesn't want any babies."

"No ducklings, either," I clarified.

"There's a female Rouen out there," he told us, as he squinted into the blinding glare.

"She won't come out until it gets dark," I said.

"I'll get her," he promised. As he walked to the nearest shore of his backyard ocean—a hardened lip of dirt sprinkled with wiry sprigs of grass—three ducks swam toward him, matching his rate of travel. The Rouen hen accompanying a pair of males resembled a slightly larger, fatter version of a female mallard. She quacked briefly and vigorously when Lestermeyer grabbed her, but I missed the miraculous moment of capture; I was transfixed by a vision of mythological proportions. A one-eared goat with a purple scarf tied around her neck appeared from the rise behind Lestermeyer's barn, followed by four auricularly intact goats so evenly spaced in single-file procession, all five might have been connected by identical invisible lengths of chain. Though I was close enough to nudge any one of them, their slitted eyes didn't register my presence as they swept along a goat-width path that rounded a rail-fenced pony pen. Just their twitching tails moved unsynchronized. It was the only example of order I had witnessed since arriving at Lestermeyer's Petting Zoo, and the sight took my breath away. I turned to share the moment with Linda, but she hadn't noticed them.

"I'm not very impressed by the way girl mallards look," she said, as Lestermeyer grappled with the wing-flapping female, and I feared another search for the mystery duck loomed. But the Rouen revealed sublime color variations when he brought her close to us. Her tan head was streaked with brown, and a thick black stripe interrupted the flow of orange across her bill. Her back was jeweled with glowing shades of brown—each feather exploded in a sunburst of gold against a raw-umber background. Her breast was creamy chestnut. Her folded wings disclosed a band of electric blue bordered by the purest white. Her tail was white. Her feet were as orange as Peggy's, and she shared Chloe's inappropriately noble bearing, along with a boisterous voice sure to harmonize with the Khaki Campbell's quacks during my extensive stretches in bed.

"She's a beautiful duck," Linda decided.

"I had no idea," I marveled, still stricken by the bovid apparition.

"Couldn't we get a donkey, too?" she asked. "He's got the cutest little one in the barn."

I could only sadly shake my head.

After we had slipped the duck inside the kitty carrier, Lestermeyer led us around a hissing gang of geese, through a small assembly of pious-faced sheep, and into a boxy, vinyl-sided farmhouse to complete the commercial transaction. All the shades were drawn, possibly in an attempt to pharisee-proof the house. The feeble glow of a table lamp in the living room confirmed the murk rather than dispersing it. We felt our way to overstuffed chairs and sat down in front of a coffee table piled with rolled-up newspapers secured with rubber bands. Either Lestermeyer was behind in his reading, or he supplemented his income delivering papers. A silent shadow that I took to be his wife rose from a couch of uncertain hue and retreated to the kitchen. Staring into my open wallet, I struggled to distinguish between the one- and five-dollar bills.

"You sure have a lot of animals, Mr. Lestermeyer," said Linda.

"It costs me more than I make to feed them."

"So, what do we owe you?" I asked.

"Eight dollars will do."

Apparently our mallard wasn't what Rupert Murdoch would have called a show duck. That also meant Lestermeyer had spent close to an hour with us for less than a ten-dollar payoff. He even refused to keep the change when I handed him a pair of fives.

"I can't do that," he told me, fishing eight quarters from a covered candy dish and stabbing them into my palm. "Thank you, but I can't take money I haven't earned. If you want to make a contribution, come back and buy more of our animals. We've got a little of everything."

"We're all through accumulating animals now," I informed him with wholly unfounded optimism. "But we'll tell our friends about you."

"You certainly are a good man," said Linda, as she leaned over to give him a hug, and my silhouette of a head nodded in agreement.

"Good luck with the pharisee," I told him.

WE SPENT THE drive back home praising Lestermeyer for his dedication to his animals. Over the next couple of weeks, he kept cropping up in conversation. Linda and I would sit down for dinner to feed Stanley, Ollie, and, to a lesser extent, ourselves. Hearing us clatter around in the kitchen, newcomer Maxine would raise her voice from the duck pen. Chloe would quack in counterpoint. Then Linda would say, "Poor Mr. Lestermeyer. He sure does love his animals." And I would answer, "I don't know where he gets his energy." Then I'd add, "I wish he was selling some of that." These gripping observations typically trickled on after dinner, but they stopped for good during a particular Friday evening when Linda spotted a classified ad in the paper that made her shout at decibel levels rivaling Chloe's, "What's this?" It was an ad placed by Jacob Lestermeyer. In addition to introducing children and their families to the pleasures of mingling with tame domestic animals, Lestermeyer's Petting Zoo provided another service. The same goats, rabbits, ducks, and chickens were also available for enjoyment as butchered meat.

THAT SPRING AND SUMMER, as visitors to the petting zoo were busy cuddling or cooking Lestermeyer's livestock, I watched helplessly as we took on additional pets from other fronts. It started with Linda grieving, "Now that Bertha's gone, I don't have a little animal to hold anymore."

"You've got Penny."

"She's your cat. And she hides upstairs all the time."

"Okay, then you've got Agnes."

"She's become an outdoor cat. And she doesn't even like to look at us." That was true. Whoever had briefly owned our small black cat before dropping her off on our property had apparently mistreated her. Whenever I scolded her for paying too close attention to the parakeets, or if I made an abrupt grab for a bag of tortilla chips sitting near her on the couch, she would cringe as if expecting a whack. She grew incrementally less fearful as time passed. Penny, on the other hand, had taken Agnes's intrusion into our house personally. She would flee from me rather than suffer the betrayal of inhaling Agnes's scent upon my person. She had developed as many hiding places as Binky, secreting herself behind the file cabinet, under the bed, or on top of a slide-projector box nestled in a storage shelf. Whenever I wanted to pet her, I was forced to lie upon the floor and stretch an arm into her hidey-hole. As long as just my fingers reached her, she would purr and roll and, at her wildest abandon, even lick my hand. Catnip occasionally lured her out into the open, though once the euphoria dissolved, it seemed to leave her with a heightened sense of vulnerability.

I didn't take Linda's assertions seriously about wanting another pet until the day I arrived home from work and was horrified to find a pair of guinea pigs occupying Bertha's old cage. When Bertha had died, both Linda and I vowed never to get another rabbit, because we simply didn't have good luck with them. From what I had read about guinea pigs, their constitutions were even more fragile, and their cranial activity, to put it politely, was significantly less intense. I raised a ruckus, and the guinea pigs promptly went back to the store. My position stressed two unassailable tenets. First, no pets were to be brought into the house without the permission of both husband and wife. Second, okay, we would get another rabbit. Two rabbits? Fine. My guinea-piggish reasoning went as follows: as long as we were falling down the rabbit hole, two bunnies would undoubtedly be less trouble than one. Rather than amusing themselves eating our baseboards and pulling up the living room carpet strand by strand, they would romp and play with each other, freeing up hours of leisure time for us. We decided to look for a pair of Netherland dwarfs.

As a starting point—and for the sheer aggravation of the exercise—Linda phoned our local Lowell pet shop, Betsy's Beasts, and asked Carl (of "No refund without fish carcass" fame) if he had any Netherland dwarf bunnies at the store.

"I only stock dwarf Dutches and French lops, and only one breed at a time. Right now, we don't have either one, but I could order one or the other, depending on which breed has the best availability."

Linda plowed on cheerfully. "I really want a pair of Netherland dwarfs like Bertha," she explained, although he could have no idea who Bertha was. "Would you happen to know of anybody in the area who raises them?"

"If I did," he answered, "I'm not going to tell you who they are. I never discuss my suppliers with the public. I don't make a profit when you buy a product somewhere else."

"What if I promise to pay you a commission on any rabbit we buy?"

"I have no way of verifying that," he told her wearily. "You might turn around three months from now, buy another ten rabbits, and I wouldn't see a cent."

"I wouldn't do anything like that," Linda said. "My husband doesn't want ten rabbits, he only wants two of them like Bertha."

"If I take you at your word that you really want just two, I can have two animals in the store within a week. But you'll have to stop in first and put down a deposit on them. That's store policy."

"But what if I don't like the two rabbits you happen to get in? They might not have a temperament like Bertha. We bought Binky without making sure he enjoyed being held, and he had an attitude. We really want a couple of Netherland dwarfs, but I can't tell which ones are right for us unless I have several to choose from."

The barrage of rabbit names brought out the worst in Carl. "A customer just walked in the door," he fumed, as if he couldn't believe the imposition of two individuals requesting his services at once. "When you make up your mind about what you want, give me another call. Actually, don't call. I'd rather you came into the store when I'm not so busy."

Carl was less busy a few months later when Betsy's Beasts gave up the ghost, leaving Lowell without a pet shop and fish carcasses with nowhere to go.

Perhaps because rabbit breeder Warren was plagued by guilt for having once sold us Binky, he acted happy to receive Linda's call and even more happily recommended a woman named Carrie who specialized in Netherland dwarfs. In contrast to Carl, Rupert Murdoch, and Jacob Lestermeyer, Carrie didn't exhibit any of the obvious eccentricities we had come to associate with people who sell animals. She might have revealed a few oddball traits had we spent more than an uninterrupted minute in her presence. Hard at work at an undisclosed project inside her house and warily attentive to the teenage son whose muscle car crouched in the driveway, she took us out to a double-stall garage stocked with a row of rabbit cages and disappeared. She returned to point out the parents of her newest batch of rabbits—or kittens, according to the rarely used technical term for bunny babies—before disappearing again. Just as we were deciding which of the young rabbits to put to the hold-and-cuddle test, she whisked between us to open the cage.

"He takes after his father; he's very mellow," Carrie told me, when I picked up a fat black rabbit with stubby ears and huge black eyes. He didn't wiggle, bite, or pee on me when I held him to my chest. In fact, he seemed to enjoy it.

"He takes after his mother, he's pretty hyper," Carrie explained, when Linda attempted to subdue a caramel-colored bunny disinclined toward human contact. She returned him to the cage in favor of a Bertha clone that briefly tolerated Linda's advances before kicking to signify his hankering for solid ground. Carrie took him from Linda. "This coloration is called Silver Marten." She blew upon a small section of fur on the bunny's back. "See the silver coloring that comes through under the black? That's how you tell a Silver Marten. Go ahead and take your time," she shouted, as she intercepted a lanky high-school-age boy wearing a basketball shirt and a sour expression, then disappeared into the house with him.

"Isn't he a doll?" Linda cooed over the Silver Marten. Bertha had been unhealthy for such a significant portion of her time with us that this bunny's bright eyes were a revelation. So were his sleek black coat with the tan stripe between his ears, his silver ring around each eye, and his silver flecks, which gained momentum as his fur flowed toward his feet. His stomach and nether regions were also silver and possibly martinized, too. I opted for the plump black charmer but was instantly vetoed.

"Can't we get the brown one instead? I don't like the looks of a solid black animal."

"Agnes is solid black," I reminded her uselessly, adding in the same breath, "Do what you want to, they're your rabbits." Before leaving with the two brothers that Linda had chosen (one Silver Marten, one brown) and a wallet forty dollars lighter (show rabbits apparently going for twice the price of show ducks), I asked Carrie if we could assume our bunnies would remain best buddies.

"It depends," she said. "Sometimes they get along. Sometimes they don't."

"Shouldn't they get along because they're brothers?" Linda asked.

"They might," she shrugged. "They might not. Puberty is when everything changes, and these guys are just a week or so away."

I hadn't even slammed my driver's-side door when Carrie's screen door banged shut and she was back inside the house. Maybe she was allergic to rabbits. I feared I had developed a weird physiological reaction of my own to the Netherland dwarfs the next day, when I said good-bye to a Silver Marten and a caramel-colored bunny on my way to work, then said hello to a Silver Marten and a fat black bunny when I returned in the afternoon. In my absence, Linda had driven the thirty miles back to Carrie's to make the exchange. She must have been plagued by guilt over my not getting the rabbit I had wanted, I hypothesized.

"The black one has a better personality," Linda pointed out.

AT BINDER PARK ZOO in Battle Creek, the cereal-producing city where Linda's mother lives, the children's zoo area includes an expansive outdoor rabbit pen. Clumps of full-grown rabbits play together on the grass, groom one another, and stretch out side-by-side for a nap in the sun. In our many visits to the zoo, we never saw a single instance of discontent among the bunnies. They appeared inherently as well suited to social interactions as ducks. And Silver Marten Bertie and roly-poly Rollo seemed headed down the path of sibling bliss. They loved jumping in and out of an Easter basket together that Linda had set up on the floor of our porch or friskily chasing each other around the dining room and kitchen. They shared the same cage, eating out of the same bowl at the same time. They were closer than two peas in a pod, more gregarious than mushrooms on a log.

One night after Linda and I had just settled into bed, we heard a loud thump from the dining room. It was the sound of hormones kicking in. After two more contained explosions, we flicked on the light to find Bertie and Rollo clawing and biting each other with such intensity, they had skidded their cage several inches across the linoleum. Then, as abruptly as the aggression had begun, the pair reverted to a peaceful coexistence that carried through the following day. By nightfall, hostilities began anew. Soon the brothers couldn't occupy a room together without uniting in a rolling ball of mayhem that left half-dollar-size patches of fur scattered across the floor and a musky wild-animal scent in the air. By then we had already purchased a second cage, ending our dreams of mutually sustaining rabbit buddies and replacing them with the burden of feuding family members that we had to sequester at all times. We had hoped that getting the brothers "fixed" would remedy the problem, but their territorialism was too deeply ingrained.

After dinner each night, Rollo got the run of the dining room and kitchen while Bertie investigated the nooks and crannies of the living room. Mornings, we reversed rooms and rabbits. Yet when both bunnies were confined to adjacent cages, they acted like the dearest friends on earth. Rollo would stick his nose through the bars and lovingly lick Bertie's ear. If Rollo lay against the right side of his cage, Bertie would press his body against the left, letting fur and flesh mingle through the wires. As long as they didn't share a common space, they were inseparable.

Back when we had first brought the bunnies home, I built a rectangular pen for them in the backyard by throwing up a run of fencing alongside the duck pen, and I use the words "throwing up" deliberately. My results looked just that professional. After the siblings became dysfunctional, I was forced to add yet another fence to divide the enclosure into separate territories for Messrs. Hatfield and McCoy.

"With this, my days of building pens are done forever!" I must have hollered as a challenge to the gods when my labors had come to an end. I have no other explanation for the Herculean construction project that was set in motion when Linda's newfound friend LuAnne phoned about an advertisement she had spotted in a local weekly shopping newspaper called the *Buyers Guide*. Linda had met LuAnne the previous year when her son performed pet-sitting duties for us during our Amish-watching vacation in Pennsylvania, and LuAnne's devotion to animals put ours to shame. Her house pets included an orphaned Green-Winged Teal named Terry who lived in her upstairs Jacuzzi. While paddling in crystal-clear water strewn with floating romaine-lettuce-leaf treats, Terry also had the option of nibbling from a row of bowls that curved along the edge of his tub. His smorgasbord included Cheerios, freshly grated filberts, succulent garden peas, sweet corn sliced off a cob each morning, and occasional dollops of pasta.

"I talked to the poor woman who placed this ad in the newspaper," LuAnne explained gravely to Linda. "She was chopping up an onion for dinner when she happened to look out the window. And can you believe the knife slipped and she nearly cut off all her fingers? She had to take a leave of absence from Amway, and now she can't afford to keep her animals, so she's giving away two ducks."

"Sweetheart," entreated Linda, "Could we maybe take a couple of nice ducks in need of a good home? Before you say no, just listen," and she told me the tearful onion tale.

Three ducks, five ducks, I didn't see what difference two more ducks could make and enthusiastically replied, "I don't know. I guess."

"LuAnne said the lady has a couple of geese."

"Geese!"

"I told her no."

"Definitely not." A goose was a vicious annoyance with wings. In my graduate-school days in San Francisco, I would hike to Golden Gate Park from my Willard Street apartment and throw stale cookies to appreciative tame ducks. I stopped feeding them the afternoon a large white goose took exception to the quality of my offerings and rose from the water to energetically bite my leg. More recently, Linda and I had been admiring a scenic pond and Victorian gazebo near the West Michigan town of Cedar Springs, when a gang, not a gaggle, of domestic geese rousted us from the area. A goose was the last thing I ever wanted to own.

A woman with a bandaged hand took us around the side of an attractive ranch-style home and into a backyard as scarred and denuded of vegetation as Rupert Murdoch's place. A ring of fencing housed a pair of the fattest ducks I had laid eyes on to date along with a clamorous pair of geese. The enclosure was so decrepit, my pathetic pens evoked the grandeur of Chartres Cathedral in comparison. A loose corral of four-foot-tall wire fencing fixed to the ground by a few wooden spears kept the ducks and geese confined by virtue of their own lack of will. More miraculous than the waterfowls' failure to push their way through the makeshift gate was their survival in this sorry jail in the face of raccoons, owls, foxes, dogs, and even coyotes. I could only guess that these nighttime hunters feared that the pen might collapse on them if they set foot inside.

Plump as penguins, the two Khaki Campbell males, Stewart and Trevor, easily lived up to Rupert Murdoch's show-duck claims. Their necks, chests, and shoulders were a buttery caramel that grew pale around their wings. Their lower backs and tails were cocoa colored. More arresting were their upper necks and heads, which appeared to be the same shade of brown as their backs, but glinted iridescent green when hit by just the right angle of light. Equally striking was the incredible roundness of their breasts, which gave each duck the bearing of a pampered pasha who expected to receive his weight in gold on his next birthday.

"Will male ducks be all right with our females?" I asked no one in particular, and no one duly answered.

"The geese sure will miss Stewart and Trevor," the woman

lamented above a din that could only have been matched by my sticking my head under the hood of a car while someone punched the horn. But I had to admit being attracted to the geese. They winningly balanced the attributes of bluster and shyness, first honking threateningly with their necks extended and their heads nearly touching the ground, then straightening to dance away on timid tippy-toes. Far from menacing her, as I had expected, they approached with embarrassed awkwardness. By any reckoning, the pair was beautiful. Caressing their necks and shoulders was a grayish white so silky that, as with Howard's back, my fingers yearned to touch it. A slightly fluffy brown-gray stripe resembling a mane slid down their heads and necks, enveloping their eyes. Their lower backs and tails were solid white. White and black played upon the folded wings. Their faces were kindly and quizzical. Their mannerisms projected a sense of vulnerability at odds with my conception of gooseness. I was hopelessly in love.

"Sweetheart, she says their names are Liza and Hailey, and they were raised with the ducks by the little girl."

"Then we shouldn't separate them," I answered, after the pretense of a meditative pause. "It wouldn't be right," I said, frowning, secretly overjoyed that I was getting the last thing I had ever wanted.

A duck pen capable of comfortably holding three, four, or even five ducks proved woefully too small, once two African geese joined the flock. At first blush, the challenge seemed to be simply a matter of maintaining reasonable standards of cleanliness. The goose sisters profusely soiled the straw bedding at twenty-minute intervals, creating an ecological disaster every two days. Weary of hauling out armloads of soggy, smelly straw, I hatched a plan for a presumably maintenance-free waterfowl pen substrate. Unfortunately, the solution demanded the two things of me I've hated my whole life: hard work and getting dirty. Decades parked in front of a computer screen had left me with the stamina of a petunia. Running the weed-eater around a few rocks ruined me for an entire day. Yet I still concocted a project that would have daunted even a healthy person.

For vague reasons that blinded me at the time with their brilliance, I decided to model a waste-disposal system based on the concept of the bed of an aquarium, even though an underwater ecosystem had nothing in common with our backyard. Nevertheless, I soldiered on with the idea, beginning with a trip to the hardware store and the selection of a dozen fifty-pound bags of sterilized white sand for the bottom filtration layer. Back outside in the parking lot, I was on my own conveying the sandbags from a wooden skid to my car trunk. The compact dimensions of the bags suggested that the manufacturer had printed the 50 LBS. boast on the label with a wink. Nothing the size of a flour sack could be difficult to heft, I figured. But once I had locked my hands around a sack, the only thing that moved when I straightened my body was vertebrae slipping. Huffing and puffing in Sumo-wrestler fashion, I managed to transfer eleven of the twelve bags to my car before collapsing in the front seat. I decided to consider the abandoned twelfth bag a tip.

While my body toyed with a state of shock, I began plopping the sandbags into the old wheelbarrow, slitting them open, and trucking the loose sand down to the pen. Our clay-hard, rock-strewn backyard soil suddenly became as unstable as swamp muck, miring my wheels if I moved slower than a gallop. Dumping the sand was sickeningly anticlimactic. My backbreaking labors yielded a granular deposit slightly less substantial than that of confectioner's sugar on a doughnut. I trudged on to the pea gravel, nevertheless.

Between the thoroughfare of Fulton Street and our barn, silhouet-
ted against a troubled sky, loomed magnificent Pea Gravel Mountain. The mighty dome had been deposited the day before by
Tip-Top Gravel Company, and like the mythical bird that given an
infinitude of time grinds down Everest by swiping its beak against
the cliffs, I commenced chipping at the base with my shovel.

The haul from the gravel pile to the maw of the duck pen—
across the side lawn, around the pine trees, past the pump house,
between the house and the milk house, through the backyard gate,
across the cement deck, down the hill, amid a knot of disbelieving
ducks and geese—became my own miniscule trail of tears. That
day, I trucked just enough gravel to cover the embarrassingly unim-
pressive dusting of sand. The following day, I lay in bed, nursing
my aching arms, rubbery legs, twitching shoulder muscles, and
locked-up lower back. The third day, I complained about how
much work was left to do as a substitute for doing the work. The
fourth day, my mind mercifully overloaded upon its reminiscence
of the initial wheelbarrow load, erasing the entire experience from
my memory.

The next five afternoons after work, as soon as I let the ducks
and geese out of their pen to frolic unemployed in the yard, I sub-
mitted to the slavery of the shovel. To ease the pain, I sang prison
work songs under my breath. Depending on how high I heaped the
stones, each wheelbarrow weighed between 175 and 250 pounds.
Once I managed to set it in motion, it was loath to stop without
banging me up in some fashion, especially during the thrilling
plunge down the backyard hill, when I switched roles from cart
pusher to dragging victim. When the task was finally finished, I
had managed to transmute a mountain of gravel into a molehill-
deep layer distributed across the pen.

Amazingly, the aptly named pea gravel functioned exactly as

planned. No matter how vigorously or how often the ducks and geese exercised their digestive systems, a quick blast of the hose dispersed the pea-green blobs and sent the unmentionable molecules hurtling through the aggregation of pebbles. Huge boulders that had belched forth from the Earth during the Precambrian Era had waited patiently hundreds of millions of years until their girth had sufficiently diminished to adequately perform these toilet duties for our pets, and we were grateful to every last little stone. We looked ahead to years of trouble-free pen-cleaning, never dreaming of the strange permutations that the gravel bedding would undergo before long. Suffice it to say that three decades hence, when developers convert our property into a gravel pit, excavation will be halted by the discovery of a mysterious rectangular artifact more resistant to air hammers than any other substance on the planet.

Even with the pen flooring suddenly clean enough that a duck could—and would—eat a meal off it, the enclosure was clearly too small for its occupants. It was partly the sheer biomass of five ducks and two geese that caused overcrowding. But the main problem was the romantic interest the male Khaki Campbells started to demonstrate toward all five females, and we knew the situation would worsen as the young lads matured. There was no escaping it. I was doomed to enlarge the pen. Given the choice between hiring Dell to abuse my intelligence or abusing myself, I decided to undertake the construction of a brand-new poultry wing, assisted by my good friend, Bill Holm, the only person I knew whose mechanical ineptitude dwarfed mine.

I first met Bill after returning to the Grand Rapids area from graduate school in 1978. I was certain that my Master of Arts degree in English/Creative Writing would be a boon to any company, and the princely offer of $3.00 per hour from a textbook publisher established the value of my education. When the publisher called with the job offer, I explained that I had anticipated a living wage. After careful consideration, he grudgingly raised my hourly boon to $3.01. Next stop was a newspaper, the weekly voice of a posh pseudo-suburb that offered me a better deal in the role of typesetter and layout artist, two positions about which I knew nothing. Bill was supposed to interview me, but couldn't be bothered to keep the appointment. I ended up working at the paper for two years, worming my way from the composing room to the editorial office, where the magnificent Mr. Holm held court. On my first journalistic assignment, covering a school board meeting, when I asked Bill a question, he held me off, saying, "The writing window is closed."

Despite this rough beginning, Bill and I became good enough friends that we ended up sharing an apartment that was complete with all the troubles old houses bring. One particularly cold winter day, the water spigot in the kitchen refused to spig because the pipe was frozen. On Bill's suggestion, we placed a space heater under the sink and blasted the pipes with incendiary temperatures for an hour without effect. That we tried this in a second-story apartment when the frozen water line hid in the bowels of the basement demonstrated not only our profound ignorance of plumbing principles, but also a pitiful lack of common sense. Later when Bill and Carol married, they requested my help building a backyard shed from a kit. We managed to use and connect all the pieces, although the lean-to appearance of the finished product failed to represent the builder's art. But helping Bill had put him in my debt. Anyway, I had no one else to ask.

In order to put Bill to his best use—lifting and holding things I was too weak to lift and hold without help—I did as much of the basic work as I could ahead of time, keeping every aspect of the project as unchallenging as possible. For example, I had decided to expand the duck pen by exactly eight feet for the simple reason that eight-foot boards were a standard length. The fewer cuts I needed to make with my brand-new circular saw, the fewer were my chances of lopping off my fingers. Half of the expansion would be for the female ducks and geese. The other half would be a separate pen for the increasingly naughty male ducks. That meant putting in a second entrance. Duplicating the plank door that Dell had made didn't seem complicated. I laid the cut boards side-by-side and connected them with crosspieces to eventually yield an approximate twin to Dell's design. But while Dell's door retained the same fixed rectangular shape at all times, mine formed a different parallelogram whenever I moved it, compelling me to add diagonal bracing that his somehow didn't require.

Observing my few bits of completed work when he arrived, Bill complained with a mixture of awe and stinging disappointment, "You've already got the whole thing done." Checking himself from delivering what could have been regarded as a compliment, he hastily added, "I see you've turned your yard into a Superfund site. Or is this a special project for the Arts Council—some sort of study in deconstruction?"

With his neatly trimmed salt-and-pepper beard, baseball-style OCRACOKE ISLAND hat with clownishly oversize brim, ST. JOHN, AMERICAN VIRGIN ISLANDS T-shirt, and military-green tech pants festooned with Velcro-closure pockets that had obviously never been opened, he was the slumming yuppie to the hilt.

Considering that our task consisted of nothing more than hammering together a few boards, hanging a door, and covering the frame with wire mesh, progress didn't go badly at all. By noon and the appearance of Linda bearing sandwiches and glasses of fizzy water, we had hammered together a few boards.

"That looks good," Linda said haltingly. Her puzzled expression only deepened when I explained that the mosquitoes had slowed us down. There wasn't a buzzing bug in earshot as we gathered around the table on the back deck. Along the fence that separated the swamp from primitive civilization, however, we had spent more time swatting insect diners off our arms than pounding in nails at crooked angles, and there weren't enough tiny bibs to go around. Actually, our division of labor was nearly perfect. While I had it all over Bill, knocking in three-inch nails reasonably straight for the first inch or so, my strength and attention would rapidly begin to wane. "Finish this one, would you?" I'd squeak, wiping sweat and mosquito bodies from my brow. Bill would finalize the job with a few absentminded whacks while formulating his next derogatory remark.

"The geese are a psychological projection, aren't they? That's why you like them. They look like you. They even sound like you, but a lot more masculine."

"They're females."

"Exactly."

After lunch and a hearty application of mosquito repellant, our pace quickened. We completed the innovatively tilted pen frame, hung the door, rehung it when it banged against the opposite post, then rehung it again after the door planks had decided upon a finished shape. Attaching the wire mesh to the frame turned out to be more time-consuming than anticipated. First there was the problem of unrolling the unwieldy roll without roll or person rolling over. Then came the painful cutting-to-proper-length with tin snips whose snipping ability would have been tested by tin foil. The geese watched our every move with an intensity befitting a hawk, honking conversationally and rustling around the pen with each fresh pratfall or collision of hammer and thumb.

"You're all right," I assured them, as we packed up for the day. "You are very good girls."

"What's that sappy voice you're using?"

"What voice?"

"'Goosey, goose, goosey,'" cried Bill in a falsetto.

"I don't talk like that," I countered.

"You've been yodeling like that all day. 'How's the goosey doing? Yo-de-lay-de-hoo!'"

"I never yodeled," I laughed in embarrassment.

"My God." He folded up the stepladder and stared at me. "I just noticed what's wrong with you. You're almost happy, aren't you?"

"No."

"You are. For all the years I've known you, you never once mentioned the animal kingdom. But here you are with your little goosey friends and a big moronic smile on your face. Either that, or it's the Zoloft."

"It's because you're about to go home."

After Bill left, I let the ducks and geese out of their pen and flopped down on a flat section of ground near the redbud tree. I spread my fingers in the warm grass and flicked an ant off my thumb as bumblebees gathered in the spirea bush behind me. Daphne, Chloe, and Maxine wandered only as far as an exquisite patch of mud just on the other side of the pen door, while the two African geese and the male Khaki Campbells chatted excitedly as they ambled up the hill. A fat white cloud released the sun, flooding the back of my eyelids with a vibrant raspberry light. Cars whooshed past the house with their radios playing. The happy grunts of the geese grew close. Though they had the entire yard to graze, they were pecking at the ground with the Khakis a few feet from my legs.

My limbs and brain felt heavy. Sleep nibbled at me—at least I thought it was sleep until I felt a distinct pecking on my shoe. Liza and Hailey were taking turns playing with my laces, while one of

the male Khakis—we couldn't tell Trevor and Stewart apart—
urged them on with whispery quacks. I sat up slowly, but still apparently too fast for Hailey, who stumbled away with a wing-flap.
Liza, identifiable by the faint yellow ring around her eyes, held her
ground. When I shifted to a cross-legged position, she honked
softly and padded closer until her abdomen rested against my calf
and she was almost sitting in my lap. I showed her my hand and
moved it behind her head to stroke the soft feathers of her neck
while she stared at me with an unfathomable eye. She stretched her
neck, grabbed a shirt button, and pulled it. On her second try, she
had the button and a clump of fabric in her beak. Hailey leaned forward to nip at my shirt pocket. The two boys were showing unto-
ward interest in my pant cuff. It was too much of a good thing.
After a seeming eternity outdoors, I stood up and walked through
a volley of disappointed honks back into the house to wash Liza's
muddy lipstick off my shirt before Linda could discover it and
jump to any conclusions.

CHAPTER 9

Creatures of Habit

P eople say you can get used to anything. Habits are habits, and repetition makes the most extraordinary events eventually seem commonplace. Back when Binky ran our lives, I learned not to bat an eye whenever I stumbled into our dining room while Linda was putting the bunny to bed. For most rabbit owners, making sure the pet has fresh food and water is sufficient. But Linda went the extra mile by treating Binky to a musical recital and me to the spectacle of my wife on hands and knees in the dining room with her head thrust through the door of the bunny's cage while singing a lullaby she had composed.

> 'Cause he's the bunny,
> The very best bunny,
> He's the bunny for
> You and me.

As she warbled the song, whose soaring melody suggested a hymn, Linda would pet Binky on the head while attempting to keep him from kicking away the pink hand towel she had draped across his

back. One or two refrains of "The Very Best Bunny" typically provided all the happiness Binky could handle. Any more and he
might bolt for the open door.

Pocket parrot Ollie's bedtime ritual was even more remarkable.
Linda would hide Ollie inside a knitted pink tam-o'-shanter she
called his "night-night hat." Clutching one end of the tam, she would
swing it back and forth in the manner of a pendulum while scat
singing a medley of American standards that usually included
"Camptown Races" and "How Much Is That Doggie in the Window?"
Eager to see the performance as well as hear it, Ollie would attempt
to crawl out of the tam. Once his head popped into view, Linda
would snug the hat around his neck and flip him upside down in her
lap. Instead of responding with his usual bad temper, he greeted this
with excited chirps whose intensity increased as Linda stroked his
head with a finger, carefully avoiding his snapping beak.

Neither wife nor parrot was shy about conducting this ritual in
front of awestruck company. Linda once even tried instructing our
pet-sitter Rhonda in the finer points of the complex ceremony, but
our helper shook her head at the idea of mastering the "night-night
hat" without months of study.

"How did you ever think this up?" asked a bewildered Rhonda.
"How did he get in the hat in the first place?"

Like an ancient traditional dance whose movements have lost
their meaning over the centuries, the "night-night hat" has origins
that are cloaked in mystery. All we know for certain is that in the
not-so-distant past, when Ollie squawked extensively while Linda
worked in the kitchen, she occasionally popped him into the
pocket of her apron, both quieting the bird and forcing him to live
up to the epithet of pocket parrot. Depositing him inside the tam
presumably evolved from there, but behavioral anthropologists dis-
agree on the precise mechanism of the transition.

Every three months I endured a less obscure ritual of my own. In order to keep from plunging into the pocket of neurosis that could open up beneath my feet, anywhere and at any time—such as in the living room after witnessing Ollie's bedtime preparations—I was obliged to visit my psychiatrist, Dr. Glaser, for quarterly updates of my Zoloft prescription. Although the Zoloft had successfully lowered my general feeling of unease, major events, such as any kind of deadline at work or an unintended slight delivered by a stranger, could still smite me with depression and anxiety, especially when the complexity of caring for two incompatible cats, two incompatible rabbits, two naughty parrots, three parakeets, a canary, a dove, five ducks, and a pair of geese wore me out. Since each fifteen-minute session with Dr. Glaser boiled down to his writing out my scrip while I pondered his Johnny Castaway screen saver, a visit every six months would have sufficed. But the office manager insisted that their computer was incapable of scheduling appointments at greater than three-month intervals. I wasn't sure if this meant that I enjoyed better mental health than the practice's other patients, exercised better sales resistance, or if all of us had fallen prey to the same bogus scheduling excuse.

A late-winter meeting with Dr. Glaser that would later turn out to be my last began like every other visit. I wandered around a waiting room whose extravagant spaciousness must have discouraged the treatment of agoraphobics. The problem wasn't finding a place to sit, it was choosing between numerous furniture groupings while wondering if concealed observers were evaluating my choice. Imagine a yawning room the size of an aircraft hanger and stock it with earth-toned couches, loveseats, overstuffed chairs, conference chairs, library tables, coffee tables, end tables, occasional tables, vegetables, table lamps, floor lamps, and accent lighting to form a dozen separate enclaves. Block the windows with opaque curtains, then sprinkle the room with a sparse population of patients pretending we just happened to be in the neighborhood and stopped by to peruse the magazines.

Dr. Glaser drifted in through a door on the distant horizon as I was absorbing an article in *Fitness* magazine on the ten best ways to sculpt my lower body, a subject near and dear to my heart. He wore a bronze-colored suit with a metallic sheen that complemented his therapeutic approach. His arms hung heavily at his sides, inviting me to forego shaking his hand as he greeted me with a brief smile and a warm over-the-forehead stare. Once I had followed him into his nondescript office and seated myself on the inevitable leather couch, he asked me the usual opening question, "Are you still taking the Zoloft?" His inflection suggested that Zoloft was my friend.

"Yes, I am," I answered confidently. Meanwhile, Johnny Castaway had just gotten bonked on the head by a coconut that had dropped from the sole tree on his island, rendering him unconscious during the passage of a cruise ship that might have rescued him.

"Is the Zoloft still effective?"

"Yes."

"Are you experiencing any anxiety or depression while taking the Zoloft?"

"Yes, a little of each. But nothing too debilitating." I did not elaborate upon the pressures of maintaining and losing pets, nor did I mention the "night-night hat," fearing he might enter the information in his database. I hated the thought of one day chancing upon an article in *Psychology Today* about psychiatric patient "Robert," who suffered dangerous delusions about headgear-wearing birds.

"Would you like to increase the dosage of your Zoloft?" he asked with weary encouragement.

"I don't think so."

"Shall I write you a prescription for the same dosage of Zoloft that you are currently taking?"

I nodded. I entertained a thought. Any thought was entertaining under the circumstances. "That's fine. But since we have a couple of minutes, I was wondering if I could ask you a question. About dreams," I added, expecting a light bulb to flash behind his eyes. Surely dreams were the filet mignon of a psychiatrist's sustenance, though Dr. Glaser's manner remained politely disinterested.

"I'll try to answer your question about dreams."

"Here's what I don't understand. Dreams can conceivably take a person anywhere. Anything is possible in dreams. I could visit different planets as easily as walking out a door. But all of the settings in my dreams are, well, incredibly ordinary. They take place at work, or in my parent's house, or garage, or in apartments I used to live in, or in my grandmother's old house. The settings repeat so relentlessly, I could probably list them on half a sheet of paper and still have enough space left over to write a grocery list. I'm just wondering if you might have any ideas why this might be so. The events in my dreams are often complicated, but the settings never are."

Dr. Glaser thought a moment, then surprised me with his answer. "Would you describe yourself as a person who values consistency in your life?" I had to agree that I would. "Then perhaps the regularity of setting is a choice that you have imposed on your dreams, indicating that you function best with routines and habits and don't necessarily adapt well to change."

His words hit me with a powerful insight about pet ownership. Rather than blaming our animals for adding complexity to my life, perhaps I should thank them for simplifying it. After all, they helped reduce the potentially unlimited possibilities of existence to a series of tedious and predictable daily routines. Nothing could suit the temperament of a timid man better. Instead of laying ambitious plans for the future or even building up a healthy clientele for my freelance writing business, I could pack each day to the brim directing ducks in and out of their pens, separating fighting rabbits, and keeping parrot-seed dishes filled. The notion that something other than folly might lie behind my acquisition of nearly countless pets brought me a tingle of joy. I overflowed with gratitude toward Dr. Glaser.

"Thank you for your help," I told him when my fifteen minutes had expired. I felt a little guilty for having underestimated his psychological expertise simply because his couch-side manner wasn't up to snuff. After he had walked me to the reception area, I turned to him and said, "See you in three months."

"Good-bye," he replied, extending his right hand. At first I thought he wanted me to shake it, but he passed me a sealed envelope, spun around, and retreated down the corridor. Out in my car, with the heater blowing and snow covering my windshield, I read a letter informing me that Dr. Glaser was leaving his practice at Psychiatric Professionals to accept a new position as director of a state mental health facility for the criminally insane in southern Indiana. The announcement concluded with the uplifting statement, "I have benefited from my association with each of you and assure you that your records will be transferred to another psychiatric-care physician in time for your next appointment." Shaken by this unexpected intimacy, I wiped away a tear as I guided my car through the gleaming office park. Every faux marble façade, each ramrod-straight, steel-jacket light pole reminded me that I had lost a consummate mental health professional who had taught me the meaning of neurosis.

IF ANYONE BESIDE myself flourished in an environment where habits and routines were deeply ingrained, it was Stanley Sue. Far from remaining the shrinking violet of her first years with us, though, Stanley Sue expanded the range of her introverted nature by exploring the kitchen drawers on the opposite side of the room. If I foolishly neglected to drape a tablecloth over the drawer handles, Stanley took the opportunity to climb from one drawer to the next until, from her perch on the hardware summit, she somehow managed to pry open the topmost drawer. Canning-jar rims, measuring spoons, and plastic cat food lids ended up imprinted with beak marks and strewn across the linoleum. On one outing she nibbled the wooden handle of one of Linda's favorite knives down to the shank.

When Stanley Sue wasn't scaling drawer handles, she stalked the tops of the bunny cages, hoping for a clear shot at pecking Bertie or Rollo through the bars. But the dining room woodwork was more at risk than the rabbits. Her love of chewing compelled me to slide a knee-high plywood board between the backs of the bunny cages and the picture window, hoping it would keep her from reaching the windowsill.

But Stanley's routine destruction of household objects wasn't so easily derailed. Seated on the edge of the board, she would gnaw a section of plywood until she had eaten away an access to the presumably sweeter material of the sill. Back before compact discs had completely phased out LPs, I regularly received albums in the mail to review for my magazine column. Folding their cardboard mailers into various shapes, I wedged them between the cages and plywood board and between the plywood board and the window as a further distraction from her intractable beavering of the woodwork. These also became grist for the mill.

If we waited too long to clean up after her, I might fill two kitchen trashbags with Stanley-generated wood shavings and shredded cardboard that she had deposited in a small space between Bertie's cage and a well-chewed cabinet that held a radio with a dangerously chewed cord.

Despite her bad habits, Stanley Sue's intelligence and good nature kept me from staying angry with her for long. In the morning she would dog my feet in the kitchen, scuttling across the linoleum as I retrieved dry kibbles from the cupboard and canned cat food from the fridge to dump into dishes on the countertop. Fearing I was bent on returning her to her cage, she would balk if I attempted to pick her up. As long as I assured her I simply wanted to take her "upstairs to see kitty," she eagerly hopped onto my hand and rode along. For a few weeks she even seemed poised to learn to "poop" on cue if I said that magic word while holding her above Penny's litter box, but my timing was frequently as poor as hers, and I gave up on it.

She shocked me one Sunday at breakfast when I told her, "Better get on top of your cage if you want your juice." She trotted across the floor, clambered up her cage, and voiced the excited *chuck* note that meant she expected a treat. On a whim I once corrected her, "Not *on* your cage, *in* your cage." She paused inches from the cage top, turned around, and ducked inside. I soon realized that she understood far more than she preferred to let on, obeying most commands only if they resulted in a reward or avoided an unwanted confrontation.

Stanley Sue formed mental connections that seemed to illustrate she was capable of abstract thought. My first inkling of this came when she mocked me with a kissing sound when I lavished praise on another pet. She demonstrated a similar leap in logic after mastering an obnoxiously accurate imitation of our squeaky oven-broiler door and erupting with the sound as soon as Linda's fingers touched the broiler-door handle. Once she lost interest in this stunt, she started making the same squeak when we opened the door to the basement. Her linkage of two completely different-looking but functionally similar objects implied that she understood the concept of a door.

Along with the blossoming of Stanley Sue's personality came a deepening bond between us. During dinner, once I had stopped feeding her long enough to try to eat from my own plate, she often left her cage top to climb the horizontal crosspieces of my chair legs and park herself under my seat. Reaching down to tweak her beak, I no longer feared a bite, at least no more often than the owner of an exuberant cat would fear a nip. If she didn't want to be touched, she turned her head away. If I insisted on picking her up when she was adamantly opposed to it, on rare occasions she would strike me with her beak rather than bite. The solution was respecting her dignity and asking her to do on her own what she would not do with my help. So, if she was happily employed reaching through the bars of Rollo's cage struggling to overturn his water dish, and profoundly resented stepping onto my hand to go back to her cage, I didn't press the matter. Instead I would tell her, "If you won't step up, you have to go into your cage on your own," and bribe her with juice if she still resisted. She would invariably comply. While my approach flew in the face of parrot behavioralists who stress that the "step up" command must be obeyed at all times, the end result was what mattered to me.

Stanley Sue's affection toward me was tempered by her jealousy of other birds. Even if she was occupied with an ambitious woodwork-improvement project, I only had to float a few sweet syllables toward Howard the ring-necked dove to drive her to a fast march across the floor, a climb up the side of her cage, and Quasimodo-like activity with her bell. But Stanley Sue's eyes turned greenest whenever I paid attention to Ollie, who enjoyed chirping, whistling, and chattering in response to a happy tone of voice. He especially savored the cryptic phrase, "Can you say?" which was a holdover from my early attempts to teach him to talk. "Can you say, 'Pretty boy'?" I would ask him, back in the days before our menagerie exploded. "Can you say, 'I'm a bitey little bird'?" While few English words ever entered his vocabulary, asking him, "Can you say?" always elicited delighted peals, which infuriated Stanley Sue, who would squawk and flap her wings as if she were going to swoop down upon the interloper. She only acted out her jealousy if I was sitting on a chair scratching her head as Linda concluded the ritual of the "night-night hat" by presenting Ollie to me with the request, "Say goodnight to Poppy." If my goodnight lasted longer than a couple of clipped words, Stanley Sue would pinch my leg with her beak.

We never got used to Ollie's squawking fits. Repetition made them harder rather than easier to bear. "I am not going to have you ruin every single meal," Linda would fume, hopping up from her chair to spoon corn or peas into his dish. He'd coo and eat contentedly as she stood over him.

"If you're not good, you're going to finish your dinner in the bathroom," I'd threaten when the squawking started again. A green bean or bit of flavored gelatin usually bought us a few moments of peace.

Fortunately, his worst tirades were confined to mealtime. The din of canary songs, dove hoots, parrot whistles, and parakeet chirps throughout the day distracted him from constantly screaming for attention. The parakeets had succeeded in wearing down his bad attitude by using the top of his cage as a gossiping spot and then effortlessly scattering whenever he approached. He grew especially tolerant of Rossy, who spurned the affections of lovestruck

Reggie in favor of perching on Ollie's cage and admiring him just out of beak-striking range.

If I placed Ollie on my shoulder, Rossy and Reggie would join him instantly. A few moments later the shy Sophie would land behind my neck—along with Elliott, the brown and white canary we had bought after Chester's unexpected death the same day we had lost Peggy to the raccoon. A competitive Howard would top the others by settling on my head, dashing my hopes of ever finding employment as a scarecrow.

HOWARD CONTINUED COURTING the parakeets with such misplaced ardor that when the opportunity arose to take in two homeless female doves, we decided to provide him with a harem of his own species. The snowy white turtledoves came to us as Jacob Lestermeyer's feud with his pharisee neighbor boiled over to include the Allegan County sheriff's department, the humane society, and a circuit-court judge. It started with the pharisee's indignant phone call to the sheriff's department when a gang of Lestermeyer's chickens scratched up his meticulously manicured backyard in search of an insect meal, then whitewashed his pristine brick patio for dessert. By the time the animal control officers arrived, a trio of uncontrollable goats was munching on the pharisee's shrubbery—possibly including a one-eared, scarf-wearing ringleader, but I'm speculating here.

"This kind of thing goes on day after day," the pharisee complained to the uniformed animal specialists, possibly with a good deal of arm-waving. (More speculation here.) "Somebody had better take a good long look at what's going on next door," the pharisee demanded, as he pointed toward the petting zoo/butcher shop.

The sheriff's department did take a look at it, and with the assistance of the humane society, determined that Lestermeyer's animals suffered from overcrowding and unsanitary conditions. We had noticed nothing of the kind when we visited his farm the previous year, but that may speak more to the way Linda and I lived than to Allegan County health standards. A judge gave Lestermeyer exactly thirty days to pare down his population of ducks, geese, chickens, pheasants, turkeys, goats, cows, ponies, horses, guinea fowl, donkeys, doves, and mythological visions to exactly one hundred edible and inedible residents.

True to his irascible nature, Jacob defied the court order up until a hair's breadth of the deadline. Linda's friend LuAnne was donating time and money to a farm that took in unwanted and abused animals, and she managed to convince Lestermeyer to part with the prescribed number of beasts, to be housed at the farm sanctuary. Her fear was that if the county shut him down entirely, none of the critters might find proper homes. The same man who had refused my extra two dollars and Linda's donation for feed insisted that LuAnne pay him three hundred dollars for the animals she was helping to relocate. He refused to part with larger livestock that might fetch earnings as steaks and cutlets, which at least made LuAnne's transportation problems easier. Two doves with insufficient meat on their bones thus found their way to our dining room. Howard's bliss was sure to follow. Or so we assumed.

We had no doubt that the new doves were females. They both proved their fecundity within days by laying lovely white eggs in the pot of a hanging Boston fern and depositing others at random in the bottom of their cage. The newcomers were a bachelor dove's dream come true. In contrast to Howard's raucous hoots, the girls cooed a softer, seductive song that all but demanded our horny ringneck come hither. They flaunted their beauty in every region of the room, spreading their wings on a scalloped chair back or strolling a placemat on the table, ostensibly in search of crumbs but in actuality trolling for a husband. What was poor Howard to do but submit to their womanly wiles?

"What the heck?" I asked Linda. "You'd think he'd be going crazy chasing them."

Instead of wooing the heavenly sisters, Howard continued making his normal rounds courting and harassing the parakeets and indulging in episodes of beak-twiddling passion with Reggie. The only interaction among our fawn-colored clown and the pale newcomers came whenever one of the sisters usurped his favorite perching place on top of the parakeets' cage. Rather than swoop down on the interloper with a masculine flourish that could be interpreted as a prelude to conquest, Howard would hop clumsily to the parakeets' cage top, driving off the female with ungentlemanly pecks.

If Linda and I had fallen in love with the doves, we would have given this budding romance the years it needed to unfold. A couple of factors hardened our hearts against the matchmaking. Pigeons, and to a lesser extent doves, have the deserved reputation as besmirchers of statues, park benches, vinyl siding, and windows. Howard was hygienic compared to his outdoor siblings, leaving discreet and easily-picked-up calling cards behind him. Without sinking to the level of giving details that might disturb a yogurt-eating reader, it must be said that the newcomers' droppings were not only plentiful, but they also possessed a sloppy quality that required an endless supply of paper towels. The girls were the miniature equivalents of geese. Added to this was their increasing pugnacity toward our smaller birds. Before long we decided that they should seek residence elsewhere, with Linda acting as their real estate agent.

AFTER LINDA HAD placed the classified ad "two doves free to a good home" in the local weekly shopping newspaper, I braced myself for the same onslaught of erroneous calls that had followed our request for a handyman. To my surprise, nobody phoned to ask about diving boards, Dove ice-cream bars, or the benefits our business offered. A dove fancier willing to drive the fifty miles from Hastings came to our rescue instead. Jonathan turned out to be a breeder who raised and hand-tamed a number of his birds for professional magicians to use in their acts.

"Magicians treat their doves very well," he assured us. Nevertheless, he promised not to sell the sisters but to introduce them to gallant males eager to encourage the laying of fertile eggs. Our pair was already too old to make good show birds, anyway, he explained.

"You have to start working with them almost as soon as they hatch if you want to win their trust," he told us.

"Just like call duck ducklings," I muttered.

Jonathan carried himself with a vibrant confidence that confirmed his claim to be an amateur magician himself. I could imagine his dark brown hair combed and styled to complement a tuxedo with sequined lapels, while his cleanly shaved upper lip cried out for the requisite neatly trimmed mustache. It all fit perfectly, and for all I knew, a cape packed with colored-silk handkerchiefs, tricky decks of cards, and collapsible bouquets huddled mysteriously in the back of his station wagon.

"Who's this guy?" he asked, as he gravitated toward Howard's cage. "You're not thinking of getting rid of him, are you?"

"Always thinking," I told him. Linda shot me a look. "But, no, we certainly couldn't deprive ourselves of Howard."

"He's a very handsome male."

"How can you tell that he's a he?" Linda wondered. "Sometimes *he's* not even sure what he is," and she went on to relate the embarrassing tale of Howard's sexual exploits.

Jonathan explained that male doves possess an apparently wider iris than the females. He held one of the girls close to Howard's cage as proof. Try as I might, I couldn't distinguish any relative difference between the colored portions of their eyes, and no other dove authority has subsequently backed up Jonathan's method for identifying dove gender—which might actually have relied upon an interspecies mind-reading stunt. Leaving us his phone number, the magician's breeder put the pair of females in a cardboard carrier, stepped into his car, and disappeared in a puff of smoke that indicated he needed exhaust-system work.

I HAD BARELY gotten used to the two doves, when suddenly they were gone. And that loss was negated by our gain of a rough-neck Muscovy duck. The day that Linda brought Hector home began pretty much like any other Sunday. After breakfast, I replenished the drinking water, pool water, and scratch feed for the geese and female ducks, let them forage in the yard awhile, then carbon-copied with the male Khaki Campbells. Agnes was rolling around on the cement back deck, so I petted her while Liza and Hailey hogged the pool and the three girl ducks looked on enviously. By the time I had wrapped up my outdoor chores, Linda was finishing braiding her hair in preparation for church in nearby Ionia. The church boasted a full sixteen members, including the pastor's family.

"'Bye, sweetie, I'm leaving now," she told me, planting a kiss on my lips and slinging her purse over her shoulder. Less than thirty seconds later, she trotted back into the house to retrieve her back cushion. "'Bye, sweetie, I'm going," she called, as she darted out the door. I was still struggling to separate the bulky *Grand Rapids Press* Sunday newspaper advertising supplements from their thin news and editorial wrappers when she returned to hurriedly heat up her therapeutic gelatin pack in the microwave. Years of pushing a vacuum cleaner, not to mention other strenuous work throughout her life, had left Linda with a pain in her lower back that marriage to me occasionally sent southward but did nothing to alleviate.

"'Bye, I'm late," she announced.

"See you in ten seconds," I said.

"No you won't." She laughed as she darted outside. Edging forward on the couch, I watched as she pulled her car toward the road, jerked it to a halt inches before its wheels hit the shoulder, flung herself out the car door and to her feet, and made a fresh assault on the house. Punctuating each door-slamming departure and reentry was a pair of baseball-size jingle bells that Linda had tied to the doorknob a couple of Christmases ago and decided to keep in place as an all-season annoyance. The thud of wood against the hoarse rattle of metal had jolted me from many a nap with nightmarish visions of plummeting headlong into a medieval forge.

Jingle! "Forgot my church collection money," she explained, as I pondered a perplexing installment of *The Family Circus* comic strip. "Bye-bye." *Jingle!*

Jingle! "I need my Bible." She grabbed it from a wicker basket perched on one of my hi-fi speakers, almost sending the basket and ten pounds of clutter crashing to the floor. "See you." *Jingle!*

Jingle! "Have you seen Grapey?"

"I don't keep track of your hats."

The errant stocking cap was exactly where it belonged, on the top tier of the coat rack next to the "night-night hat."

"That everything?" I asked.

"Drink of water." She thundered into the bathroom and out again. "'Bye!" *Jingle!*

Jingle! "Don't forget, I'm going to try to talk that farmer into giving us that duck."

"Jeez." *Jingle!*

I had forgotten all about the duck. Ceasing to purchase new animals no longer saved us from acquiring new animals. Without warning, we had slid across an unmarked border into the territory of animal rescuers. It was a realm that demanded a high state of alertness lest we join a group that thought nothing of devoting every waking moment, dollar of income, and square inch of property to caring for the unstoppable tide of unwanted pets. As pet owners, we were way over the edge of excess with our bird, cat, and rabbit menagerie. I couldn't see myself joining the ranks of animal rescuers without descending into a bottomless hell of crabbiness. But I did find myself agreeing to take in animals, especially when their lot in life was as pitiful as Hector's.

The drive from Lowell to Ionia along M-21 always provided a wealth of interesting sights. My favorite was an ancient Standard Oil gas-station sign embedded in the bank, or perhaps the Dumpster built to resemble a miniature house. Linda's favorite had been a complex of pens containing tame white-tail deer near the village of Saranac, until the owner blocked her view with a stockade fence to protect them from trigger-happy, beer-besotted hunters. She also enjoyed a barnyard where white Charolais cattle ate constantly from their trough. One Sunday, as she drove to church, she noticed a tiny enclosure on the Charolais property with a large bird inside. On her way home, a closer look revealed a dirty white Muscovy duck confined to a cage so small he didn't have room to flap his wings. Never one to shy away from promoting animal welfare—especially when it involved the chance to knock on a total stranger's door and engage in conversation—Linda decided to ask the farmer to sell her the duck.

I met Linda in our driveway after church. Peering through her car window, I noticed that the animal carrier had migrated from her trunk to the backseat, but I couldn't tell for sure if the duck was inside. "Did you talk to him?"

"He was a really nice guy."

"Then why was he keeping a duck in a cramped little cage?"

"We might not know what to do with him, either," she answered.

"Why is that?"

"He didn't want to sell him to me. I offered him ten dollars, but he wouldn't take it. He said he was a really mean duck that they originally got as a Christmas present for the grandchildren, and they used to fuss over him all the time. Then when he got bigger, he started hissing at the kids—he hisses at everyone—and chased them around the yard. He became such a nuisance trying to bite people, he eventually had to put him in a cage. He used to be in with another duck, but he thinks he might have killed it, because they woke up one morning and the other duck was dead."

"Well, we don't want that kind of duck, either."

"He looked so pathetic in that cage, I asked the farmer, 'Would you sell him to me?' and I tried to give him ten dollars, but he told me no. He said the duck was only worth twenty-five cents, and that's all he would take. He made me give him a quarter. But he told me not to take any chances, to keep the duck away from us and keep him away from the other ducks. So you'll have to put up a fence to keep him separate."

"What do you mean, 'a fence'?"

"Like the loop you put in the pen to separate the call ducks," she answered cheerily. "I want to call him Hector."

"I don't want him at all. He sounds too dangerous to keep."

"He looks like a Hector."

"I've still got the loop," I conceded. "I saved it."

"Make sure he can't get out of it," Linda said. "I don't want any of our ducks getting killed."

With trepidation, I trudged briskly to the lower level of the barn, where I had left the wire loop curled up next to the disassembled tree-branch "teepees" that had supported Linda's pole beans the previous year. Even the geese seemed nervous when I dragged the fence into their pen, and honk restlessly as I nailed it to the wooden posts with poultry staples. Finishing the task with a couple of hammer whacks, I brooded about a sociopathic twenty-five-cent Muscovy possibly disrupting our peaceful duck and goose society. Hector's introduction also put my own well-being at risk, as defined by Dr. Glaser. Despite the occasional bouts of animal injury or illness, pet care had settled into a series of routines and rituals, from bedtime vocal concerts to elaborate parrot feedings. Hector stood poised to add an element of chaos. He threatened to complicate rather than simplify my life. What would come next after taking in a killer duck? Living with bears in the hollowed-out side of a hill?

"It's done," I told Linda, who waited outside the duck pen with the animal carrier in tow. "You might as well grab him out and bring him in."

"I'm not picking him up!"

"Then put the carrier inside the loop."

The carrier entered the circular enclosure as I stepped out of it. Leaning down, I popped the latch with as little finger contact with the front grate as possible. Clutching the top handle and the smooth plastic back, I tipped the carrier forward, releasing the Muscovy in the same way I had released the raccoons. My first glimpse of Hector shocked me. He was as wiry and tough a duck as I could have imagined. His feathers were white but soiled by streaks of dirt. Patches of yellow on the flat of his tail suggested a recent dabbing with iodine. But his face was the immediate attention getter. While Daphne wore a demure mask of bare facial skin, the entire front of Hector's head was encased in a bright red fleshy, knobby mass that no stretch of the imagination could term visually appealing. He didn't need defenses against rivals or predators. Appearance alone would discourage attack. Compounding the effect of this visceral hood, a narrow crest of feathers rose from his head in a series of connected spikes. Beak wide open, steely eyes flashing, he panted a gravelly succession of hisses whose vehemence made me retreat from the fence, swallow hard, back out of the pen, and wish the other residents the best of luck.

The spectacle of Hector compelled me to reconsider Dr. Glaser's insight to my dreams. Maybe they didn't reflect my love of habit and routines after all and were as bland as unbuttered toast for a far more obvious reason. My days included such improbabilities as a parrot that could reason, a dove-breeding magician, bunny songs, the night-night hat, a duck that personified a raging id, and my role as a tree for our birds. With waking hours that outrageous, who needed an excursion to Xanadu after dark?

CHAPTER 10

Let's Talk Turkey

Sweetheart, come out here quick! Hurry, sweetheart."
A fresh layer of snow tried to muffle Linda's voice. But her summons still reached me upstairs from the backyard, penetrating two panes of glass, thirty feet of diagonal space, and the pleasant *whoosh* of heated air through the furnace duct. I was lounging in my office enjoying a cup of ginger tea and savoring the fact that Linda was taking care of the ducks on a frigid January afternoon while I read a detective novel with a warm cat pressed against my leg.

"Sweetie, come quick, it's Hector!"

Bolting out of my chair, I thudded down a flight of stairs, dodged a twenty-five-pound bag of rabbit food in the living room corridor, and bounded toward the basement. Various unpleasant scenarios crowded my brain. The farmer who had sold us Hector three months earlier was right about our Muscovy's mercurial personality. Hector could have injured one of our ducks, though so far he had reserved his aggressive attitude for people. That meant he might be chasing Linda. When gripped by a darker mood, he would not be deterred from latching on to a leg or article of clothing with his wickedly serrated beak. Or the blowhard could have clashed with our neighbor's dog or a raccoon on snack break from hibernation. Clomping across the basement floor, I expected the worst as I threw open the back door. Nothing could have prepared me for what I saw.

Dressed in a nylon jacket and crowned with the inevitable stocking cap, Linda stood beaming on the back deck with a large white duck perched on her shoulder.

"What is he doing up there? Are you okay?" I demanded, fearful that Hector might have bitten my wife silly.

"He flew up there himself. Well, he didn't exactly fly. I was bending down to pick up the hose, and he sort of climbed up all on his own."

"You must be very proud," I muttered above the hammering of my heart. "Both of you."

"Take a picture of us, sweetie!"

WE HAD AT FIRST treated Hector with such extraordinary caution, he might as well have been a fer-de-lance. Isolated in his wire loop, he was safely prevented from inflicting any evil on our geese and ducks that his Muscovy mind might devise. I was especially wary of him. When dangling an arm into his loop to give him water or a fresh bowl of feed, I moved in exaggeratedly slow motion, speaking in the same reassuring voice that Dr. Glaser had used successfully with me.

"Now, I'm just giving you something nice to eat, Hector," I'd quietly explain. "Here, I'm setting down the bowl, and in no way should my fingers remind you of edible pink worms. They are far too bony to enjoy, not succulent like Linda's, if you get my drift."

After a couple of days of keeping Hector in solitary confinement,

Linda complained, "This isn't any better than the way he lived before. He needs room to move around."

"How about Idaho?"

"Just let him out. He looks utterly harmless to me."

"So did Ollie, and Hector's a lot bigger."

But the next time the ducks were grazing in the yard, Linda deemed it a good opportunity to test Hector's social skills, despite my whining protests. "It's a huge area," she pointed out. "He shouldn't feel territorial or hostile toward the ducks or geese."

"How about toward the person who picks him up?"

With a dismissive sigh, Linda reached into Hector's pen, pulled him out without incident, and deposited him on the grass near our geese Liza and Hailey. I took two long steps sideways that simultaneously took me closer to the geese in order to protect them in case of an attack and also closer to the basement door should I decide to run for it instead. The geese continued nibbling at the lawn as Hector waggled his tail and waddled a few steps toward them. The female ducks busied themselves patrolling the area near the spirea bush in search of fresh patches of gourmet mud. Stewart and Trevor shadowed the females at a distance, confused by their low autumnal hormone levels as to what they should do next. A tanker truck thundered past the house. A sulfur butterfly fluttered in a splash of sunlight on the border of our woods. Hector moved closer to Liza, flapped his wings, and ambled off on his own in another direction.

Once back inside the pen, the story was different. The geese and female ducks gave the liberated Hector a wide berth, as if they were noticing him for the first time, while Stewart and Trevor quacked in whispered gratitude for the fence that separated them from the Muscovy. Hector walked to the water bucket, towing a perimeter of empty space around him. Looking bored, he gave the feed dish a perfunctory peck, toddled toward Maxine, who scurried away from him, then began preening the base of his neck with his beak. From the open basement door, I leaned toward the yard, expecting a ruckus at any moment. During dinner, deafened to the outside world by the indoor birds, we peered through the windows. A placid white shape stood by as the geese splashed in the pool. Then it was dark. There was no trouble the next day, either.

Hector turned out to be a complex Jekyll and Hyde of a fellow who seldom socialized with the other ducks. For days at a time, his behavior was innocuous almost to the point of invisibility, as he kept silently to himself while brooding over weighty matters known only to a waterfowl who doesn't enjoy the water. His antipathy toward the pool was responsible for the dirt-streaked feathers that gave him the air of a tough from the wrong side of the marsh. Even by Muscovy standards, the preen gland at the base of his back wasn't up to snuff. Try as he might to groom his feathers, his beak either came up dry or globbed his tail and lower back with yellow spots. Once Linda realized how agreeable our "Ducker Jekyll" could be, she occasionally whisked him into the basement, plunked him in the laundry tub, and lathered him up with baby shampoo. "I think he likes it!" a soaked Linda would holler up the stairs to me, as Hector thrashed in the basin. She never quite got him clean—industrial solvents would have been required—but he looked substantially better after a bath and sported an agreeable Johnson & Johnson scent.

Hector's Mr. Hyde aspect would descend upon him without warning. One day he'd be docile and withdrawn. The next day, without so much as the portent of a full moon, he would undergo a personality cataclysm. As if seized by the spirit of a rabid lapdog, he would follow us around the yard panting with great gusto, his crimson-masked head thrown back, beak thrust open, crest raised, and glassy eyes lit with incomprehensible intent. "He just wants to be petted," Linda explained, and against any prediction I would have made, he huffed and puffed contentedly in place as she stroked the back of his neck. If she sat down in the grass, he would actually climb upon her lap in search of affection.

But petting him could be risky. His hissing just as often gave way to aggression, as he defended what he considered his territory. When Hector was out of the pen and out of sorts, I seldom ventured into the backyard without a pushbroom to push between my body and his jagged-edged bill, capable of inflicting frighteningly hued hematomas. If he was bent upon attack, there was no cowing him. On one occasion, each time he came at me with bloodlust on his brain, I picked him up and tossed him in the air, but he would not be discouraged. Fluttering to the ground, he resumed the attack unceasingly and tirelessly. When he was in such a state, there was no herding him back to the pen with the others. Carefully avoiding his snapping beak, I picked him up, clamped him against my chest, and plunked him down inside the pen. But he never transferred this hostility to his fellow inmates. He wandered sullenly but nonviolently among the ducks and geese, as disconnected from their social order as a tortoise at a bridge tournament.

Though Hector's good days and bad days were evenly doled out, we doted on his outgoing personality most of the time and found more comedy than threat in his rages. He was mysteriously selective in his judgments about people. Whenever my parents and sisters, Joan and Bette, came for a Saturday lunch, we inevitably lured them into the yard. Without hesitation, Hector would bypass my well-nipped legs in favor of launching beak strikes at my mother. She was, in fact, the first of us ever to suffer a Hector attack, and because she was so engrossed describing a friend's latest ailment, she didn't even notice that a large duck was chewing on the hem of her dress until I pulled him away. Just as quickly as Hector categorized my mom as beak fodder, he tagged Linda's friend Deanne a romantic interest.

"Isn't he sweet," cooed Linda, as Deanne sat under our hackberry tree holding and stroking the love-struck miscreant. "I hope he decides to become Daphne's husband. Rupert Murdoch said that Muscovies make the best mothers."

"What a thought. That would mean more ducklings," I pointed out.

"I would love it if we had some baby ducklings."

"Muscovy ducklings," I added, but Linda still didn't get my drift.

"Growing up into big Muscovies. Like Hector," Deanne prompted. Sensing that he was being insulted, Hector scuffled his clawed feet until Deanne set him on the ground.

WE DID END UP with baby ducks, but Daphne wasn't the mother. Before the first snowfall of the season arrived—and a month before Hector turned himself into my wife's epaulet—Daphne grew listless and stopped eating. Linda brought her indoors late one afternoon to spare her from a cold and windy night, and by morning she was dead.

"I think she was older than we knew," Linda said. "She looked old when we first got her." And it was true that even in death she seemed worn down rather than at rest. She had carried the heavy burden of ushering us into the world of poultry and had witnessed the passing of three friends—Phoebe, Martha, and feisty little Peggy. She was not only our first duck, she was our sole mouse-devouring duck, and her passing saddened us.

Although our waterfowl dormitory was segregated into male and female residences, we frequently allowed the boys and girls to mingle in the yard once spring had passed and Stewart and Trevor were no longer constantly chasing the hens—and I use that word correctly. Female ducks are hens. Male ducks are drakes. And duck owners who permit unchaperoned conjugals are asking for unplanned embryos. We were accustomed to Maxine and Chloe disappearing into their doghouses and sitting on a nest of unfertilized eggs for days on end, rarely abandoning their vigil to eat, drink, or upbraid our lawn. So we didn't take the latest round of incubation behavior seriously until the morning we were greeted with the sound of peeping from the pen. Maxine jealously guarded four brown-and-yellow gobs of fluff. Chloe had just one duckling of her own. Considering her broken leg and limited mobility, one youngster was probably all she could handle. Chloe proved that she could handle me just fine when I reached for the tiny brown baby and she flew at my face. Miraculously, she missed my nose—only to catch my wrist with two rattlesnake-quick bites.

Linda was ecstatic about the babies. She laughed when they came out from their shelters to peck crumbled duck meal, whooped when they flapped their stubby, featherless wings, and nearly exploded when three of them tried swimming in their water bowl. But she also felt the weight of worry that any new mother undergoes. "What if Hector's mean to them?" though he was too self-absorbed to even acknowledge their presence underfoot. "What if they get stuck in the swimming pool and drown," she fretted, but they were too small to climb over the rim. "Do you think they'll be safe out in the yard?" Behaving like miniature adults, they followed the other ducks around the lawn, the synchronized twitching of green sprigs betraying their presence in the tall grass.

Even I got caught up in the excitement, phoning my friend Brian in Washington, D.C., to brag, "We've got baby ducks!"

"So do we," Brian replied. "We've got them in the pond behind the condo."

"But these are ours," I emphasized. "We're raising them."

"We've got all kinds of them," Brian bragged. "You've got to come out here and see them."

By midsummer, the ducklings had grown as large as their parents. They had also sprouted adult feathers and acquired determinable genders. Chloe's Clara was her double. Via one or both of the male Khaki Campbells, Maxine had produced the mostly brown Gwelda, who wore a mallard's white and blue hashmarks on her wings, and the miraculous Marybelle, who accessorized a coat like her sister Gwelda's by adding a beige ring around her neck.

"Are you sure Howard didn't get out into the duck pen?" I grilled Linda. "That ring looks like his work."

The two male ducklings had rather plain brown-and-cream bodies offset by the dark green head and roguish curlicued tail feathers of a male mallard. We shuttled them into the boys' enclosure lest further demon-seed hybrid offspring appear, but son and nephew fought so vigorously with father and uncle that we rapidly returned the newcomers to the female sector, figuring we could postpone dealing with their housing until spring when they would receive their first full wallop of duck testosterone. The addition of five ducks to a pen already occupied by Chloe, Maxine, Hector, Liza, and Hailey might have crowded the female side of the fence if the entire group hadn't gotten along so well. But we threatened the harmonious atmosphere when we unexpectedly took in a quartet of birds vastly more unruly than the greenheads and several magnitudes bulkier.

THE FREDERIK MEIJER GARDENS was a botanical garden fifteen minutes from our house. Linda and I particularly enjoyed visiting the rain forest conservatory on weekends, when members of the Great Lakes Aviary Society showed off their pet parrots against an ersatz jungle backdrop. One Sunday we had been admiring a sulfur-crested cockatoo with a louder voice and far more demanding personality than Ollie's and were gleefully reminiscing about the sad expression on the owner's face as we started back home. No sooner had we pulled onto Bradford Street alongside the Gardens when Linda blurted, "Pull over! Pull over! Right here! Don't you see them?" Remarkably, I hadn't. On the side of the road, a trio of black and bronze–colored turkeys with flashes of green iridescence on their backs surrounded a fourth turkey huddled on the ground. They yipped like dogs as we rolled to a stop.

My only experience with wild turkeys had occurred a couple of months earlier at the house of our friends Tam and Steve on the Flat River. Squatting in their living room, we had peeked through a window at turkeys so shy, they scattered at the movement of a curtain. These, on the other hand, refused to budge when Linda and I climbed out of the car. Instead, the three standing turkeys advanced on us as Linda knelt next to the downed bird. Two made warbling cooing sounds while the third pecked insistently at my shoe. If their behavior was unlikely, so was the setting, which favored neither wild nor domestic poultry. Though evidence of woods and meadows lay all around us, their habitat was broken up by a subdivision. Behind a stand of trees that at first glance appeared to be a woods, the newest homes concealed their wealth. An elderly woman across the street watched the turkeys mob us as she tended a neatly coiffured hedge. Linda trotted up the front walk, and with her usual enthusiasm, inquired whether the woman knew anything about the birds.

"Oh, them," the woman chuckled. "They make their rounds every day. They like to go from yard to yard and visit us. They're crazy about people."

"Where did they come from?" asked Linda.

The woman gestured vaguely toward the thicket where the turkeys were gathered. "The Oostdykes. They had a lot more of them, but these are all that's left."

I had tentatively moved toward the conversation, then backed off for fear that I might end up in the backyard touring a ceramic-frog collection. After a long interval during which civilizations rose and crumbled to dust, Linda finally returned to fill me in on the story. A young couple called the Oostdykes had spotted a few wild turkey stragglers upon moving to their upscale suburban neighborhood and decided it would be great ecological fun to supplement their number. They bought thirty-six turkey chicks, hand-fed them for several weeks in their cavernous garage, and when the birds got too large to handle, unleashed them upon the world. The young toms and hens explored the area but did not successfully colonize. Within three months, the three dozen had dwindled to the four individuals here on the shoulder of the road. Contributing to their troubles in the wild, we later determined, was their lineage as hybridized birds bred for dinner-platter delectability. Engineered for maximum body weight and minimum initiative, they had about as much chance of making it on their own as our pasta-eating parrot, Ollie.

"John—that's the husband—said that foxes got most of them. Some broke their legs falling out of trees," Linda told me. She grimaced. "He ended up shooting them. We better see if we can get the injured one some help."

I often find myself wondering how my college-age self of the 1970s would regard what I have become. He might have forgiven my move out to the country. He would not have accepted my adoption of ducks and geese. And if a time traveler from the 1990s had materialized in front of College Bob to play him a video of Married Bob struggling under the weight of a thirty-pound turkey, while

three more turkeys followed him up a curved driveway behind a
scrim of trees, it's safe to say that I/me/he would have joined a Tibetan
monastery to prevent such a catastrophe from coming to pass.

While I did my best to hide behind the unexpectedly placid
turkey, Linda rang the Oostdyke's bell. It resounded with an au-
thoritative Westminster chime designed to signal that we were
darkening the doorstep of people with oodles of money. The three
turkeys pecked at the lawn near a Tiffany gas lamp, where rem-
nants of scratch feed showed signs that the area served as a feeding
station. They didn't seem inclined to wander, so I set down the
fourth upon a bed of exotic Sulawesi Island hardwood mulch. Ex-
tracting a sales slip from her purse, Linda wrote a note explaining
that we were willing to take the turkeys, added our phone number,
and wedged the folded note into the solid platinum doorframe.

AGAINST ALL ODDS, I genuinely liked turkeys. Shortly after
we were married, Linda and I took her mom to the Kellogg Bird
Sanctuary near Battle Creek. As we walked from habitat to habitat
watching swans, geese, and ducks, a turkey tagged along for no apparent reason other than that it enjoyed our company. Staying just
behind us on the walkway, it even ignored the corn we flung at the
waterfowl. More recently, Linda and I had stayed overnight in a
blue caboose at the Choo-Choo Motel in Strasbourg, Pennsylvania,
in the heart of Amish country. A de facto petting zoo on the premises included turkeys that perched unperturbed on a split-rail fence
as I posed among them for a snapshot. The turkeys were far more
trusting than any other bird I had ever encountered, and I found
an unexpected sweetness in their faces. Their large eyes, miniscule
heads, comically massive bodies, and clumsiness when attempting
to do anything other than standing in one spot struck a responsive
chord.

Although I was eager to help the Bradford Street turkeys, I was uneasy about taking on a full quartet. For one thing, we had no clear idea where to put them. The barn seemed like the natural place, but they couldn't live entirely indoors. Our fenced-in backyard was a good three hundred feet from the closest entrance to the barn, and I knew that the turkeys wouldn't herd any better than the indomitable Hector. I also wasn't keen on acquiring an injured bird in need of immediate medical help. That matter, at least, was cleared up to Linda's satisfaction when Nancy Oostdyke called her the same night.

"I would be absolutely thrilled to have you take the turkeys," she told Linda. "They've become real nuisances, chasing the children around the yard. There's only one problem."

"I wanted to ask you about that," said Linda. "What happened to the turkey that can't walk?"

"Which one can't walk?"

"The one we left laying down next to your yard light."

"They were all walking around when we came home from the cottage. They wouldn't leave the kids alone."

I was thunderstruck when Linda reported this to me. "What does she mean all four turkeys were walking around? Did she actually see them walking around?"

"I asked her about it twice. I said, 'Are you sure all four turkeys are okay? Are you positive?' And she told me there wasn't anything wrong with them as far as she could see."

"That doesn't make any sense," I complained. "Unless they're just trying to dump an injured turkey on us."

"That's not it," Linda said. "The husband doesn't even want us to take them. Nancy—that's the wife—has to talk to John and get back to us tomorrow. He wants to keep them, but she thinks she can convince him they'd be better off with us. And she also said they'd only give them to us if all of them were healthy," she added, to forestall further pointless arguments from me about the fourth turkey's ability to walk.

Later that night, Nancy Oostdyke called Linda back and agreed to give us the turkeys. John would even bring them over himself. It turned out his reluctance to part with them had little to do with attachment to the birds. His kids had their hearts set on taking a turkey to school for show-and-tell when Thanksgiving week rolled around, and we had to give our word to lend them one for the occasion.

"Did you ask her again about the injured bird?"

"Her husband said the turkey was fond of lying down."

"Fond of lying down?" I sputtered. "That's ridiculous. It couldn't even stand up."

"We'll see for ourselves tomorrow when Mr. Oostdyke brings them here," she told me, in the patient tone of voice used with a slow-on-the-uptake child.

John Oostdyke arrived right after dinner with a refrigerator-size cage containing all four turkeys in the bed of a gleaming dollar bill–green pickup truck. Not only was he filthy with money, but he was also sickeningly healthy. I didn't realize what a big guy he was until he stood next to me and took my robin's foot of a hand into his massive paw. While I had struggled under the load of a single turkey, Oostdyke grabbed two of the birds, pressed one under each arm, and whisked them down to our duck pen. He carried them as easily as one would two bags of groceries, with almost as much regard for his cargo. Two children trailed behind him. I hadn't seen them earlier, presumably because they had been engulfed by his shadow.

"That's the four of them," he boomed, as he released the last two birds. Our ducks and geese huddled together in a corner on the far side of the pen. Even Hector seemed cowed by the bustling visitor.

"Daddy, it's a goose," the blond-haired girl observed, as she pointed at Liza.

"All of them standing," he offered, with a generous smile in my direction.

"Are those your geese?" the girl asked me. The boy entered the pen to bid one of the turkeys farewell by stroking its neck. Then he jumped back, shielding his face as two of the turkeys flapped their wings and hopped clumsily to the top of a squat shelter resembling a failed bookcase that I had built for the ducks.

"Come on kids, Mom's expecting us."

"Thanks so much for the turkeys. We'll take good care of them," Linda assured him. "Call us before Thanksgiving if you want to borrow one." The little boy nodded happily as his father grasped the cab of their pickup truck, lifted the vehicle to shoulder height, shook open both doors, and set it back down on the gravel—or if he didn't actually do that, he looked as if he could have. With a couple of toots of the horn and strands of blond hair trailing out an open window, the Oostdykes were gone.

"We've been visited by a god," I mused, but Linda was already down at the pen yelling at me to come quickly.

Imagine a square divided into four smaller squares. The boys' enclosure consisted of a single square with its own door to the outside, while the more numerous girls occupied the remaining L-shaped enclosure. To accommodate the turkeys overnight, I had blocked the leg of the L at foot level with a board. Higher up, I had stretched an old wool blanket between two vertical pen supports to discourage border transgression by flight. The cobbled-together divider would have worked fine with a duck, because a duck would never try to breach what appeared to be a solid barrier. However, I had vastly underestimated the strength, stubbornness, and unusual worldview of a turkey. The gobblers completely ignored the flimsy blanket in favor of launching themselves at the wire pen walls like feathered cannonballs.

"They're not used to being cooped up," Linda told me, as the entire pen shook around us. Each time a turkey threw its weight against the wire, it sounded as if a monstrous tennis racquet had served up a wet Saint Bernard.

"We can't let them roam loose!" I said. I had to holler to hear my own voice above a cacophony of turkey yips and goose honks.

"They can't stay in here, either. They'll wreck the pen."

"We'll have to put them in the barn."

"They'll hate that even more. But at least they can't knock it down."

"We'd better do it now!" I urged Linda, gallantly allowing her to precede me into the poultry maelstrom. Fortunately, the turkeys' unruliness was wholly directed at the enclosure. They probably regarded us as fellow prisoners pitching in to help them escape. Linda and I each picked up a bird. They protested no further than to make a few pro forma flaps of the wings and some halfhearted foot-thrashing as we toted them out to the barn, into the same enclosure that Daphne had hated so much. But instead of massing for a punishing attack on the plank walls, the turkeys settled down and acted right at home, as if a propensity for barns had been lurking in their genes all along. One by one they half-hopped, half-flew up to the wooden stanchion rails and settled in for a peaceful snooze.

That left us with the problem of what to do with them during the day. In the back of my mind stirred the idea of somehow shuffling the ducks around and acclimating the turkeys to a section of their pen. Then they could amble around the yard while the ducks strip-mined our few remaining patches of healthy lawn. This seemed to be the easiest solution. They certainly couldn't lead a dual life on the eastern and western extremities of our property with terra turkey incognita in between.

After the turkeys had assembled in the backyard to suitable arm-waving and shouted encouragement from us, we released the female ducks and geese. Disaster was immediate. As soon as the birds had waddled out of their pen, the turkeys took off after them. The fury they had shown the previous night toward the walls of the duck pen was nothing compared to the vigor with which they lit into the waterfowl. While I didn't witness them actually land a single peck, the terrorism of their pursuit was punishing enough. The ducks and geese must have felt like Roman soldiers upon seeing Hannibal's elephants bearing down on them. Hollering for them to stop, Linda and I added our bodies to the mêlée. College Bob would have abandoned all hope for the future at the sorry spectacle of Married Bob chasing turkeys that were chasing ducks, and sympathy stirred in my bosom for me/us. Once again, the turkeys didn't struggle when we caught them. They were grateful to be removed from the company of their inferiors and happy to return to their beloved barn. Clearly they would have to live there, and clearly I would have to add another round of fence-building to my résumé.

Just in time, the following Saturday, to prepare for Bill Holm's appearance as my caustic construction assistant, I had my first visit to Psychiatric Professionals for the renewal of my Zoloft prescription since Dr. Glaser's departure. Dr. Jerold Rick could hardly have been more different from his predecessor. He introduced himself with a hearty handshake, tarried in the doorway of a kitchenette to ask if I wanted a cup of coffee, then led me to an office whose picture-covered walls had more personality than I did. Dr. Rick opened our session by devoting a couple of minutes to giving me his background: College in upstate New York in the late 1970s. Travels in Central America and Eastern Europe. Medical school in

Illinois. Primary practice in Okemos, just outside of Lansing. Gig at Psychiatric Professionals two days a week. House in the country. Passionate about woodworking and music. As he talked, I read the driftwood-framed Thoreau quote above his head, admired a Martin guitar nestled in a metal tripod near his desk, and examined the picture on his computer screen of an Amish barn raising for any sign of Johnny Castaway–type activity.

Dr. Rick slouched in an overstuffed chair with his legs crossed. I could easily imagine his curly, greying hair extended to shoulder length and his fingers pinching a fat doobie. Appearances to the contrary, he turned out to be anything but laid-back. Unlike the pharmaceutical companies' best friend, Dr. Glaser, he immediately expressed an antipathy toward a pill-popping approach to mental health.

"How long are you planning on taking the Zoloft?" he asked abruptly.

"As long as I need to," I told him. He had not made it sound as if the Zoloft were my best friend.

"It doesn't bother you that you could be taking this drug for the rest of your life?"

I shook my head. "I don't consider myself any different than a person who needs thyroid medication. Besides, I'm taking an awfully low dosage, so I don't think I have to worry about long-term effects too much."

He leaned forward in his chair. "What makes you think a low dosage of Zoloft would have fewer long-term effects than a higher dose? There hasn't been any long-term research on Zoloft or Prozac or any of the other SSRI drugs, because they haven't been around long enough for extended studies."

"So you're saying I should stop taking Zoloft even though it's helping me," I said, as a flush of anger rose to my face.

"No, I'm not saying that at all. I just wanted to understand your attitude toward the medication."

"Would you like to recommend an alternative?"

"Relax," he told me. "No, not at all. You're doing fine." But he left me feeling unsettled and confused, which is probably how a clever psychiatrist guarantees repeat business.

The prospect of assembling yet another fence did little to lift my spirits. The armload of fence posts needed for a six-foot-high, dog-proof enclosure filled the interior of my car from its back deck to the dashboard, and the sharp metal ends of the posts gouged figure-eights into my glove-compartment door as I trucked them home. I first tried to carry, then ended up rolling, two heavy bails of fifty-foot fencing from our driveway to the barn, gasped for breath at the exertion, and was splashing my face with water from the pump when Bill Holm arrived.

"Sink broken? Or are the turkeys using your bathroom?"

"They're just over there," I told him, pointing to the enclosure. "Go on in and introduce yourself."

"Really?"

"Absolutely. They like people a lot." I neglected to mention that their expression of affection included launching amorous pecks at the arms and legs of admirers. Each turkey was the equivalent of Hector with a sharp beak, and commingling with four at once kept a person on his toes. "They love being petted on the head," I suggested.

"They are kind of pretty up close," he called back. "Aren't you beautiful?" he cooed to one of the girls. Linda and I had determined that all four birds were females by studying pictures in our birding field guides and noting the absence of fleshy dewlaps. It didn't take long for Bill to experience the full glory of turkey behavior. "Ouch!" he hollered. "One of them's biting me. Yowch! Two of them. Stop it! How do I get out of here? I'm surrounded!"

"They'll do that," I told him blandly, as I left the barn and headed for the basement to fetch the tools.

In theory, putting up a poultry fence was simple. You mapped out the shape of your enclosure, pounded in the metal posts at three-foot intervals, and hooked the fencing under the tabs on the posts, unrolling the bail as you went. Then you gave each post a couple of final whacks with a hammer to tighten its grasp on the fencing. But success depends on being able to sink your posts more than an inch into the ground. The barn seemed to have been built on top of a heap of boulders sprinkled with a cosmetic layer of dirt. As a result, Bill and I were forced to significantly alter the enclosure shape. I would begin by positioning a post at an ideal location, beat on it in vain with a hammer, then shake my head to relieve the ringing in my ears produced by metal striking rock. With the greatest optimism, I would move the post two inches in each compass direction. In the end I would have to deviate a foot or so off the parallel before I managed to slip the post into a crevice between adjacent boulders.

"Weren't we trying to make a rectangle?" Bill snorted.

"This follows the natural contours better than a static rectilinear form," I said.

"'Natural contours' is right. It's shaped exactly like your head, if you can call that natural."

I shushed him. "Hold it a second."

"What?"

"You hear that?" Off and on throughout the morning, the turkeys had erupted into doggy yips from the other side of the barn door. "Somebody's looking for you," I told him. "You better go to her. But this time don't lead her on with talk about how beautiful she is unless you plan on making an honest turkey of her."

The turkeys took to their outdoor pen at once. It was large

enough that they didn't experience the kind of anxiety attack that had gripped them in the duck pen, which was fortunate. I didn't think I'd have much luck convincing Dr. Rick to give me four more prescriptions for Zoloft. Even though they now had three hundred square feet of weed-infested, stony ground to explore, Linda was afraid they'd miss the rambling lifestyle of their Bradford Street days. Their love of the barn outweighed their wanderlust, however. Some days, in fact, even after Linda pushed open their door, they didn't bother to hop down from the stanchion rails until she went back to the barn, shooed them to the floor, and hustled them outside.

Because the turkeys were essentially self-contained—coming and going from barn to pen as they pleased—I didn't expect that Linda would have an opportunity to spoil them. But she managed. She decided that apples would be good for their health. At night after she had closed up the barn and the turkeys were on their perches, Linda would go from bird to bird holding an apple in her hand, allowing each turkey to peck at it. One evening she told me, "I don't think the girls are happy about having to bite into a whole apple." I had no suitable response. I merely watched as she diced the apple and put it into a bowl, which she presented to their highnesses in turn. And to insure that no turkey felt left out, she would offer each bird only a bite at a time so that she could make several rounds. The fussier turkeys might let the bowl pass them once or twice before they deigned to take their treat.

One night after she came in from the barn, I told her, "I can't believe anyone thinks turkeys are stupid."

CHAPTER 11

Who Cooks for You?

I knew I never should have called the owl into our yard. I don't consider myself particularly superstitious, although it's true I won't go anywhere in my car without buckling the seat belt first, and I have a phobia about running red lights or driving in reverse on the freeway. Automobiles aside, I like to think my decisions in life are guided by the rudder of common sense rather than blown willy-nilly by folkloric hokum and balderdash. But something about owls gives me the creeps. They're secretive. They inhabit dark and lonely places. Their cries are eerie and foreboding. They see better on a moonless night than I do in full light of day huddled in front of my computer screen. They can zero in on prey using their hearing alone, swooping down on huge wings that make less of a rustle than an ant crawling on a napkin. Not for nothing are owls considered potent symbols of the invisible realm and harbingers of death.

But I couldn't resist calling one into our yard. It was a barred owl, and ever since I had first moved into our house, I would hear its distinctive cry in the spring. You can't mistake a barred owl for anything else. "Who cooks for you?" it demands in the middle of the night, after even the telemarketers have gone to bed. "Who cooks for you all?" it repeats in dialect, betraying its identity as the spooky old hoot owl of Southern swamps. Though I had heard the barred owl several times, I had seen one exactly once—an hour before an owl aficionado came over for dinner, strangely enough. On my way to the grocery store to pick up a head of broccoli in the late afternoon, the sight of a large bird fluttering in the bare tree branches less than a quarter of a mile from our house stopped me dead on the road. I went back for Linda, and we sat in the car watching his deep black eyes watch us. When he tired of the rubbernecking, he launched his heavy body off the tree, laboriously flapped his wings, and sailed across the street.

"You can call an owl pretty easily, you know," Jason told us over dinner that evening. He was a college student who had worked for us cleaning up our duck pen a couple of times, and because of his interest in birds, we had invited him and his girlfriend over for a meal.

"How do you call them?" I asked.

"Jason does great owl impressions," said his girlfriend, Kathie, who preferred exotic snakes to birds. When Jason had first met her in the dorm, a rough green snake was peeking through her hair.

"Do the screech owl," she said.

He made a warbling whistling sound that may or not have been a perfect rendition of an owl that I had never heard before in our woods, though Jason insisted that we lived in prime screech-owl habitat.

"Do you do a barred owl?" I asked, envisioning a nightclub career for Jason.

Jason took a preparatory breath, flicked his eyes, and paused. Too embarrassed to turn his mimicry into a medley, he suggested instead, "You can also use a recording of an owl's call. They're very curious, and they'll come to investigate."

My own pathetic rendition of the barred owl's call a few nights later resembled a six-year-old boy imitating a trombone, and the sole answering hoot was unmistakably derisive. The following week, I was outside after dark bringing in our bird feeder to keep it from raccoons, when an owl not more than one hundred feet away inquired about my dinner. "Who cooks for you?" it demanded. "Who cooks for you all?"

Darting upstairs, I returned with a flashlight, a pair of binoculars, and a boom box with a tape of a barred owl call. Out on the back deck, I cranked up the volume and let a few repetitions rip into the night. The swamp below our back fence was swollen with water from recent rains and added an unsettling metallic echo to the calls. The owl didn't reply. I rolled the tape again. Across the swamp, beyond our barn, and within a chain length of the river, our neighbor's chocolate brown Labrador retriever responded with an explosive volley of barks. Then from somewhere in our yard, somewhere close, the barred owl's throaty, sliding call came back to me, a cross between a fanfare played on a muted trumpet and an animal growl that prickled the nape of my neck.

"Linda! Linda!" I ran upstairs, summoning her with a hoarse whisper. "There's an owl outside. He's talking to my tape." She looked doubtful. On previous occasions when I had dragged her outdoors, a glorious song would invariably sputter to a halt the moment her feet crossed the threshold. This time, I played the tape again, and the owl astonished me by answering immediately. The final, drawn-out syllable of his call descended in an icy vibrato that mimicked the quavering "hoo" of a classic Hollywood ghost.

Linda turned to me with wide eyes. "He's right in the yard," she whispered, enunciating every word.

"I think he's in the walnut tree," I said. Switching on the flashlight,

I swept its beam up a tree about fifty feet away. A weak circle of light caught an owl perched on a low branch with his flat face turned directly toward us. Linda kept the barred owl illuminated as I peered at him through binoculars, then I held the light again and let Linda gape at him. The intensity of his unblinking stare unnerved me. It was as if the bird were training twin lasers on me whose wattage dwarfed the candlepower of my feeble flashlight. I felt the pressure of his eyes even as I leaned down and fumbled with the tape recorder controls.

"Who cooks for you?" the boom box demanded.

Hearing another owl within pouncing distance, he leaped off the branch to soar directly at me, zooming between the house and the milk house with his five-foot wingspan not five feet above my head before circling back into the yard, landing in another tree, and hooting his response. His approach had been so quick and so unexpected, I didn't even have a chance to curl up into a cowardly ball. For only the second or third time in my life, I experienced profound gratitude that I hadn't been born a field mouse.

"He thinks you're his girlfriend," Linda lamented. "The poor guy. "

"Or a rival," I countered, puffing out my chest. But the truth was that my initial elation over luring him into the yard had soured into embarrassment. It's one thing when a black-capped chickadee hops from the pine tree to our bird feeder to get a close look at the idiot who is mangling his simple, two-note song. It's quite another bothering a solitary predator whose life depends upon determining if another owl has invaded its territory and whether that invader is a prospective mate or a probable foe. What must our barred owl think, I wondered, to follow the call of a fellow owl to its source only to find a guilt-stricken skinny guy and his disapproving wife? Summoning such a formidable creature merely to see if it could be done was akin to uncorking a bottle and disturbing the thousand-year sleep of a fierce genie and then telling him, Oh, never mind, go back to bed. Parrots don't forget when they've been teased. They wait months for just the right moment to take revenge upon their tormentor. I doubted if an owl would be any more generous. You underestimate the strength and patience of a bird at your peril. I learned this when the shy duck Chloe bit my arm bloody defending her nest and again when Hector kept coming at me in a savage hissy fit no matter how many times I flung him from me. An annoyed barred owl could easily tear my clothes and shred my flesh with a few twitches of his knife-sharp beak and talons. Cold, hard logic told me this would never happen. More likely he would wield his influence with supernatural forces to teach me a lesson instead.

"That's the last time I'm ever doing this," I vowed loudly enough for the owl to hear, as I unplugged the tape recorder and wrapped the cord around my wrist. "Sorry," I hollered to the owl. But it was too late. The damage had been done, and I prickled with unease that I would pay for playing tricks on an emissary of the unseen world.

The next morning, in a haze of sunshine, Linda flung open the door to the girl ducks' pen. Ducks Maxine, Chloe, Clara, Marybelle, and Gwelda trotted out into the yard with goose Hailey bringing up the rear. But goose Liza stayed behind, suddenly unable to walk or even stand.

For two weeks, Liza had been waddling with a limp, but we hadn't thought it was anything more serious than a pulled muscle. The green-headed mallard–Khaki Campbell males had taken advantage of her condition by chasing her around the girls' side of the pen until they had flattened her into a corner or she had retreated into a doghouse.

Since Liza's mobility problem hadn't descended on her all at once, like Chloe's broken leg had, we didn't think a traumatic injury had occurred. Dr. Carlotti agreed, but that was all that he could say for certain. Although he kept a pair of picturesque horses in a tidy corral in back of his country practice, he was by no means a country vet. He mainly treated dogs and cats, and his experience with poultry was limited.

"If I had to guess, I would say that it's a temporary nerve problem," he sighed. "If she's been sitting on eggs like you said, it's possible that one or more eggs in her oviduct have been pressing against a nerve, temporarily paralyzing her leg. I don't see any sign of injury. Let her rest, and if I'm right, she should be walking in a couple of days."

This hypothesis seemed reasonable and reassuring. After venturing a few steps into our woods, I shouted my thanks to the now invisible owl for visiting nothing worse than a scare on us. Maybe mimicking a mate was equivalent to a parking infraction rather than a felony in the owl behavioral code, I reasoned. But when four days passed without Liza showing any improvement, we grew concerned enough to set up an appointment with the knowledgeable Dr. Hedley.

I had bought a beagle-size pet carrier that we often used for duck and rabbit duties, and it sat on the floor beside my chair in Dr. Hedley's crowded waiting room. Hoping to reduce the stress on Liza, who wasn't accustomed to being folded up and shoved into a plastic box, I had draped a towel over the front grate. The shrouding succeeded in piquing the curiosity of a dachshund on a long leash. "What kind of dog do you have in there?" asked the woman on the far end of the leash, just as her dachshund poked his snout behind the towel and Liza responded with a startled honk. I grinned uneasily, then stared intently at the floor tile pattern as a pungent scent resembling tincture of highly concentrated grass

clippings seasoned with a dash of boiled cabbage wafted up from
Liza's carrying case. A man seated across from me with a kitten in
a cardboard box on his lap coughed. The kitten coughed, too. My
mind grappled in the dark for the barest beginnings of an explanation, and in despair utterly abandoned the attempt.

The receptionist finally banished us to an examination room. I
had expected Dr. Hedley's appearance to cheer me, but he wasn't
himself when he walked in. His usual outgoing personality had
been turned inside out. He gestured at me as one might nod
vaguely to an unfamiliar silhouette in the dark and he mumbled an
introduction to the college-age man at his side. "This is Mr. Dalton.
He's a veterinary school student who is making the rounds with me
today. You don't mind if he observes us?" he asked.

I wanted to tell him that if he needed something to observe, he
should have witnessed the scene in the waiting room, but instead
I murmured a quick, "That's fine."

Dr. Hedley's detached attitude puzzled me. But after having
taken too many animals to too many veterinarians on too many occasions, I've learned not to judge the mood of a vet on any given
visit too harshly. He might have lost an animal in surgery that
morning, or he might have been forced to euthanize a client's beloved
pet when nothing else could be done. Maybe Mr. Dalton depressed
him. Whatever had happened to Dr. Hedley earlier, his robustness
had evaporated along with his enthusiasm for getting to the bottom
of a problem. The mysterious burden he was carrying increased as
he peered sadly at Liza, pressed a stethoscope against her chest,
and told young Dalton in a teacher's voice, "We have here a very
sick little goose. Do you see how her bill opens and closes as she
struggles to breathe?"

The observation took me by surprise. "I hadn't noticed that," I
said. "I thought she just had something wrong with her leg."

"How has her appetite been?"

"I don't know. I assumed it was okay. She has her own bowl of food in her pen."

"She's very weak." Directing his attention back to the student, he explained. "She's suffering from pneumonia. They don't last long in this condition." His expression was grave, but he shaped his lips into a calming smile and told me, "I'll give you an antibiotic to take home with you. It might possibly help, and it certainly won't do her any harm."

Liza hadn't comprehended the judgment against her and felt no worse after Dr. Hedley's virtual death sentence had been issued than before. I felt miserable, though. She was a wonderful goose, and I couldn't imagine walking out into our yard without her and Hailey blistering my ears with their happy greeting.

Three days of giving Liza antibiotics did no discernible good. I gained little from the experience, either, other than the adventure of prying open a goose's beak and finessing a syringe between her serrated mandibles without losing a finger in the process. Thankfully, Liza took the abuse graciously.

Linda suggested we immediately get a second opinion from Dr. Fuller, the veterinarian who had told us that Stanley was actually Stanley Sue. In the examination room, Dr. Fuller beamed at the sight of his first goose patient. Liza sat placidly on the table with her head bent sleepily toward the blue towel that I had arranged beneath her into a nest. "She's beautiful," he told me, stroking her neck. "What seems to be the trouble here?" he asked Liza. "Aren't we feeling well?"

Translating and elaborating upon Liza's honk, I told him the full story of her illness, from the first sign of her limp through her inability to walk and Dr. Hedley's diagnosis of pneumonia. I omitted my encounter with the owl, fearing that the sordid details might muddy his scientifically trained mind. Dr. Fuller took it all in with brisk nods of his head. Dr. Fuller was tall, rather lanky, and projected an enthusiasm worthy of an Edwardian stage actor in a musical revue. He exuded buckets of intelligence, topped a personable sense of humor with a fluttery laugh, and was an absolute stickler for process. The gears began whirring as soon as he beamed a light into Liza's eyes and listened to her breathing.

"You hear that?" he asked me, laying down his stethoscope. "There it is again. You can hear a definite click whenever she breathes. Dr. Hedley was certainly correct prescribing Baytril for pneumonia, but I don't think we have that here. From her labored breathing and weakened condition, I suspect she's suffering from aspergillosis. It's common among waterfowl and raptors. Many of them are carriers, and the acute stage can be brought on by the type of stress that the male mallards probably caused her. To be certain, we would need to perform an aspergilla titer."

My head was swimming. "What was that you said she has?"

"She probably has aspergillosis," he repeated. "It is a fungal infection that birds can pick up in damp conditions that favor mold growth, especially if their immune system isn't working like it should. Wet straw usually provides favorable conditions for the fungus, which is why we sometimes see this in animals kept in barns. Humans can get aspergillosis, too, so you have to be careful if you·have close contact with an infected bird. It is not something you want to get," he cautioned. "It resembles tuberculosis and it is very stubborn to treat."

"Is it fatal for a bird?" I asked, trying not to gulp. I stretched out a hand and placed it on Liza's back for moral support.

"Not necessarily," he told me, with a rise in his voice that indicated it usually was. "What I would suggest is that we keep Liza overnight for observation. She's pretty weak, so I would like to do a tube feeding to get some nourishment in her, and we'll give her a vitamin injection. Aspergillosis is difficult to positively diagnose. We need to take a blood sample and send it to a lab in Chicago for an aspergilla titer. The result can take four or five days, so I would recommend that we assume she does have aspergillosis and begin the appropriate treatment immediately with an antifungal medication."

I didn't know what a titer was, but I nodded my head while groping for a suitably intelligent facial expression. I left Liza in Dr. Fuller's hands with far more optimism than the situation warranted. But his thoroughness impressed me with the belief that if anyone could turn the situation around, he could.

Back home I hopped onto the Internet and posted a question on a pet-bird newsgroup, asking if anyone had successfully treated a bird stricken with aspergillosis. A few hours later I received an e-mail from a woman who called herself Toucanlady. "I treated an Amazon parrot that had the acute generalized form of aspergillosis. He was emaciated and very ill. He eventually recovered, but it is a long hard road. Good luck."

I headed back to the vet's the next day to pick her up. The staff was all smiles once I stated my name and was recognized as the goose person. "We just love Liza," a technician told me. "She's so sweet."

"She didn't try to bite anyone?" I asked.

"Liza?" asked the technician incredulously. She reacted as if I had disparaged a lifelong friend with whom she used to share a carton of milk in kindergarten. "Liza wouldn't bite anybody."

"No, no, of course not," I assured her, recalling the muddy beak prints she had embossed on various shirts I owned. "Not Liza."

Dr. Fuller greeted me in the examination room, then led me through a secret doorway and into the inner recesses of the clinic.

Guided by flickering torchlight, we trudged through miles of winding corridors before ending up in a squeaky-clean hospital area
where hard-luck cases received constant care. Liza trumpeted a
hello before I spotted her in the second tier of a shiny aluminum-
sided high-rise of pens that somehow reminded me of restaurant
ovens. I half expected to find our goose resting on a bed of wild
rice.

"Liza has been doing very well, haven't you, Liza?" Dr. Fuller
asked. She answered with an enthusiastic volley of staccato notes.
The technician handed him a clipboard, which he glanced at
briefly. "She took the tube feeding with no problem, and she's been
eating on her own. Aside from her getting her medication on
schedule, her recovery depends on making sure she receives sufficient nourishment each day."

"Linda has already set up living quarters for her on our porch,"
I told him. "Or maybe those are for me, and she'll be moving into
the house. At any rate, we'll wait on her hand and foot until she's
well."

"In that case," he said, while writing on the lab report, "I would
list her prognosis as 'Guarded' upgraded to 'Fair' "—he circled both
words with ballpoint whorls—"as long as she receives the proper
care. And I see that she'll be getting that."

"She is our golden goose from now on," I replied.

That remark proved frighteningly accurate once I totaled up the
bill for Liza's treatment and lab tests, then added the cost of a pricey
prescription that we couldn't get filled just anywhere. Her antifungal medication wasn't an off-the-shelf item. It needed to be com-
pounded, meaning its chemical constituents had to be carefully
measured and mixed by hand. Apparently, few pharmacists in the
area did anything more ambitious than transferring pills from large
containers to small bottles and filling out insurance forms. The

closest drug store staffed by pharmaceutical initiates skilled in the ancient alchemical principles of compounding turned out to be a drug store located on a nearly impossible-to-access triangle-shaped block of businesses in the Grand Rapids suburb of Walker. Cars whizzed past me as I gathered cobwebs in the shadow of a stop sign on the busiest side street in America. From the condition of the drug store's archaic glass-brick façade, its neon sign promising a soda fountain, and a yellowed portrait of Speedy Alka-Seltzer, few motorists apparently braved the left-hand turn to the Park Hills parking lot.

The slatted wood floors inside the Park Hills Drug Store squeaked and groaned like a patient in a sickbed as I threaded my way through narrow aisles stocked with unfamiliar palliatives and elixirs. Ahead of me in line at the pharmacy counter stood an elderly woman so frail of frame, I wondered how she had ever darted through the traffic out front until I realized from the slow pace at which Park Hills conducted its business that she had un-doubtedly been waiting for her prescription since Reagan's first inaugural. When my turn finally came and I informed the pudgy pharmacist, "I'm here to pick up a prescription for Tarte," he couldn't have been more excited to meet me.

"You're here for the goose?" he asked, blinking his large eyes.

"Yes, prescription for Tarte, please," I repeated.

"Matty," he called to the sixty-something woman rattling glass vials behind him. "It's the man with the goose."

"How's the goose doing?" Matty brightly asked me.

"We put her medication in a liquid medium as your veterinarian requested," the pharmacist explained, as he removed a small plas-tic bottle from a refrigerator next to the cash register. "I tried to choose a flavor that I thought your goose would like. This one is liver. We had a fish-flavor base, but I didn't know if geese cared for fish."

"Not as much as they love liver," I assured him. "Anyway, she won't have much of an opportunity to taste it. I pretty much squirt it straight into her crop with a syringe."

"You use a syringe?" he asked in wonderment, widening his eyes so far, he seemed positively owlish. Who cooks for you, I wanted to ask him, but I didn't want any trouble. "I guess you couldn't use a spoon." He chuckled as he popped the medicine into a bag with a handful of pro bono syringes.

"I hope your goose gets better," Matty told me. "We've done cats before, but never somebody's goose."

"That would explain the liver and fish flavorings," I replied, as I edged away.

Linda set up living quarters for Liza on our enclosed porch that would have been the envy of any housebound goose. Filling a wading pool with straw, she topped it with one of several bed sheets that she changed and washed throughout the day. After dark, she tossed a lightweight blanket over Liza's back and would have offered her a pillow if she could have wrested mine away from me. A space heater took the chill off the May nighttime temperatures.

Within easy reach of Liza's pool were bowls containing water, scratch feed, and mud, though she preferred us to hold the bowls whenever she ate. She required dirt for the strictly utilitarian purpose of grinding and predigesting the raw corn kernels in her gizzard, but she attacked it with the vigor of a gourmand devouring a sinfully rich dessert. Half submerged in mud, her beak snapped open and shut almost too rapidly for the eye the follow, and in her eating frenzy she would all but knock the dish out of my hand. To supplement her bowl foods, I gathered dandelion leaves from the yard.

"Look at these beauties," I'd brag to Linda. "I found them near the mailbox, mixed in with some annoying grass."

Liza relished dandelion leaves even more than mud, tootling her appreciation with alto-saxophone slurs while yanking an entire handful from my fingers at a time. "Liza, you made me drop them all," I'd complain, and she would honk gleefully between mouthfuls.

Despite her good spirits, Liza remained too weak to walk or even rise to her feet on her own. If the sun was shining, and we didn't want her to have to spend all day on the shaded porch, we would carry her down to the duck pen and set her in an area on the girls' side that I had fenced off. Sequestering her discouraged the others from their genetically-imprinted urge to pick on the weak, and it also kept them from getting close enough to catch her aspergillosis. Once or twice I carried Liza out to the front lawn and placed her in the middle of a virile cluster of dandelions, hoping that she would help herself. But even after twenty days on her antifungal medication, she remained gravely ill.

"Sweetie." I looked up from the newspaper on a cool June evening as Linda came into the living room from the porch. She spoke softly, breaking bad news gently. "I don't think Liza's going to make it through the night. She's having a lot of trouble breathing."

I took a cushion onto the porch and sat on the floor next to our goose. She rallied briefly when she realized that I was there, even favoring me with a conversational honk, but a few seconds later she lowered her head to her chest and squeezed her eyes shut. I tried tempting her to eat with a fresh bowl of mud and a handful of tender dandelion leaves, but she wouldn't take any food. Her entire body strained each time she took a breath, and her wheezing was unusually loud. "I'm sorry, hon," I told her, petting her neck. Linda came out to spread a blanket over her and adjust the space heater. Finally both of us told her good night and went back into the house.

"She sure has been a nice goose," Linda told me sadly, as we settled into bed. "I sure have enjoyed our time with her. I like it when we're watching TV and she honks because she wants us to go out and fuss over her."

"I just hope she isn't suffering too much," I said.

In the swamp below the backyard, the last of the spring peepers were singing. Only five or six were still left in the shrinking seasonal pond, and each time a car rumbled past our house, they immediately fell silent only to resume their chirping several seconds later. Ever since moving to the country, I had loved the song of the frogs, and despite my aversion to fresh air, I'd occasionally crack the window open on chilly spring nights to bring their voices closer. But as I lay in bed worrying that Liza was dying, I wondered how I'd feel about the frogs the next time I heard them. Bertha had died at the height of katydid-calling frenzy, and hardly an August night went by when their *zip-zip* song didn't evoke a memory.

I awoke the next morning with my stomach knotted by dread. Crawling carefully out of bed so as not to disturb Linda, I eased shut the bedroom door and unlocked the door to the porch. I was still twisting the knob and hadn't even taken my first step outside when Liza was already honking hello. She peppered the air with excited bleats and attacked her scratch feed with gusto when I held the bowl. It took two trips to the front lawn to gather enough dandelion leaves to satisfy her hunger. I was so thrilled that her vitality had returned, I generously waved at a passing motorist who was rude enough to beep his horn at your average everyday pajama-clad man squatting in the grass plucking weeds.

We experienced a few more shaky nights with Liza, when she barely had sufficient strength to breathe, but by the end of the fifth week, she would occasionally succeed in struggling to her feet after soaking up the sun on our front lawn. She even managed a wobbly step or two to great vocal encouragement from her caregivers. One morning during week six, Linda called me from the bedroom to witness Liza standing proudly at the threshold to the porch all the way across the room from her wading-pool bed. That same afternoon, as the ducks and Hailey fanned out across the backyard while we changed their water, Liza rose from her spot in the warm grass, walked to the front gate, and honked at us to let her join the others.

"Should we let her go?" Linda asked me. "I can't see what it would hurt."

"Let her through!"

Few sights would seem to hold less drama than a goose waddling through a garden gate, but to us the occurrence was every bit as monumental as if the Sphinx had climbed down from the Giza plateau and moved into our barn with the turkeys. Walking slowly, Liza honked nonchalantly to Hailey and joined her grazing under the redbud tree. Toucanlady had been correct. The short trip from our front porch to the backyard had turned out to be a long, hard road indeed. Our goose had been so sick for so many weeks, I had never expected her to get better, and I felt overjoyed at her recovery. Liza's return to health apparently affected her emotionally, too, since she immediately underwent an unusual form of amnesia.

A year and some months earlier, our geese had come to us from their previous owner habituated to human company and not yet in the throes of hormonal changes that would later cement their interests exclusively to members of their small waterfowl society. Gone were the days when I could plop down on the lawn and find a goose in my lap without a favorite food item to tempt her there. After Liza had fallen sick enough that she had lost her ability to walk, however, she placed her care in our hands with unstinting confidence, not merely tolerating but welcoming physical contact with us. The touch of a hand reassured her, and she no more feared our approach when we walked over to her pool to feed her than would the family dog. But once a healthy Liza strolled back into the pen with her sister, Hailey, and her duck accomplices, all memory of the niceties of human contact fled. The very next day when I let the girls out for a romp around the yard, I headed toward Liza to give her a pat and wish her well. She honked and skittered away as if to say, "What on earth are you doing? What kind of a goose do you take me for?"

"That's good," Linda answered. "She's really back to normal." And she was right.

From time to time after Liza's recovery, I would hear the barred owl hooting from our woods. On more than one occasion, it sounded like the owl was calling from the walnut tree on the edge of our backyard, where I had caught it in my flashlight beam on that fateful spring night. "Who cooks for you?" the barred owl inquired. "Who cooks for you all?"

I was tempted to hoot back with my boyish trombone imitation. After all, a summons from such a magnificent and powerful bird was an honor that deserved a reply. But remembering my manners, I restrained myself and muttered to the window instead, "Forget it, owl. What kind of a superstitious fool do you take me for?"

CHAPTER 12

Comings and Goings

A voiding pet stores wasn't enough to keep our animal population from expanding. Neither was snipping the phone line to block requests that we take in yet another winged or long-eared orphan. Occasionally a new animal would literally drop from the sky.

One summer afternoon, Stanley Sue sounded the shrill alarm-call whistle that usually indicated she had spotted a hawk from the dining room window. I peered into the yard and up through the skylight, but didn't see anything more threatening than a nuthatch, until a tan-and-white pigeon plopped down from our hackberry tree onto the flat roof of the milk house. While pigeons are as common as in-laws in most neighborhoods, they never visited us in the country. A few shy mourning doves pecked the ground under our bird feeders in frigid seasons when natural food was scarce, but we were definitely far removed from pigeon thoroughfares. In an attempt to satiate every bird within a two-mile radius of our house, we usually supplemented the food in our bird feeders by dumping vast quantities of seed on the ground and on the milk-house roof. Ground-feeding birds such as blue jays, along with finch flocks, attacked the scattered seed with gusto, but with nothing resembling the desperate greed exhibited by the tan-and-white pigeon. Once the bird had eaten its fill, it stayed put even as I grimaced at it though different windows and from different angles, attempting to assess if anything was wrong.

"I think it might be someone's pet," Linda concluded. "Maybe it's a racing pigeon that got knocked off course by a hawk."

I pooh-poohed the idea even as I considered the possibility that it might be true. Wherever the pigeon had come from, it didn't demonstrate overt fear of humans—or at least not of me, failing to budge from the roof even after I had unfolded the stepladder next to the shed, clomped quavering to the top, and sat upon the eaves not three feet away from the presumed stray. Reaching out to tweak its beak proved a step too far. The bird flew to the metal strut on the second story of our house that buttressed the chimney of our basement wood furnace. Once I returned to ground level, the pigeon's love affair with the milk-house roof resumed.

"I think that bird might be someone's pet," I explained to Linda patiently.

"She looks like a Tillie," Linda surmised.

Deciding that the pigeon sought our help, I sent her flapping back to the chimney support by lugging our trusty Humane Live Animal Trap to the top of the milk house and loading it with a virgin pile of scratch feed sweetened with a pinch of the parakeet seed that Howard loved. I watched with Stanley Sue through the dining room window as Tillie dropped down to the roof, paced in front of the open door of the trap bobbing her head with each step, and after a moment of indecision, hopped inside. I worried that she didn't weigh enough to trip the trigger, but a few seconds later she fluttered her wings in panic as the door snapped shut behind her.

Tillie showed more annoyance than unease as Linda transferred her from the raccoon trap to a cage on the front porch. Less than a month earlier, Liza had abandoned her straw-filled pool to rejoin the backyard ducks, and it seemed natural to once again have a living creature outside the living room to keep the mice and spiders company. Uncertain what sorts of exotic microscopic creatures might be clinging to an apparent bird in distress, I took her to see Dr. Fuller after a few days.

"She does have lice," he told me, as he began examining her.

"She's a Birmingham Roller Pigeon," I blurted out in her defense.

"Son of a gun," he chuckled politely. My dubious identification was based on three minutes spent with a guide to doves and pigeons at a local remaindered-book outlet. I had wanted to buy the half-priced reference book, but was easily dissuaded by an expansive "Disease and Injury" appendix brimming with color photographs of bizarre growths, pustules, and swollen internal organs.

"She certainly doesn't look like any wild pigeon I've ever seen," I insisted.

"I don't know," he answered gently. "I've seen lots of color variation, including all-white birds. But they usually don't last long in a flock. They stick out like a sore thumb to predators."

Except for the bloom of lice scheming beneath her feathers, Tillie received a clean bill of health from our vet. Back home on the porch, I was shaking a can of bird insecticide from the pet store until my arm hurt when Linda came out to determine what the moaning was all about.

"Too much exercise," I complained.

"What are you going to do with that?" she asked.

"Delouse Tillie."

"Put her somewhere else while you spray her cage."

"You're supposed to spray the bird. That's the whole point."

"But that's insecticide."

"See the label? See the picture of the happy bird on the label? 'Safe for birds.' You have to spray the bird to kill the lice. Dr. Fuller recommended this brand."

"It's still insecticide," Linda pointed out. "It will make her sick."

"'Safe for birds,'" I repeated. "I'll spray the cage. But I have to spray her, too."

"Don't spray her with insecticide. You'll make her sick."

"You're supposed to spray the bird."

We went around and around like that until both of us were giddy. Releasing the bird from the cage to flutter around on the porch, I took the cage outside and liberally doused it with the spray. Linda watched, then went back to her business in the house. I chased down the bird, put the bird back inside the cage, and lightly sprayed the bird with insecticide. More of the insecticide dribbled onto my fingers than ended up on either cage or caged bird. I licked my fingers with no ill effects other than a sudden hankering for an arachnid canapé.

The longer we kept Tillie, the stronger she became. She also grew less satisfied with captivity and increasingly intolerant of her captors. For a few days we tried putting her in the dining room with the other birds, thinking that once she had gotten a taste of the pampered life, she would reclaim her identity as a pet bird. The only joy she eked out of perching on a cage top near the ceiling was launching pecks at Howard whenever he landed near her. In the larger free-flight area of the porch, she spent the majority of her time fluttering from window to window in search of a way outdoors. Gradually, we came around to realizing that Tillie was undoubtedly a wild bird after all. Dinner at my sister Joan's house clinched it when Linda and I studied the sky-darkening flock of pigeons that had descended on her lawn around her bird feeder.

Sprinkled amid the standard-issue blue-grey city pigeon uniforms were pigeons clad in brown, white, and green color mixes.

THREE WEEKS HAD elapsed between Tillie's capture and the afternoon I took her cage outside and opened the door. "You can leave if you want to," I told her, hinting that it would be ungrateful to actually fly away. With an energetic chugging of her wings, she rose as high as the second story chimney strut and stayed there. Throughout the remainder of the summer, she stayed close to the yard. She might disappear for hours at a time, but by evening we would always find her roosting on the chimney support as close to the house as possible, for protection against hawks. Sometimes when Linda and I were taking care of the ducks and we left a hose running on the lawn between pens, Tillie would swoop down, grab a drink, then return to the safety of the milkhouse roof or our hackberry tree.

A few days after Tillie's release, Linda ran into Tam and Steve at the Food City supermarket. The couple shared a house even smaller than ours with eight orphaned cats and owned a patch of land overrun at various times with wild turkeys (we had watched a flock from Tam and Steve's living room window), deer, Canada geese, and raccoons. An industrious muskrat usually busied itself in the pond on the other side of their gravel driveway, while a fat possum they dubbed Electrolux had taken possession of a back corner of their garage.

"A friend of ours has a really nice rabbit in need of a good home," Tam told Linda. "She's getting married and moving away, and she can't bring the rabbit with her."

"Bob won't let us have any more rabbits," Linda said.

"The poor guy sits out in a cage in the barn all by himself."

Faster than the eye could register it, Linda wrote down the telephone number of the rabbit owner. As if swept in on a tide of history, I found myself the following Saturday walking into a barn owned by Tam and Steve's neighbor, Judy. I had spent the morning rehearsing any number of excuses in my mind why we couldn't possibly take a third male rabbit, but I found myself laughing out loud when I laid eyes on Walter. As soon as he saw us, he hopped into the battered cardboard box that Judy told us was his favorite spot to hide. Hiding didn't equal concealment, however. He couldn't quite squeeze his entire body into the shadow of the carton. Compared to Bertie and Rollo, Walter was huge, a Checker Giant mix, tipping the scales at just over eight pounds. Despite the epic proportions of his rump and haunches, his head appeared comically oversize, and his jet-black eyes topped with an exuberant thatch of eyelashes added an irresistible element of pathos.

"He's beautiful," Linda beamed.

Beautiful and silly. After a minute or two, Walter determined that we didn't represent enough of a threat to discourage him from abandoning his shelter for the feed dish. This gave me the opportunity to step back and attempt to take in his whimsical magnificence. It was as if a careless breeder had spilled a can of grey paint on the back and head of a pure white rabbit, and the paint had fanned out in symmetrical patterns on his right and left sides like ink on blotting paper. Before deciding to take him home, we tested to see if he would allow us to hold him without squirming and kicking. He failed, but the test was moot. No person of sound mind would pick up and cuddle an eight-pound rabbit, and neither would we. When Linda set him down on top of his large wood-and-wire cage and started petting him, however, he immediately hunkered down in anticipation of a prolonged spate of pleasure. That earned him a passing grade.

Received wisdom in rabbit circles speaks of bonding that can

occur between rabbits of vastly different sizes. While bunny brothers Bertie and Rollo fought voraciously on the few occasions that
they shared a room without benefit of a wire grid between them,
we held faint hopes that Walter and Bertie or Walter and Rollo
might buddy up and simplify our lives. As it turned out, Walter
showed no trace of aggression toward Bertie. He liked Bertie. No,
he loved him. Eagerly and incessantly, he tried mating with the rabbit that was a mere one-third his size. Bertie was invisible beneath
Walter's bulk, and we marveled that he hadn't suffocated before we
could reach them amid the tangle of dining-room table and chair
legs.

Burdened with three rabbits that required constant separation, I
created a triad of fencing loops in the basement anchored to a central pillar. Outdoors, I subdivided one of the rabbit runs, leaving
the largest of the three for our Checker Giant. On temperate days,
the boys enjoyed a romp in the fresh air during the afternoon and
a romp in the moldy basement air after dinner. Then Walter was
free to explore the kitchen while Bertie gnawed up the living room
and placid Rollo sat upon my lap for an hour of television (his
choice of program). Next, we would catch Bertie and return him to
his cage in the dining room, allowing Rollo his turn desecrating the
living room furnishings. After twenty minutes or so, we retired
Rollo to his cage for the night and removed the board between the
dining room and living room so that Walter could blunder in and
rub his chin on every object in view, scent-marking them until the
next day when the entire wearying process would begin all over
again.

As if simple logistics didn't keep us busy enough with the
rabbits, we discovered that Bertie suffered from a malocclusion, a
condition in which the teeth do not meet properly but overlap in
bucktooth or underbite fashion. Though dental defects are cute as

can be on waifish supermodels, they're potentially lethal to a rabbit, whose teeth grow more than a quarter-inch a week. Unchecked, Bertie's upper incisors would curl in on themselves like a party blower, while his lower incisors would ultimately pierce the roof of his closed mouth, though he'd be unable to eat long before that occurred. An unhelpful book I found on dwarf-rabbit varieties, written by a German expert, recommended euthanizing any bunnies with tooth problems, but this struck me as counterproductive. Instead, Linda would haul Bertie into the bathroom about once a week, wrap him in a towel, and pry open his mouth while I clipped his teeth.

Initially I used a tool designed for trimming dog toenails, abandoned it for human toenail clippers that didn't fit the contours of rabbit dental anatomy much better, then, upon advice from Dr. Fuller, settled on the smallest pair of wire cutters I could find. The trick was to quickly truncate the teeth in two or three clips before Bertie decided to clamp his mouth shut. If I took off too little of the tooth at the wrong angle, I ended up sculpting knife-point fangs and creating an attack rabbit. If I took off too much at a single clip, I risked the stomach-turning consequence of splintering his teeth down to the gumline. Apart from causing eating difficulties, splintering an upper incisor could also inflame the rabbit's tear duct and even lead to pasteurella, a potentially lethal bacterial infection. When done correctly, the amputation apparently hurt Bertie less than it did me. Rabbits' teeth lack the nerve endings that ours have and more closely resemble thick versions of our fingernails, but the procedure never failed to set my own teeth on edge.

Meanwhile, backyard lodging became a few feathers less crowded when I unexpectedly found a home for our pugnacious greenheads. For weeks at a time, the Khaki Campbell–mallard hybrids shared the same pool with their Khaki Campbell father and uncle without a single incident of domestic abuse. But proximity to the females in the adjacent pen would suddenly send duck testosterone levels soaring, forcing us to confine the youngsters to the inevitable wire loop in order to give Stewart and Trevor respite from pecks, bites, and wing-flapping. I carped about the situation on an Internet poultry newsgroup, for some reason populated mainly by English farmers. Average Americans were probably too busy trimming rabbit teeth to spend much time on-line. Richard and Jeri Pellston not only sympathized with our excess-duck problem, but also offered to take the greenheads off our hands. Remarkably, they lived in Michigan. Though their home was near the tip of the "thumb" region, clear across the Michigan "palm" from us, Richard's job as a database consultant occasionally took him to, of all places, Lowell.

"We got a couple hens. Two Barred Rocks and a Rhode Island Red," Richard told me in an e-mail that made me wonder how much the ability to count figured into his government job. With heartbreaking innocence he added, "We want to try some ducks."

After promising to build a raccoon-proof pen complete with a non–Ninja Turtle plastic swimming pool, he and Jeri showed up on a late July afternoon when the weeds in our yard were at the peak of ripeness. I thought of them as weeds, but Richard begged to differ. Shortly after stepping out of a shock absorber–challenged station wagon that cleared the ground by as much as a few millimeters, he immediately started stabbing greenery with his cane. "That's lamb's-quarter," he pointed out. "You can cook it or shred it in a salad." Jeri nodded in agreement. "That's pokeweed over there."

"I love the purple berries it gets in the fall," Linda told them.

"I like to eat it. You ever heard of poke salad?"

"I've heard the song 'Poke Salad Annie,'" I offered, though Richard was fifteen years too young to recall the song.

"They eat it down South," said Linda.

"I eat it," he repeated, as he hobbled across the yard two steps ahead of us. His sparse brush of a chin beard and truculent tone, which I interpreted as shyness, suggested he could spend an afternoon grazing an overgrown meadow in goaty bliss. "I bet you've got all kinds of edibles out here," he marveled.

"You are keeping the ducks as pets?" Linda ventured.

Richard turned his head in surprise.

"You're not planning on eating them?" I clarified.

"We might breed them," Jeri answered, "But we would never kill a duck. We don't eat our chickens, either."

"We eat chicken," Richard explained with a burst of gusto. "We just don't eat *our* chickens."

With his battered military jacket and wide-wale corduroy pants with whole sections of cord worn away, Richard didn't strike me as particularly fastidious. But his first comment about the greenheads voiced an aesthetic concern. "What's the mark on that one's beak? It looks like his beak's peeling." Sure enough, if you studied the duck with microscopic intensity, a fleck at the edge of his upper bill disclosed a darker shade of olive than the rest of his beak.

I shrugged helplessly. "I don't know. The Khaki Campbells get that, too." Either Stewart or Trevor—we had no idea which twin duck was which—betrayed a similar nearly imperceptible cosmetic flaw. "There's a thin layer of tissue that coats their beaks, and sometimes it gets worn away," I bluffed.

"So it will grow back," he frowned.

I shrugged again. "I don't see why not. It's never gotten any worse."

Satisfied that the greenheads had a reasonable shot at attaining perfection, he agreed to take the pair, though Linda insisted on further assurances that the ducks would be housed properly, kept as pets, and spared a seasoning with savory herbs. Richard leaned thoughtfully on his cane and supervised while Linda and I packed the greenheads into a cardboard box and loosely sealed it with the obligatory duct tape. Jeri opened the tailgate of their cluttered station wagon and managed to clear a few square feet of space by rearranging a dozen or so heavy cartons containing dot-matrix computer printouts presumably brimming with confidential government data. Just as the couple was about to drive off, Richard smiled at us for the first time. "Maybe we'll stop by again next time we're in town," he told us. "Maybe we could have a cookout."

The pair did prove good on their word to take good care of the greenheads. Within a week, Richard e-mailed me a photo of the ducks frolicking in a floral-print wading pool inside a high-walled chicken-wire pen.

TILLIE THE PIGEON had witnessed the greenheads' exit from her perch on the chimney strut. She seemed fully dependent upon the scratch feed we tossed onto the roof of the milk house each day, and as summer gave way to a chilly, windy fall, we wondered how she would cope with the coming snow. Hiding in a pile of scrap lumber in the barn was a crudely made wooden box that looked as if it had a full year of life still ahead of it. One of the small children of the former owners of our house had apparently cobbled it together with a native carpentry skill that I could admire but never duplicate. Taking exceptional care not to stress the workmanship, I looped a rope through a handy knothole in the most reliably solid slat and slowly hoisted the box to the gently sloping roof above our dining room, positioning it just under Tillie's favorite roosting spot.

"I hope she's smart enough to use it once the weather gets cold," I told Linda. Our visiting pigeon turned out to be even smarter. When the first blustery day arrived, Tillie was nowhere to be found. Judging that a good thing had reached its logical end, she apparently flew off to petition for readmittance to her flock.

Not all departures from our bird community were happy. One fall afternoon, Linda called me out to the barn to try and help one of our turkeys that was thrashing in pain on the concrete floor. By the time we got back to her, she was already dead. "Some animal chewed up her wing," Linda said, and we also discovered wounds on the bird's right side. There was no indication an animal had climbed over or burrowed under the five-foot-high fence, and the other three turkeys appeared as unruffled as ever. We couldn't figure out what had happened, unless a hawk had been bold enough to swoop into the enclosure. But a raptor was usually far too wary to enter the relative confinement of an outdoor pen except under circumstances of extreme hunger, and in that case a hawk wouldn't waste its time on prey too large to carry away.

Puzzling over the unexpected death of our turkey kept us occupied off and on as a snowy fall blew into a frigid winter. We certainly had sufficient time to mull the mystery over, since we were no longer visiting pet shops, answering the phone, shopping for food, or glancing out our windows for fear that another addition to the circus would land at our feet. But I couldn't avoid my job; in early January I received an e-mail at the office from my sister Joan, which set a flurry of events in motion.

"MY GIRLFRIEND B.J. IS SEEING A BIG WHITE DUCK AT RICHMOND PARK SWIMMING IN A LITTLE CIRCLE OF WATER THAT HASN'T FROZEN YET," Joan wrote me before her discovery of the caps lock key. "B.J. DOESN'T THINK THE DUCK CAN FLY. HER NEIGHBORS NEAR THE PARK ARE WORRIED THE DUCK DOESN'T HAVE ANYTHING TO EAT."

Little comprehending the force I was about to unleash, I casually mentioned the e-mail to Linda over dinner. "From Joan's description, it sounds like a White Pekin, and she said a Canada goose that also doesn't seem to be able to fly is keeping it company."

"It's going to get really cold this week," said Linda, with alarm in her voice. Her fork hung in midair between her plate and mouth. "What's B.J.'s phone number?"

"How should I know? I've never even laid eyes on her. Anyway," I added irritably, "I don't trust people who go by initials."

"That's not true. How about M.C.? My mom's friend named M.C. is an awfully nice lady."

"Then call M.C. and ask her for B.J.'s number," I suggested. I didn't like where this was going, and I didn't like where I knew I was going. Two hours later, after we had put the animals to bed, warmed the car up to hockey-rink specs, and driven twenty miles to Richmond Park on the west side of Grand Rapids, I stood shivering in eight-degree air with a wind chill of minus twenty under a bank of floodlights that crisply illuminated each flake of blowing snow, making me even colder. The few diehards still in the park were surrendering to the darkness and the steadily falling temperature. Parents and smiling children with glowing, wind-burned faces towed toboggans behind them as they trudged toward the parking lot. A mother and a tiny girl paused to watch Linda as she paced the edge of the frozen pond searching for a way to reach the duck and goose that swam unconcerned a few dogsled lengths away. The weather didn't bother them a bit.

"Do you think I can walk out on the ice?" Linda asked.

"God, no!" I told her. "Not if there's still a thawed spot in the middle."

"I threw a branch out on the ice and it didn't crack."

"I think you weigh a little more than a branch," I said, surprised my ears hadn't cracked and tinkled to the ground.

"I wish I had a net," Linda lamented. "If I had a wide enough net, and a person on each side of the pond held one end, and a third person shooed them out of the water, we could probably catch them." Her eyes darted up the slope of the sledding hill and down again to the parking lot as if someone in his haste might have accidentally dropped precisely the net we needed in the snow. "How about if I crawl out on the ice on my stomach?"

"I wouldn't do that, either."

"I'll just crawl out a little ways."

"Let me remind you that I can't swim, and I especially can't swim in really cold water." I hugged myself tighter, even considering the possibility of my shivering flesh coming in contact with anything wet. "If you start to drown, you're on your own."

"Hold on to my ankles, then," she told me, as she got down on her knees and leaned twin purple mittens upon the ice. Startled by her intrusion or simply rattled by the inexplicable sight of a well-bundled hominid on all fours, the white duck and the Canada goose fled with flapping wings to the far side of the frozen pond.

"They'll be okay," I told her, as we stood staring into the floodlit gloom of swirling snow. Eventually the duck and goose began sidling toward their water sanctuary, convinced that they must have experienced a winter hallucination. I was sorry for the birds, even though they didn't seem particularly vulnerable at the moment. But Linda was probably right that once the pond completely iced over, without the ability to fly, they would be at the mercy of stray neighborhood children and boisterous dogs. We were peculiarly helpless to help them. Far from feeling defeated by the futility of the situation, I was beginning to experience a faint glow of happiness as I recalled the comfort of the beckoning living room couch. We retreated to the relative warmth of the car and slid on icy roads in the direction of home.

Linda didn't give up on the Richmond Park duck. She had

started calling him Richie. Through B.J. she learned the phone number of a woman named Lesley who lived near the pond and had tried to catch the duck. When she wasn't plotting strategy with Lesley, Linda was conspiring with energetic animal-shelter employee Bruce, whom Lesley spoke to almost daily about the icebound duck and goose. Bruce had made two after-midnight attempts to sneak up on the birds, in addition to a number of daylight pursuits. During her own visits to the pond, Linda enlisted the aid of gamboling grade-school-age kids, who leapt at the chance to chase the waterfowl without incurring a frown or swat from an adult. But the birds always eluded capture.

Linda's worries about Richie and his friend increased as temperatures plummeted. I devoted a tiny corner of my mind to the Richmond waterfowl, but our own ducks and geese were my immediate concern. One Saturday morning when I waddled out to the pen swaddled in sweaters and a ski parka, all of the birds except Hector trotted out into the snow. Although he hissed and snapped his beak, Hector was rooted to one spot, unable to walk away. Like our first Muscovy, Daphne, his feathers didn't repel water as efficiently as the other ducks', and after splashing himself from the bucket the previous evening and failing to shed the water, he had ended up frozen to the ground. Only a few feathers imprisoned him, and I managed to quickly free him with a couple of deft tugs. When Linda "defrosted" him with a hair dryer, she noticed an odd lump of flesh the diameter of her thumbnail protruding from the middle of his back. "We'd better have that looked at," she said. "It's some sort of growth that might need to be cut off."

The news from Richmond Park turned dire. When Linda called Lesley for an update the following Monday, she learned that the pond was almost completely frozen over. A few adventuresome children had begun skating on the thickest ice around the edges, frightening the birds into retreating to the bushes until after dark, when they returned to their tiny dwindling patch of slushy surface water. "In a day or two," Lesley said, "there won't be any water left." Linda barely slept that night. Around 4:00 A.M. I awoke to blearily notice light leaking through the crack of the closed bedroom door. I found Linda on the couch. "I've been up since two," she told me. "I can't stop thinking about that duck."

After work the next day, I took my boots off on the porch rather than stomping off the snow on the mat in the living room and quietly set them on the floor. I opened the front door gently enough to avoid triggering the oversize jingle bells still tied to the doorknob and shut it with the same care. I expected my exhausted wife to be in the throes of a ferocious afternoon nap. Instead she whooshed in from the kitchen enveloped by a beatific glow. "Bruce just called!" she cried. "He caught Richie last night. The Canadian got away. It turned out he could fly."

"He caught Richie?" I marveled. "How?"

"Bruce had a net of some kind," she told me, though presumably not the two-person pond-wide variety. "He was able to get right out onto the ice and snuck up on them when they were sleeping. The Canadian flew away, but get this. When he took Richie to the animal shelter, it turned out that they already had a Canadian goose, so they put Richie in the same pen with the Canadian, and he feels right at home. It's a miracle from the Lord!"

"What'll happen to him?"

"They've got to decide at the animal shelter. We might get him, so keep your fingers crossed."

RICHIE STAYED AT the shelter for just over a week while the staff veterinarian evaluated his health. After passing the treadmill test with flying colors and promising to watch his cholesterol levels, he was first unleashed on an area farmer who occasionally took in orphaned animals. But Richie turned out to be one duck too many for his flock once his penchant for fighting with other males emerged. We agreed to take him and try housing him with our females, figuring that a large White Pekin couldn't mate with our smaller Khaki Campbell females any more successfully than Walter could sire another rabbit with Bertie. We did wonder whether a feral duck accustomed to the unfettered grandeur of Richmond Park pond would adapt well to drab captivity. His most recent interactions with humans had consisted of them chasing him with or without a net, and we worried that he might not tolerate us performing duck-pen chores at close quarters, especially when one of us could conceivably be singing "Camptown Races" as she worked.

Richie's impressive gooselike stature and radiant white plumage immediately intimidated both our hens and drakes when we introduced him to the girls' side of the pen. Stewart and Trevor muttered dire threats from the safety of the opposite side of the wire. The females danced away whenever the behemoth took an awkward step in their direction. The girls' nervousness infected the geese, who maintained a respectful distance even though they stood a full head taller than the puzzled newcomer. As the day wore on and important matters such as quacking incessantly for ice-free swimming pool water supplanted lesser concerns, the girls came around to blandly regarding Richie as just another duck. For his part, Richie decided that while freedom had its place, bountiful females and plentiful food were what he really wanted in life.

With a dollop of trepidation, we released Richie and the girls into the forty-inch-high snow pack that covered our backyard while we changed their water and replenished their scratch feed. Instead of bolting for the perimeter fence at the sight of Linda dragging out a hose from the basement, Richie dutifully stayed close to the girls as they paddled through the powder and obediently followed them back into the enclosure when their exercise time and our tolerance for frigid wind blasts mutually expired. He meshed so easily with our other ducks, I wondered if he hadn't been pining for a stable home environment during his seemingly carefree months at Richmond Park.

"What was he even doing there?"

"He can't fly," Linda said. "He couldn't have gotten there himself, so somebody probably dumped him."

That meant we were building a community of waterfowl misfits.

Our main misfit, Hector, accompanied Linda on a late-winter visit to Dr. Fuller, who delivered the bad news that the growth on the Muscovy's back was an inoperable tumor rooted to his spine. I took the information in stride, figuring that any negative consequences loomed far off in the future. The previous winter, Dr. Fuller had x-rayed our friendly female parakeet, Rossy, and discovered a tumor tucked inside the recesses of an air sac that was responsible for her intermittent breathing difficulties. Sometimes in the evenings when she grew tired, her tail flicked with every breath and she wheezed loudly enough that we could hear her in the next room. Still, she remained active and happy for a full year. On her last day of life, she flew to my shoulder as usual during dinner, snuggled against my neck, and pecked at a scrap of bread, weak but apparently otherwise untroubled. If Rossy could survive for months carrying an insidious tumor deep inside a vital respiratory organ, then Hector's external tumor didn't strike me as immediately life threatening.

His freezing to the ground earlier in the winter had apparently been an omen, however. He began to stumble and move around

more slowly. One spring morning shortly after the lavender cro-
cuses had replaced the last patches of ice on the ground, the girls
streamed out of their pen to nibble greedily at the damp backyard
dirt. When Hector didn't follow at his usual diffident distance,
Linda discovered her favorite duck stranded inside the pen, unable
to stand up. By tensing his wings and using them as crutches, he
managed a degree of locomotion across the gravel floor but not
enough to get him anywhere. The hot pride in his yellow eyes
dared Linda to feel sorry for him, and he thrashed unhappily when
she picked him up and carried him into the house. We commandeered Walter's fenced-in enclosure in the basement, wrapped
straw around a sheet for use as a bed, and kept Hector as comfortable as possible. He disliked being indoors and might have tolerated the porch with better humor, but Linda worried that it was too
cold for him.

Linda's friend LuAnne brought over a small laminated picture of
St. Francis of Assisi with a prayer to the saint printed on the back
—we called them "holy cards" when I attended Blessed Sacrament
School—and hung it on a ribbon over the convalescent's pen. "It's
been blessed by Father Andresiak," she told Linda. "I brought a bottle of holy water, too." While Linda held Hector in her lap, LuAnne
looped a rosary around the duck's neck, sprinkled him with the
holy water, and prayed with my wife for his recovery. As always,
Hector loved receiving attention from Linda, though I suspected
that LuAnne's Catholic rituals perplexed a duck whose disdain for
water had always ruled out baptism.

Despite their prayers, Hector grew alarmingly weak over the
next few days and finally stopped eating his scratch feed. I wrestled
with the question of whether we should euthanize him, while
Linda held firm to her belief that as long as he didn't appear to be
suffering, he should be allowed to live out his final hours. I knew

she was right, because Linda made sure that Hector's last impression was of her love for him. If any duck died happily, that Muscovy did. While I went to work as usual, Linda spent a large part of the morning with Hector. "I could tell by the look in his eye that he wasn't going to make it through the day," Linda told me later. She placed him outside so he could enjoy the sun. When he tried to flap his wings and acted agitated, she picked him up and he calmed right down. "I sat back down and held him for a while," she told me. "He gave a shudder, and I knew that he was dying then."

I was incredibly touched by Linda's dedication to an animal that most other people would simply have ignored, if you could ignore a duck who was busy calculating the most auspicious angle for latching on to your leg with his beak. We were comforted by our friends, especially Linda's friend Deanne and our pet-sitter Betty MacKay. The previous fall, while we were on vacation, Betty's husband, Wayne, could hardly believe his wife's description of our hissing, panting duck and had come over to our house to see the beast for himself. He had immediately hit it off with Hector, Betty had told us, and had gotten a kick out of the way the Muscovy followed him around the yard. When Linda phoned Betty to break the news that Hector had died, Betty paused. "I sure hate to have to tell Wayne," she said. "He was just crazy about him." I can't think of another duck who had as many admirers as our twenty-five-cent Hector, and I just hope that the next world is solid enough for him to bite.

Other backyard developments helped distract us from grieving too much for Hector. Our Richmond Park duck, Richie, entered the spirit of spring full throttle and began pestering the females. We tried talking Stewart and Trevor into sharing their space with the newcomer. Though they reluctantly agreed to give the lad a break, they failed to factor in their own elevated hormone levels. Feather-tugging fights erupted within minutes of Richie's entry to their pen.

"They'll sort it out and be best buddies pretty quick," I predicted. Instead, tempers flared to such an extent that interloper Richie hung back near the feed dish while the Khaki Campbell brothers duked it out between themselves. The fights disturbed the females next door, who lodged a formal complaint with their landlords by boisterously honking and quacking their disapproval. The only remedy was returning Richie to the harem in which we figured he was effectively a eunuch. To be on the safe side, we zealously discarded the females' eggs as a surefire method of birth control. The last thing we needed was yet another duck.

Because ducks cannot crossbreed with geese, we never bothered to examine Liza and Hailey's nests of infertile eggs, and that was our mistake. We permitted the two sisters their motherhood fantasies and let them each enjoy their nests. We only took away their eggs if one broke and interfered with the natural perfume of the pen—or if the geese grew obsessive about their nests and refused to leave them even to eat. Liza was getting close to this point when she started clinging to her nest with unusual vigor. We saw so little of her that I started to fear she might be having an aspergillosis flare-up.

"Liza?" As I bent down and peered into the doghouse, I confronted her thatch of white tail feathers. "Liza, are you okay?" I touched her between her shoulders. A soft double honk answered me from the shadows, but she showed no sign of budging. "Come on, you need to get some fresh air," I told her, as I pressed my hands around her body and eased her through the portal, being careful not to bump her head as she extended her neck and shot me a surprised look. Once I set her on the gravel floor, she tooted indignantly and for a moment seemed poised to pop back into the doghouse. At the sound of an answering honk from her sister out in the yard, she changed her mind and trundled through the duck-pen door. As I followed her, I thought I heard a tiny unfamiliar voice. I stopped and surveyed the trees around the pen and the dense thicket of thorny bushes that leaned over the back fence in hopes of snagging me. I prided myself on knowing the songs, call notes, and squawks of two dozen or so species of birds that visited our property throughout the year and wondered if an exotic warbler was about to reveal itself. But when the briefly detected peeping didn't recur, I put it out of my mind.

The next day Liza stayed behind once more while Hailey and the ducks fanned out across the lawn. Deciding it was probably time for her eggs to disappear, I urged her off her nest with a few encouraging words and a firm two-handed grab. After I had pulled her out of the doghouse, I was shocked to find a black and yellow puff of fluff racing back and forth and cheeping for the goose. I immediately let go of Liza. I could hardly have been more surprised if Howard, our dove, had laid an egg himself. Back inside the house, as I nursed a cup of coffee and tried to figure out how Liza had ended up with a baby, I remembered that just before Liza had taken possession of the doghouse, Marybelle had occupied it for a few days. Hidden among Liza's baseball-size eggs had obviously lurked the fertilized product of an unholy tryst between Richie and our brown duck.

Too excited by the notion of a goose rearing a duckling to fade into my usual midafternoon nap, I planted myself in the living room, where I could keep an eye peeled for Linda's return from a housecleaning job as I scanned the pages of *Entertainment Weekly* in vain for any dish about Pat Sajak and Vanna White. When my wife's station wagon finally lurched into the driveway, I rushed to her door and greeted her with a malicious grin.

"What?" Linda demanded. "What's going on?"

Grinning wider, I crooked my finger. "There's a surprise for you out back." Dropping her purse and keys on the front seat, Linda followed me out to the duck pen and gasped when I reached into Liza's doghouse and presented her with a squirming, buggy-eyed duckling with enormous black feet and stubby gesticulating wings.

"Oh, my gosh!" Linda squealed. "Where did that come from?"

"Liza hatched it," I told her. "She's the surrogate mother. Richie's the father."

"Is that your baby, Liza?" Linda asked the goose and got a happy honk in return.

I wouldn't have dared grab a duckling from a mother duck, but either Liza trusted me, or she knew that she was merely acting as a nanny. She didn't try to bite me as Chloe once had and guarded the little one from the other females more with her sheer bulk than with any aggressive behavior.

Timmy, as Linda named him, definitely needed guarding and stuck close to the goose both in and out of the pen. Female ducks may be fanatical protectors of their own brood, but their maternal instincts do not extend to other ducklings. Any time Timmy stepped too far out of Liza's shadow and a female was in nipping distance, he was in danger of receiving an unkindly poke from a beak. I thought that Marybelle might recognize the duckling as her own and volunteer as baby-sitter, but she was as ornery with him as the others.

I didn't blame Marybelle for failing to recognize Timmy. Within a couple of weeks, he shot up out of pecking range until he stood only a tad shorter than his dad. By no stretch of the imagination did his coloration resemble either of his parents. His blotchy black and yellow down covering had yielded to jet-black adult plumage, with splotches of pure white on his breast. His feet, legs, and bill were also black, in contrast to Richie's orange and Marybelle's olive brown accessories. We had seen a duck like Timmy at Jacob Lestermeyer's farm and wondered where he had come from, since none of the other petting zoo/meat department ducks were black. Now we knew that black-and-white was the hallmark of a White Pekin–Khaki Campbell domestic mallard mix.

It didn't exactly roll off the tongue. But it seemed all of a piece with the complicated comings and goings of a year in which we had found and released a dove, given away a pair of Khaki Campbell mallard males, taken in a rabbit, lost a turkey to a mysterious animal attack, lost our parakeet Rossy and Muscovy Hector to cancer, gained a White Pekin duck, and ended up with a mixed-up duckling that had been brought up by a goose. In days gone by, if anyone had asked me if I owned any pets, I could readily rattle off their names. To answer that same question now, I would have to excuse myself, find a pen and sheet of paper, sit by myself for several minutes, and try to sort the problem out.

CHAPTER 13

Hazel Eyes

It hardly seemed that a mere eight years separated my love-hate relationship with Binky from my embrace of all manner of feathered creatures and a few furred ones. I had gone from railing at a rabbit who hid placidly on the other side of a plasterboard wall to barely raising my eyes from a joke in *Reader's Digest* to mumble to Linda, "It sound's like Stanley's chewing up the cupboard door again." Where our pets were concerned, chaos just didn't bother me the way it used to. The ceaseless demands of Ollie had long ago raised my threshold for tolerating noise and property destruction, while matching wits with bunnies, doves, and ducks had taught me the foolhardiness of trying to exert my will upon even the most seemingly innocuous creature. In the end, the intensive bother of dawn-to-dusk animal care had become so deeply embedded in my daily routine that from time to time it all felt like coasting.

And along the way, I had lost a good deal of the squeamishness that had dogged me since earliest childhood, when I had chickened out of fishing out of revulsion at having to touch a worm.

When I was a teenager, a mouse nibbling on an issue of *Playboy* hidden behind my dresser had kept me awake in terror until I had finally collapsed in exhausted sleep, or possibly fainted. In my thirties I'd used a pencil to transfer a clammy washcloth from the bottom of the bathtub to the laundry basket, lest I contract the smorgasbord of bacteria, mold, and mildew it had cultivated over-night. Nursing animals through sickness eventually sent most of my fussy phobias packing. My résumé included squirting anti-fungal medicine down a goose's throat; draining bunny abscesses; swabbing Betadine on the torn-up back of a ring-neck dove blind-sided by our parrot; massaging the bright yellow oil gland above a Muscovy duck's rump; clipping bird wings, nails, and parrot beaks; trimming rabbit teeth; plus administering assorted injections, nasal drops, eyewashes, ear medicine, and antibiotics. Bathroom humor still made me blush, but assisting with animals' bodily functions had become second nature, as I routinely picked up, sponged off, and sprayed away animal droppings of all sizes and shapes.

It was tempting to credit the Zoloft with these attitude adjust-ments, but its effectiveness muffling the chattering of my nerves was dwindling over time. A sick pet was often enough to bring on the morning shakes. And occasionally I would wake up in the mid-dle of the night and begin worrying about the animals in general. What was I doing with so many of them? Why did we keep taking in new ones? Three rabbits, two cats, three parakeets, a dove, two parrots, three turkeys, two geese, a canary, and nine ducks at last count were just about what Noah had started with, and he never brought his animals into the house. Once I started fretting about the pets, I would lie awake for an hour or more trying to shut off a deluge of nagging concerns that in full light of day seldom seemed serious. After a few months of this, I suggested to Dr. Rick that I might need a slight boost in my Zoloft. Rather than lecturing me again on the questionable long-term effects of the drug, he surprised me by immediately agreeing.

"Most people who take Zoloft for several years find they need to increase the dosage. Let's double the amount you're taking."

"No, that's way too drastic," I said. "I've had trouble with large dosages before. Just bump me up from fifty milligrams to seventy-five."

"They don't make a seventy-five-milligram pill."

"Do they make a one hundred fifty? Give me that, and I'll just break it into two."

"If we're going to make a change, let's make it significant," he insisted. "I'm writing you a prescription for one hundred milligrams." Reassured by the acoustic guitar chords that rippled from the speaker on his desk, against my better judgment I agreed to give the double-potency pills a try. It was tough to argue with a jazzy version of John Lennon's "Norwegian Wood," complete with faux flamenco flourishes. "Call me in a month with a progress report," he told me, as he escorted me to the payment desk.

Oh, how I paid for my suggestion. Exactly as before, the drug at first enveloped me in a deceptive calm before summoning up a seratonin cyclone that battered every nerve-ending in my body. I was simultaneously hyper-caffeinated and drained of every last drop of energy, wielding just enough strength to lie lifelessly on the bed but too jittery to do so. The most humdrum occurrences suddenly seemed fraught with danger. A visit to the Food City produce department with its seductive leafy greens and round ripe shapes felt as unnatural as crunching broken glass beneath my shoes. The fluorescent lighting saturated the store in merciless uniformity, plunging all into a clinical blandness without shadows. The aisles had the gall of metaphor as they swept me toward an inevitable fate at the romaine lettuce bin. The sheer number of items that each blink of an eye took in troubled me with essential questions about separateness and individuality. When the checkout clerk spoke to me as my lettuce, bananas, cat food, and batteries silently rode the conveyor belt, I thought so hard about making an appropriate response, I barely heard what I was responding to. "No coupons today," I answered, with a hopeful smile. Before the Zoloft could completely immobilize me, I cut back to fifty milligrams.

I phoned Dr. Rick at the end of the month and reported my poor reaction to the increase. Rather than clucking sympathetically, he barked at me. "You did this without asking me?"

"I didn't know I needed your permission."

"You should have called me up immediately and I would have prescribed another drug to see you through the transition."

"I don't even like taking one drug that alters my brain chemistry," I told him. "I'm certainly not going to take two of them."

"I'm not saying you did anything wrong," he replied without much conviction. "I just wish you had let me do my job and help you out."

Doing one's job and job security were both iffy issues in the psychiatric field. Shortly after my conversation with Dr. Rick, I received a letter in the mail from the director of Psychiatric Services —Werner Klemperer, or something like that—informing me that due to skyrocketing health care costs, recent decisions by insurance carriers to deny coverage of previously supported mental health services, and the ever increasing difficulty of recruiting seriously silly therapists, Psychiatric Services was regretfully closing its doors. The letter signed off with a postscript inviting me to drive fifty miles to Okemos for the pleasure of continuing my relationship with Dr. Rick. Instead, I asked our family doctor in Lowell to renew my prescription.

It would have taken more than Zoloft to blunt the emotional impact of the cold April afternoon when Linda rushed me out to the barn. "Something terrible has happened to one of the turkeys," she told me, as we hurried through the wet grass. "I don't know what happened to her. I think she's in a coma." I had been working on my music column for *The Beat* and was in one of my usual stupors, running phrases over in my mind and wondering why none of them sounded any better than the CD I was reviewing. Heavy clouds hung low in the slate-grey sky. We hadn't seen the outline of the sun for over a week.

I still wasn't particularly engaged as I followed Linda through a wooden gate to the old cow stanchion that we had converted into turkey quarters. I had never developed the same close rapport with the turkeys that I had with our geese. I took pleasure in their repertoire of sounds, from classic gobbles to doggy yips, liked the way they would cluster around me when I stepped into their pen and showed them off to visitors with tongue-in-cheek earnestness. But I always thought of them as "the turkeys." It was all but impossible to tell them apart. Their coloration was essentially identical, and the subtle differences we noticed seemed to change from week to week, such as a few extra bristly feathers flecking one bird's knobby pink head.

I half expected to find the stricken turkey up and about and happily pecking at her plastic tub of scratch feed—the victim of nothing more serious than a nap. Instead, she lay stock still where Linda had left her on an elevated bed of straw against a fieldstone wall, her neck ominously limp and outstretched. I couldn't see any signs of trauma at first. As my eyes adjusted to the darkness, I made the shocking discovery that her entire head had turned a smooth shade of featherless black, as if it were encased in a snug leather hood.

"She looks burnt," Linda told me, as I gaped at the turkey in disbelief. "I found her in the outside pen next to the fence. One of the girls was standing over her making crying noises, like she had done something to her and was ashamed of herself."

The turkey's breathing was so labored, I expected each breath to be her last. But when I noticed her eyes, or the puffy slits where her eyes should have been, I forgot about her breathing. I touched her face and was startled to find that the scabby flesh felt hot. Linda poured a trickle of water on the injured area. The air was cold enough that wisps of steam curled up from the bird's head. I turned away.

I retreated through the Dutch door facing our neighbor's gravel road and walked the perimeter of the turkey pen, searching for a clue to what could have happened. Our neighbor had complained of strange cars driving down the road at night and turning around just before they reached the house. Two miles from us, another farmhouse had burned to the ground, and I'd heard gossip at the feed store that arson was to blame. I scanned the remnant of last season's weeds on both sides of the fence for matches, a Zippo lighter, a can of lighter fluid, a charred patch of dirt, or anything that might have suggested arson—if that's an appropriate term for setting a turkey on fire. Mostly I was just killing time, hoping that the turkey would have quietly passed on before I returned to the barn.

"We've got to get her out of the cold," Linda told me. "We've got to get her into the house."

The turkey gurgled as I picked her up. I carried her across our property past a cluster of tiny rock-topped graves in back of our house marking the resting places of a rabbit, a duck, a canary, and a parakeet. Linda threw open the basement door. Unable to see my feet, I ran into a mound of unwashed clothes while walking well out of my way to dodge a collection of empty birdcages. Inside the largest of the three bunny-exercise pens, I placed the turkey on a nest that Linda hastily prepared from a bedsheet peppered with holes, courtesy of Stanley Sue. Under the sheet was a plush sheepskin sleeping mat that neither of our cats had taken to.

Our turkey was nearly unconscious, barely clinging to life, and we did what little we could for her. Linda dabbed her head with Betadine. Using a syringe, I coaxed her beak open and got her to take a few swallows of water. Linda phoned Marge Chedrick, a DNR-accredited animal rescue volunteer whose residential backyard concealed recuperating geese, ducks, squirrels, chickens, a white peahen, and a one-winged blue heron, all behind a stockade fence. Marge suggested we hang a light bulb a foot or so above the bird for warmth during the night. "She'll move away from it if she gets too warm," she told us. But our turkey showed so little awareness of her surroundings, I doubted if she would be inconvenienced by anything as trivial as a sixty-watt lamp.

During dinner we picked at our plates while our parrots ate voraciously. Taking advantage of our subdued mood, Stanley Sue and Ollie lorded it over their shell-shocked owners by demanding one variety of food after another and throwing corn, toast, bits of enchilada, and tapioca pudding to the floor with exuberant wastefulness.

"One of the other turkeys had blood on her beak," Linda told me, as Stanley Sue mimicked gagging when I presented her with a spoonful of pinto beans. "It was the same one who looked guilty about what happened."

"Why would she attack another turkey?"

"They get real territorial this time of year. When they find a spot in their pen where they want to sit, you have to just about pick them up to make them move, especially if they lay an egg. Maybe she was sitting in a spot the other one wanted."

"That would explain the turkey we lost last year," I said, trying to wrest the spoon from Stanley Sue's grasp. She had fastened her beak on the handle just below the bowl of the spoon and was doing her best to dump the beans on my pants. "Something really went after her, and it was probably the same turkey that pecked the one downstairs."

"But why would a turkey sit still and get pecked to death? I still think there's a firebug in the area and somebody burned her head."

"But why would anyone bother to set just the head of a turkey on fire? She's not burned anywhere else, if that's what's wrong with her. And why would she sit still for that, either?"

Only one thing seemed certain out of all of this. It was silly to keep referring to "the turkey in the basement" when we finally had a way of positively distinguishing her from the others. Being awarded a name under such dire circumstances didn't constitute much of an honor, but at least whenever we referred to her from then on— posthumously or not—we would call her Hazel, the name Linda suggested.

Around 10:30 P.M. we trooped downstairs for the final time that night to say our good-byes to Hazel. Her head felt hotter than ever when I brushed a finger pad against her face. I was tempted to give her another drink of water, but she was blissfully unconscious, and I didn't want to awaken her to a world of pain. She raised her head slightly off the sheet when Linda draped a calico blouse over her body, then she sunk back into oblivion.

The next morning I lay in bed exhausted by a long, repetitive dream. Stanley Sue had escaped from a bamboo cage into a thickly forested version of our backyard. She kept flying within arm's length before taking to the trees again whenever I approached too closely. As I tried to put the dream aside, Hazel's injury came crashing back like a steel door blocking my release. At least, I thought, the gravely injured turkey would have died quietly while we slept. In stocking feet I walked down the bare wood basement stairs for an official check on her status before delivering the news to Linda. But the poor bird was alive and breathing, making a watery noise resembling a drinking straw chasing liquid around the bottom of a glass. She had rotated a quarter of a turn during the night and had managed to throw off Linda's blouse. Then I saw something else that made me turn and bound back upstairs.

"Linda!" I called from the living room. "Linda." She was just getting out of bed. "Come down and look at this," I told her.

"What?" Her voice was tinged with dread.

"Just come here and look," I hollered, as I trotted back to the turkey.

As Linda stood warily at the bottom of the basement stairs, I held out an object at arm's length. It was oval shaped, exaggeratedly pointed on one end. White, almost beige, and spattered with brown speckles. It was the egg that Hazel had laid during the night, in a totally unexpected affirmation of life. Upon hearing Linda's delighted laugh, the turkey surprised us by struggling to her feet. I raised a water dish to her chest and urged her head down until her beak met water. She took a couple of swallows, then sank back to the floor.

"Maybe she's going to be okay," Linda suggested, though we both knew Hazel's chances for survival were almost nil. The black scab that covered her entire head had sealed up her eyes, except for two small openings that expelled a milky substance. Using cotton balls, we carefully dabbed her eye slits dry without holding any hope for the damaged tissue behind them. I could see that she was totally blind. She couldn't even detect the light from the bare bulb I waved in front of her. More immediately alarming was the sound from her nasal cavity indicating she had come down with a respiratory infection. The infection could kill her within a day or two unless we treated her with an antibiotic; that was usually the way it went with birds. Unfortunately, it was Saturday, and Dr. Fuller's practice was closed, as was Dr. Carlotti's.

But Linda got an answer when she phoned Dr. Colby, the vet who had treated Bertha. The receptionist balked at the idea of the doctor seeing or even discussing a turkey. "Dr. Colby just doesn't have any time this morning," she told Linda. "I'm very sorry about your turkey, but there's nothing we can do for you."

As I sat frowning into my oatmeal, a drastic change overtook me. Shucking my well-studied philosophy of life, I decided to take action for once, and confrontational action at that. "She may not be willing to see Hazel," I told Linda. "I wouldn't want to move her anyway. But she's going to give us an antibiotic." The fact that a turkey, of all our animals, had motivated me to assert myself was one of those ironies that I just had to accept. But I found it impossible not to fight for Hazel. She exhibited a will to live that I lacked on the sunniest, Zoloft-inflated day, and the least I could do was cop the chemicals she needed.

I fumed all the way to Colby's Animal Clinic, barely hearing NPR's *Weekend Edition with Scott Simon* over the drone of my interior monologue, as I practiced what I was going to tell the vet. The steep green hills, winding curves, and rain-filled air conspired with a construction crew setting up orange traffic cones to keep me from organizing my thoughts. The best opener I could come up with— "Exactly why is a common meat-production turkey any less deserving of your care than an AKC registered pure-bred champion Jack Russell terrier?"—seemed to lack the proper sting. But striking a tone of justifiable outrage was what really mattered, I told myself.

Just past the village of Hubbs, I overshot the gravel road that led to Colby's Animal Clinic, turned around in a convenience store parking lot, crossed a culvert bridge barely longer than my car was wide, and navigated the brush-choked driveway to a boxy farmhouse on the edge of a horse pasture. A side door marked CLINIC opened straight into a vestibule, where a knee-high accordion gate blocked me from continuing into the family's laundry room. A handwritten sign directed clinic visitors sharply to the right and down a precipitous flight of stairs.

Except for the college-age receptionist who had taken Linda's phone call, I was the only person in the pine-paneled waiting area when I presented myself unannounced. If only to spare herself prolonged contact with a man demanding medicine for his pet turkey, the receptionist raised the hinged section of the front counter and ushered me inside the sole examination room.

Before I had a chance to inventory the glass display case packed with Beanie Baby animals, I heard the scrape of footsteps behind the wall as Dr. Colby came through the door from the adjoining lab. "What can I do for you today?" she asked with politeness, smoothly concealing her annoyance.

I faced her with rising indignation and mental fingers poised to clutch a rational argument as I suddenly found myself fighting back tears. I lost further ground as I struggled with the truth that the emotional outpouring wasn't in defense of the grey parrot whose head I had rubbed each night for years, the green parrot who snuggled against my neck in between bites to my shirt collar, the cats that rolled on my carpeted floor or cement slab as I bounced baby talk off them, the dove who loved to perch upon my head and coo at me, the fat black rabbit who sat on my lap licking my hand when I wasn't petting him, or even the goose Linda and I had nursed through a deadly illness on the porch—but of a turkey that until two days ago I couldn't have picked out of our group of three.

"It's about our turkey," I answered, my voice starting to crack.

"I'm sorry," she told me in a way that suggested she regretted my visit more than my turkey's ill health.

"She's been injured. Either pecked very badly by the other turkeys, or someone burned her head."

"I see."

"That's okay," I stammered stupidly. "It's her respiratory infection I'm worried about. If we don't get her on antibiotics, I'm afraid she'll die."

Looking at me steadily, Dr. Colby asked, "And what would you like me to do for you?" as if I'd ventured into the tire center in the middle of town by mistake. I reminded myself that this was the same vet who wouldn't let us have deworming pills for our cats unless we brought in a section of the worm. Either she suspected us of hoarding deworming pills, or she was collecting feline tapeworm segments for mysterious purposes of her own.

"I'd like to get an antibiotic for my turkey."

"How much does she weigh?"

While I thought about it, I looked down at her arm. A fresh scratch joined a myriad of hairline scars revealed by the fluorescent light. "Well, she's big. Turkey-size big."

She nodded wearily, turning her back to reach for a bottle of medicine. "It's important that I get an estimate of weight in order to calculate the dosage."

Comparing Hazel to a sack of black oil sunflower seed, I told her, "More than twenty-five pounds, less than thirty."

"So between twenty-six and twenty-nine pounds, you think. I'll prepare a broad-spectrum antibiotic to give her orally twice a day —if you can do that," she said with a questioning look.

"I did this," I sniffed, glumly basking in my minor triumph.

As I waited for my prescription in the aptly named waiting room, I saw no hint of the flurry of patients that had supposedly prevented me from bringing in the turkey. One woman breached the steep stairs to inquire about boarding rates for her Lhasa apso and was speedily dispatched with a rate card.

The receptionist handed me the antibiotic and uttered a phrase that she undoubtedly had never used before: "I hope your turkey feels better soon." I almost gave her the phone number of Matty the pharmacist at Park Hills Drug Store so that the two of them could commiserate, but I beat a hasty retreat instead.

Hazel certainly didn't feel good about taking her medicine. The procedure was fairly straightforward. Get the bird's beak open, then carefully push the syringe down her throat and into her crop to administer the antibiotic. We'd had previous experience dosing Liza. But Hazel weighed more than twice as much as Liza, wielded wings that could knock us across the room, and possessed a formidable beak that was already well acquainted with our flesh. Even in her weakened state, she had little difficulty dragging me around her basement pen as I hung on for dear life. When I tried pressing her down into a sitting position using both hands, I ended up splayed on the floor. Linda helped by bracing herself against a hefty support pillar and clutching the turkey to her body while I applied my feeble musculature to restraining Hazel's head and working the syringe between her mandibles. We soon learned to mix the powdered antibiotic with as little liquid as possible, since one shot was literally all we got each session. Though she proved to be an expert in passive resistance, she never once pecked, nipped, bit, clawed, or otherwise throttled us. I wondered if she understood our intentions despite the discomfort they inflicted.

Successfully administering the antibiotics solved one problem. But Hazel hadn't eaten a speck of food since her injury. She needed sustenance to fight off her respiratory infection, but offering her scratch feed was out of the question when she couldn't see to peck

at her dish. Since she would occasionally, with coaxing, drink water, our strategy was to concoct a nourishing liquid of some sort.
My efforts at mixing water and scratch feed created a grainy sludge
of no interest to anyone except a bricklayer. Acting on Marge
Chedrick's suggestion, Linda picked up a powdered rice cereal
for infants along with Pedialyte, an electrolyte-packed liquid, in
the "Baby" section of the supermarket. (A "Turkey" section was
strangely absent.) Hazel drank a smidgen of the watery gruel, but
she wouldn't slurp up enough to fill her stomach. Hazel had to go
to the veterinarian. I called in sick, feigning a nonspecific stomach
ailment and sparing my coworkers the particulars of my increasingly eccentric existence. No way would Hazel fit in our goose carrier, so we set her inside a curbside recycling bin that apparently
had a poor effect on her morale. Hazel's head was just about the
same size as Stanley Sue's, and the brain inside her thicker skull
was no larger than an acorn. Keeping tabs on the geographical location of the various feathers and appendages attached to her massive body left her precious little cranial activity to waste on reason
and common sense. Despite this mental handicap and her blindness, she still recognized the insult of being conveyed via a trash receptacle. By the time we lugged her into Dr. Fuller's clinic, Hazel's
neck hung limply and she showed little interest in staying conscious. Her depression was contagious. No sooner had Dr. Fuller
swept into the examination room to relish his first ever turkey patient than the wind was expelled from his lungs by her distressing
state.

Linda described how she had discovered Hazel in her pen and
the treatment we had given her so far. Dr. Fuller discounted the
theory that a vandal had set her head on fire by explaining that her
injuries were consistent with a pecking attack by the other turkeys.
"They were definitely going for her eyes," he told her.

"Why would they hurt her like that?"

"Chickens and turkeys do strange things when they get upset. It could be that a hawk flew over their pen, causing them to panic, and they attacked her."

"Or maybe a stranger scared them," suggested Linda, a version of the firebug still dancing in her head.

I was relieved when Dr. Fuller suggested that he keep Hazel overnight to tube-feed her and give her a booster shot of antibiotics. The seriousness of her condition actually filled me with a peculiar confidence. Two years earlier, at the moment that I had walked away from the clinic leaving our goose Liza in Dr. Fuller's care, I didn't believe that she would die. This time, I didn't believe that Hazel would survive. These opposite poles somehow seemed equivalent, and with a tremor of calm and no nagging expectations, I smiled at Linda, assured that we had finally done all that could be done.

When I returned to pick up Hazel on Tuesday afternoon, I found a changed bird in her place. She stood straight up in her recycling bin, head erect and turning from side-to-side as she tracked sounds in the examination room. Her nasal cavities barely whistled when she breathed. Dr. Fuller told me that the antibiotics from Dr. Colby had probably saved her life, but he wanted her on a different antibiotic for another ten days. "The good news is that I don't see her sinus infection as being a significant problem now," he told me. "But I'm afraid her long-term outlook isn't good. She will probably never regain her eyesight, though we won't know for sure until the scabs come off. The problem with birds is that they are so visually oriented toward their food, they don't like to eat what they can't see."

"Couldn't we learn to tube-feed her the way you did?" I asked.

"You could," he answered hesitantly. "But if it comes down to that, you really have to ask yourself what kind of quality of life she'll have. Under those circumstances, it may be best to euthanize her."

Although I could hardly consider Dr. Fuller's message upbeat, Hazel's progress so delighted me that I sailed home above the rush hour traffic on a pair of turkey wings, buoyed by the realization that for the first time since her accident, she wasn't in imminent danger of transitioning to the big roasting pan in the sky. Keeping her anchored in our world wouldn't be an easy job, I knew, but I figured we had a grace period of a day or two before worrying about finding a way to get her to eat. From the condition of the bottom of the recycling bin by the time I pulled into our driveway, I could tell that the animal clinic had filled her with plenty of food. I had imagined that they would treat her to an exotic high-protein wonder formula, but according to Dr. Fuller they had given her the same scratch feed that we had fed her in the barn. Tube-feeding her the scratch feed had done the trick. In fact, it was like priming the pump.

SHORTLY AFTER THE homecoming fanfare wound down and we reinstalled Hazel in the basement, I presented her with the Pedialyte-and-rice-cereal mixture, gently lowering her head until her beak touched the liquid. She wouldn't drink it. Without a hope of success, I grabbed the metal bowl containing her scratch feed, shook it to tantalize her ears with the seductive scrape of cracked corn and grains upon curved aluminum, and placed the bowl under her head. To my astonishment, she immediately pecked at the food. She raised her head to swallow and, not being able to see the bowl, lowered her head and pecked in a different spot, missing the bowl and forcing me to quickly shift the food to meet her beak. Each time her head rose, I tried anticipating where it would land next time, so I could be there with the bowl. Popping the bowl back and forth provided a nice visual metaphor for the excitement I was feeling that our never-say-die turkey had cleared another serious hurdle.

"She ate feed from her dish!" I announced to Linda in the kitchen. "She ate the scratch feed," I added for clarification, when Linda failed to perform handsprings on the linoleum.

"I know. She ate some for me a little while ago. She drank her Pedialyte, too."

"But she *really* ate for me," I told Linda, as my altruism turned to pettiness. "She ate so much, she didn't have room for your Pedialyte. She really ate a lot."

In the days that followed, I tried imagining a system that would allow Hazel to feed herself, but there didn't seem to be a substitute for the handheld metal bowl. I mentioned one idea to Linda. "What if we build her a long, narrow pen out in the barn that barely gives her room to turn around. But she'd have plenty of space to walk up and down."

"Uh-huh."

"Along both sides running the entire length of the pen, there would be a trough full of scratch feed. And that way, she could peck almost anywhere and never miss her feed dish. What do you think?"

"What's she going to do about water?" Linda asked.

"I don't know." I considered the problem. "We could flood the barn."

Even if my inspiration wasn't up to snuff, my motivation was solid. After all, a turkey didn't exactly make the ideal house pet. Linda kept the washer and dryer running almost constantly in an attempt to keep up with the number of clean sheets we needed for her bedding. Still, it took far less effort to gather up a sheet and shake off the turkey poop than it did hosing down, scrubbing, and disinfecting the cement floor every twenty minutes. We tried spreading straw inside her pen, but it continually needed changing and tended to scatter throughout the basement, cling to the bottom of our feet, and appear on the living room rug. No matter how hard Linda worked keeping Hazel's quarters clean, a turkey smell pervaded the basement and occasionally invaded the upstairs, and that strong, sour odor made me long for the comparative perfume of the duck pen.

On the first sunny day after Hazel's strength had returned, Linda decided we should put her outdoors in the bunny pen where she couldn't wander off or run into anything that might hurt her. "A little while in the fresh air will do her good," she said.

Lowell only gets around sixty days of cloudless sunshine a year, and the sky was such an oceanic shade of blue, I could imagine the dome of stars huddled behind it waiting jealously for night to fall. The birds were unusually silent in the trees. The titmice, cardinals, orioles, and song sparrows were too dazzled by the gorgeous afternoon to sing. I set Hazel down in the grass, wishing that she could enjoy her surroundings as much as I was. But the scab that enveloped her head and hid her damaged eyes sealed her in a total eclipse. She took a few steps forward and lurched to the left until her wing pressed against the fence. She raised her neck and cocked her head. The wisp of a breeze carried the scent of our freshly cut lawn to her nostrils, along with the bacterial decay of the evaporating pond just down the hill. She twittered nervously.

"You okay?" I asked her.

She erupted in a string of piercing yips. Everything was quiet, and then she started barking again. Maybe being outdoors was upsetting her after weeks of security in our basement. I was about to bring her back into the house until it hit me what was going on. She was calling to our other turkeys. If Linda hadn't found Hazel in

the barn shortly after her injury, and if it hadn't been for our subsequent struggles giving her the medicine, food, water, and all of
the other treatment she desperately needed, she would have died.
Despite this, Hazel's feelings for us didn't run particularly deep. We
barely existed in her world, because her world was her flock. Unleashing another volley of barks, she called again to our other
turkeys, the very same turkeys that had nearly pecked her to death.
I was horrified. From the opposite end of our property, a turkey answered her. Hazel called back with unbridled passion. I walked
into the house and shut the door.

 While Hazel continued to improve, the scab on her head was
stubbornly slow to heal. Rather than crumbling away in patches,
the sheath of thick, dead skin began to loosen around her chin like
a hood that had been unlaced. One afternoon as I was feeding her,
I noticed that I didn't have to move the dish around as much as
usual. She pecked her food with surprising accuracy while I held
the bowl in place. Crouching on my hands and knees, I peered up
into the gap between the clinging scab and the left side of her face
and thought I saw an animated glint. I ran upstairs and grabbed a
small pair of kitchen scissors. Holding her head as best as I could,
I cut an arc of dead skin from the bottom of the scab, then another,
then another, until a naked eye surrounded by pink flesh looked
back at me. I drew my hand toward it. She pulled her head away. I
picked up the bowl of scratch feed and out of sheer habit shook it.
She blinked and regarded it blandly.

 Hazel could definitely see.

 The orbital tissue was misshapen and her eyelid drooped, but
the eye itself worked fine. The scab on the right side of her head—
the side that had been more severely injured than the left—hadn't
loosened enough for me to risk a trim. But one good eye was fine.
No, one good eye was great. One good eye made all the difference

between a turkey we would have to wait on hand and foot and a turkey that could live a nice life on her own. And a good eye it truly was. I sat down on the basement floor beside her, marveling at its beauty and amazed by the fact that an event involving a turkey somehow added up to one of the happiest days I could remember. I definitely needed to get out of the house more often.

"You don't want to put her with the other turkeys," Dr. Fuller told Linda when she phoned him a week later. I had finally succeeded in cutting away a section of the scab on the right side of Hazel's face, uncovering the remnant of an eye that seemed to respond vaguely to light, but was useless for resolving objects. "A turkey that's blind in one eye is susceptible to further injury," Dr. Fuller warned. "You want to keep her by herself." That had been our thinking, too. I sectioned off a separate pen for Hazel in the middle of our barn leading to an outdoor pen of her own, adding two more entries to my fencing résumé. Just like our three bunnies, who couldn't bear to share the same room but cuddled through the bars of their cages, Hazel would often sit close to the fence while her sisters parked themselves nearby on the other side of the wire.

It took me weeks before I could walk down to the basement without expecting to find Hazel on her blanket in the bunny pen. Although caring for her had involved an impressive amount of work—most of which I was thankful Linda had undertaken—I still missed Hazel's presence in the house. I missed the way she would stand up when she heard our footsteps on the stairs and occasionally talk back to us with soft warbling sounds. I missed her enthusiastic stabs at her bowl of scratch feed. I missed the turkey feathers I carried to work on the seat of my pants. And I missed the quizzical eyebrows of the men who delivered our water-softener salt. Because I found myself missing Hazel, I visited her in the barn, and she still enjoyed it when I held her bowl while she ate. It was the least I could do. Linda and I may have provided the care she needed at a crucial time, with important help from Drs. Fuller and Colby, but Hazel alone had supplied the courage and patience that had pulled her through.

One afternoon about two months after we had moved Hazel from our basement to her new pen, Linda found one of the other two turkeys dead on the barn floor. She lay sprawled on the cement with her wings outstretched, suggesting she had leaped from the stanchion rail, missed the cushioning straw, hit the floor wrong, and died on the spot. That left us with only Hazel and one other turkey. That turkey needed a name, and because Linda identified her as the bird with blood on her beak the day of Hazel's injury—and also because we figured she was behind the fatal attack on our other turkey the previous fall—I dubbed her Lizzie. Lizzie Borden. Considering the suffering that Lizzie had caused Hazel, I made a feeble effort to dislike her, but even that didn't last.

CHAPTER 14

Weaver in the Weeds

I was lying in bed listening to an early evening rerun of Art Bell's "Coast to Coast" paranormal-topics radio talk show when I heard something that I couldn't believe. Art's guest was a ghost hunter from Pennsylvania who was playing back voices of the dead he had recorded at haunted houses, cemeteries, and Civil War battlefields. During a commercial break, I yawned and turned down the volume only to hear Linda on the telephone in the living room.

"Sure, we'd love to raise some baby starlings for you," she said. "We've been wanting to do this for a long time."

Hardly trusting my ears, I scrambled out of bed and thudded into the next room, where I found Linda stretched out on the rug. Because of her worsening back problems, she rarely used furniture any longer except when she was eating or sleeping. Waving my arms, I managed to catch her eye as she unhitched her head from the receiver to tell me, "Guess what, sweetie? Marge Chedrick has seven baby starlings, and she's going to let us raise them for her!"

I shook my head so hard the vertebrae in my neck popped. "Tell her we have to talk about this first."

Linda nodded at the phone. "Tomorrow afternoon? Do we need to bring anything?"

"Another husband," I muttered, as I scuttled in defeat back to my world of powerless disembodied entities.

In truth, I was a weak man with a weakness for starlings ever since seeing a newly molted adult up close at a pet-bird show. In contrast to the undistinguished black-and-brown birds of city lawns that are frequently lumped with squirrels, rats, and high school children as unavoidable urban pests, the European starling in his snappiest attire is an engaging dandy. His plumage resembles an outlandish costume made of cloisonné, from his black flight and tail feathers encircled by ocher borders to his white-tipped breast feathers, brown-speckled back, iridescent shoulder coverts with a hint of green, and white-flecked brown and black head. "People keep asking me what kind of bird he is," the woman we met at the bird show told us. "They think he's some kind of imported exotic. They're like, 'What?' when I tell them he's your run-of-the-mill starling."

If a stunning seasonal display were the starling's only attribute, I might have mentally filed the species away with Christmas trees and Fourth of July artillery as merely an attention grabber. But the bird also brandishes a wickedly appealing talent. It can talk, and talk as adroitly as a parrot. This fact was drilled deep into my consciousness when Linda frustrated my attempts to turn the pages of a Dashiell Hammett novel by reading long passages aloud from Margarete Sigl Corbo and Diane Marie Barras's pet literature classic, *Arnie, the Darling Starling,* describing the titular bird's verbal abilities. With all due deference to Hammett's *The Glass Key,* Arnie's chatty, friendly ways ultimately captured my attention, and I ended up reading the book myself.

"Someday, maybe we'll have a starling of our own," I would dreamily tell Linda now and then when my blood sugar dipped dangerously low. Along with the house sparrow and the rock dove (better known as the city pigeon), the European starling is one of three wild American birds that can legally be kept as pets, because all three are introduced species. Never mind that all three species have lived in the country long enough to have earned residency status. Starlings were brought to America in 1850 by a man intent on populating New York City's Central Park with every bird mentioned in Shakespeare's plays. No one bothered to tell the birds they were to stay within the park, and they quickly fanned out across the country. Over 150 years later, starlings are still considered interlopers. "Conservation laws in the US do not protect nongame, non-native species," sniffs the "Conservation" note on the page devoted to the European starling in the Smithsonian Institution's *Birds of North America* handbook.

Marge and George Chedrick apparently hadn't read the Smithsonian guide, however. The European starling enjoyed strong conservation at the Chedrick house, as did the small but vocal goose that served as gatekeeper to their bustling backyard. Once we had stepped through, a quick glance in search of Marge located a flightless seagull named Hannibal, a noisy white peahen, chickens, swans, Canada geese, and assorted domestic waterfowl. Marge stood near the back porch sucking on a cigarette as she suspiciously eyed a squirrel.

"Back here again?" she demanded, as the creature stood up on its hind legs. "It isn't feeding time yet." At the sound of her voice, a one-eared squirrel scampered down a tree and joined the first near Marge's foot.

"Watch out for Ginger," Marge warned me. The beefy Rhode Island Red rooster circled behind me as he scratched at the ground ostensibly prowling for worms. I was his real prey. Ginger loved nothing better than launching a flying peck at the small of my back

that felt as if my spine had been bonked with a hammer. I learned
never to crouch down to talk to the tamer ducks and geese when
Ginger patrolled the area.

"Why's he always in such a bad mood?" I asked her.

"You'd be in a bad mood, too, if you saw both of your parents
killed by hawks."

George breezed by, a strong wedge of a man carrying a fifty-
pound bag of scratch feed under one arm and a sack of mesquite
wood chips under the other. He wore on his shoulder a squat white
bird that sported a swiveling periscope for a head and neck. A charcoal grill that had seen better days spewed happy clouds of black
smoke toward the stockade fence that kept the foundlings in and the
predators out. Beyond the fence, the weathered bricks and large rectangular windows of the Victorian-style house next door hinted at
a quiet city neighborhood in another world. A pair of male Muscovy
ducks paused to hiss menacingly at George when he whisked past
them toward a metal barn containing triple-decker cages of recuperating critters. Last time we had visited, a muskrat and two foxes
were among the patients.

"Is that a —?" I gestured in befuddlement at the bird on George's
back, as he disappeared into the barn.

"That's Ricky," Marge replied. "He's a two-week-old baby turkey.
George's crazy about him. Get back, Muff." A Labrador retriever/
American bison hybrid accessorized with a red bandana tried to
squeeze past us as we followed Marge up the porch steps and into
the kitchen. The aluminum door squeaked shut behind us. A blue
jay landed on the porch railing and begged raucously for the blueberries on the kitchen windowsill. Across the room—beyond a
table piled with DNR paperwork and littered with plastic containers with holes punched in the lids—pork chops nestled in a bowl
soaked up a watery marinade. Marge lifted the dish towel cover-

ing an opaque rectangular box and said in a quiet voice, "Come look at my babies." We peeked in at four tiny squirrels sleeping on a bedding of napkins and paper towels.

George came through the screen door with Ricky still perched on his shoulder.

"I love that little turkey," cooed Linda.

"Isn't he beautiful?" said George.

Marge shoved a shoebox toward us. "Here are *your* babies," she told us, as she popped the hinged lid. A cluster of brown, feathery lumps instantly transmogrified into bright yellow flowers of wide-open beaks accompanied by a chorus of demanding squeals. Half in jest and half in genuine shock, I backed away and turned to face the sink. Spotting me through the screen, the blue jay on the porch raised his head and squawked again.

George laughed at my reaction to the starlings. "When you're done with them, Bob, come out behind the barn." He walked into the living room to glance at a football game on TV. "I want to show you the pond I'm digging for our heron and swans."

"You feed them every two hours," Marge instructed us. The hand wielding a syringe moved expertly from beak to beak, squirting yellow liquid down their throats.

"Every two hours?" I whined.

"From seven in the morning until nine at night. Just be glad you're not doing the squirrels. They have to be fed all through the night."

"How do you ever manage to leave the house?"

"The animals come to school with me," Marge said, turning to Linda. "I've been there so many years, no one's going to complain, and the kids love to see me feeding them. When your babies get a little older, you train them to eat worms, and you let them go. That's all there is to it. Starlings are pretty easy."

A crow croaked from the dining room. George reluctantly

abandoned his short-lived post at the television to feed it balls of cat food.

"Does it go on like this all day?" I asked him. Though we had visited Marge and George a couple of times before the yearly baby-animal boom had started, we had never seen them in full caregiver mode.

"We didn't eat dinner until, what, midnight last night?" Marge asked.

"We both still work," George explained. "But when I retire in another year, this is what I'll do all day."

"Is that something you're looking forward to?" I asked in disbelief.

"I love it," George answered, with a wide grin and no trace of irony. "There's nothing I'd rather be doing than this."

"Do you guys have syringes?" Marge asked us.

"We might have a few at home," said Linda.

"Take some. I've got syringes up the ying-yang." She grabbed a handful from a jar and presented us with a margarine tub of starling-food goop from her refrigerator. Linda copied down instructions for mixing up a batch of our own. Kitten chow, chicken entree for infants, liquid vitamins for children, plus water were mystically combined and mushed up in a blender to yield the hummus-colored concoction, which I hoped would never end up on my dinner plate by mistake. Just as we were about to leave, a woman met us at the door. She had talked to Marge on the phone earlier that day, and here were the eight baby starlings her husband had found in a nest on their trailer hitch. She had packed the nest and birds inside an inkjet-printer box.

"Want some more starlings, guys?" Marge asked.

Both of us vigorously shook our heads.

After feeding blueberries to the blue jay on the porch, we returned home to our slightly more manageable menagerie and tried getting through our first day with the starling chicks. The process wasn't as easy as Marge had made it look, and I was grateful to be relegated to understudy status. Linda wanted to care for the starlings on her own and, taking her cue from Marge, she even took them to work, carting the birds and food goop to her housecleaning customers' homes via a miniature version of our faithful cat/duck carrier. She bravely resisted my assistance until the middle of day three, when the unruly tykes began to wear her down.

"Two hours seems like a long time when you're doing something you don't like," Linda lamented. "But the two hours between feedings seems like about five minutes."

I could see her point as I tried my hand at the job. The complicated process began with fetching the plastic carrier that contained the starlings, opening it, and standing back in disbelief at the shrill cries of the birds as they clamored for their meal. The noise was actually loud enough to cause my ears to ring, if I bent my head too close to them for more than a few seconds at a time. Our eight starlings were neatly arranged in three napkin-padded margarine tubs inside the carrier, but they didn't stay in their bowls for long. Being unable to fly in no way impeded the hopping ability of these animals that seemed to consist of nothing but open beaks on legs, and if I were slow on the draw with the syringes, several chicks would inevitably pop out of their plastic nests.

Getting the food into the birds presented little problem, since few easier and willing targets exist in nature than the mouths of hungry starlings. Keeping the food in their mouths was another matter. No sooner did I feed a chick than the bird would shake its head and spatter itself, its neighbors, and our kitchen wall with unswallowed food. Once the birds had eaten, they would raise themselves up and hoist their posteriors over the rim of their bowls to release an impressive amount of poop. The trick was waiting until all birds had relieved themselves before removing the soiled napkins from the carrier and tubs, cleaning the plastic surfaces with a washcloth, and replacing the napkins. Miscalculating the timing of two chicks forced me to have to scrub one of the bowls three times. When I had finally finished, closing the carrier lid on the birds and returning them to the back room where Ollie slept at night was one of the most satisfying deeds of my entire life.

"This will drive you nuts," I told Linda with frazzled awe, as she wiped droplets of thrown food off the wall and countertop. "I don't know how you stand it."

Later that week, I feared that caring for the starlings had sent her over the edge when I strolled into the kitchen to find her waving a hair dryer over the birds.

"Are you okay?" I asked her in a reasonable imitation of a calm and soothing voice. "If you wanted to lie down for a while, I could finish, um, styling and setting the birds."

"Their heads were caked with dried food," she said.

"That would explain the hair dryer," I suggested gently. "I'll bet the dried food comes right off if you get it warm enough."

She shot me an unhappy look. "I've already washed them off. But their feathers weren't drying, and I don't want them to catch cold, so I'm using a blow-dryer."

"Sorry," I said. "That makes perfect sense." But just to be on the safe side, I sneaked into the bathroom and hid the curling iron.

I didn't remember seeing a blow-dryer in Marge Chedrick's kitchen. Clearly she hadn't told us everything that we needed to know about our task. Unfortunately, she was so busy coping with the endless stream of baby birds and injured animals people brought to her door at all hours of the day that returning phone calls from harried starling stepparents understandably occupied a low priority. With time, we figured out a few essentials on our own, such as feeding each bird only a small amount of the yellow goop per syringe shot, which greatly reduced the incidence of food flung around the room. Simple common sense—and the displeasure of retrieving flapping birds from the crack between the wall and microwave or the narrow space beside the refrigerator, where the vacuum cleaner just about fit—told us when it was time to transfer the birds from their plastic bowls to a cage.

HAVING TAUGHT OURSELVES to feed the starlings, it was time to teach the starlings to feed themselves. Marge had told us to simply scatter a few live crickets on the bottom of the cage. "They're attracted by the motion, and it just comes naturally that they start pecking at them." Following avian instincts hadn't ever seemed to occur to our birds before. They didn't even comprehend the principle of perching without extensive coaching. Grasping a wooden cage perch with their feet was as alien to them as learning to strum the strings of a lute. Linda managed to get one of the older starlings to wrap its toes around the perch, but that merely necessitated a separate set of lessons on posture, balance, and gracefully recovering from a fall. This didn't bode well for their hunter-gatherer skills.

The crickets supplied by Marge came in a mesh container with, of all things, an open top. Crickets, unlike starlings, are incapable of jumping straight up, and so the insects were trapped in the tube as if sealed inside a tin can. True to Marge's word, the starlings were indeed fascinated by the movement of the crickets. I placed their cage upon a porch shelf that a few years earlier had borne the burden of holding homemade ceramic mugs, vases, plates, and other unsaleable items from our basement pottery studio. Then I shook a few crickets into my hand and dropped them through the top grate of the cage. The starlings stopped all other activity, trained their eyes on the insects, and watched with deep interest as the crickets by trial and error wriggled through the bars to populate remote regions of our porch. I tried blocking the insects' egress by threading adding-machine tape in and out of the bars, forming a two-inch-high stockade fence around the bottom of the cage. This did in fact slow the crickets down, but given an infinite amount of time by the uncomprehending starlings, the bugs parlayed their random jumping and crawling into other means of successful escape.

Mealworms proved easier to deal with than the crickets. Although the birds were just as clueless about their ability to eat these visitors, the worms weren't jumping anywhere. The best they could do was crawl to the edges of the cage and slip beneath a folded sheet of newspaper, where we could retrieve them and try again. To kick-start their gourmet instincts, Linda picked up a mealworm with a tweezers and thrust it into the open mouth of a pleading starling. The eager youngster instantly clamped shut his beak, opened it again in bewilderment, and allowed the worm to fall out and crawl.

Despite these setbacks, after just under one debilitating month with the birds, the day finally arrived when they were dining on worms from the bottom of the cage and we could set them—and ourselves—free. Marge suggested that we move their cage out to the barn and let them leave at their own pace and return to the cage if they couldn't find food on their own. All of the birds elected to leave at once, though it took them a bit of flapping and cricket-style hopping to locate the yawning barn door. With syringe in hand, Linda checked the premises a couple of hours later to fortify any recidivist with goop, but the barn was empty except for yipping turkey Hazel and her sequestered sister, Lizzie.

I was pleased that the starlings had gone. Their departure was not only proof that we had nurtured them correctly, but it also considerably lightened our load, since feeding them every two hours had bent our regular animal-chore schedule to the breaking point. After dinner, buoyed by a mood of blissful release, I volunteered to go out to the barn and treat Hazel and Lizzie to their evening apple while Linda relaxed by washing the kitchen floor for the fourth time that day. I fed both turkeys by hand without losing a finger. On the way back to the house, I took a detour around the huge pine tree out back to check on the progress of Linda's vegetable garden. Although I carefully avoided the sprinkler, two of our released starlings had been less savvy. I found them fluttering in a patch of weeds soaked to the hollow bone, unable to fly, and potentially easy catches for our outdoor cat, Agnes. Popping them back in the birdcage that I retrieved from the barn, I placed them on their familiar porch shelf overnight for release in the morning after their feathers had dried.

When Linda opened the cage the following day for a test flight on the porch, both birds propelled themselves into the air, but only one of them managed to stay aloft. The aerodynamically challenged starling skittered across the floor like a spring-loaded mouse, while his brother flew in frantic circles against the nearest window. Linda snagged the floor flapper and confined him to his cage, then flung open the porch door and allowed the airborne bird the opportunity to soar into the wild blue yonder. He soared only as far as the front yard hackberry tree, joining three of his siblings, who apparently defined freedom primarily in terms of boundless dining privileges.

"It was a scene from Alfred Hitchcock's *The Birds*," Linda said, shuddering, when I returned home from work that afternoon. "Here I thought we were finally rid of the babies, then I went outside to work in the garden, and two birds suddenly landed on my head and started pecking me. Then two more landed on my shoulders. I had to run inside and get the syringe to feed them."

"I don't suppose they left after that."

"Didn't you hear them out there?" she asked incredulously. "They've been hanging around all day. I'm surprised you made it from your car to the house without getting dive-bombed. I can't even tell you how many times I've had to feed them. Oh, no," she groaned. Her expression darkened as she glanced out the kitchen window. "They're on the gate again, begging."

"I'll feed them," I volunteered, recalling the noisy but otherwise well-mannered blue jay that haunted the Chedricks' porch. I didn't see the problem. A few hungry birds on our property couldn't possibly be as difficult to deal with as a cage full of clamoring starlings in the kitchen. My thinking changed as soon as I stepped outside the kitchen door holding the tub of yellow goop. Starlings hovered around my head, hammering their needle-sharp beaks into my scalp. When I tried to brush them away, they clung to my hand with their toenails, pecking my knuckles as I pumped food into the bird that had settled on the gatepost. One by one, as I filled the bottomless mouths with the syringe, the birds returned to their tree almost too heavy to fly.

"At least they're out of the house," I gasped from the safety of the kitchen.

"No they're not. Didn't you notice the one on the porch?"

"What's the matter with him?"

"He still can't fly, and I don't think he sees very well. Every time I try to feed him, he bobs and weaves his head around, and I keep missing him with the syringe."

Weaver, as we came to name the miniature ostrich, would flap his wings like mad without gaining an inch in altitude. Even Ollie, the worst flier we had ever seen, could make it across the room on sheer gliding power. Weaver fell like a crumpled wad of paper whenever we urged him to give his innate abilities a fresh try. Fearing he had an insidious wasting disease, I took him to Dr. Fuller, who spread one of his wings and made the diagnosis, "Poor feather development." And it was true. His flight feathers resembled porcupine quills dipped in fluff, and they leaked more air than a window screen.

"It was probably caused by a vitamin deficiency," he said.

"But he ate the same food as everyone else."

"The deficiency may have come at a crucial stage of his early development."

I left before he started quoting Freud and resigned myself to the fact that we couldn't release Weaver until he had gone through a molt. But by then, I knew, he would probably be too tame to ever adapt to life on his own outdoors. That meant I had moved from reading about *Arnie, the Darling Starling* to suddenly having an Arnie of our own, though the darling aspect was definitely up for grabs.

Although he couldn't fly, Weaver still insisted on coming out of his cage to scamper around the top of the kitchen table in search of imagined caches of his beloved mealworms. If we didn't accede to his demands for freedom, he would throw himself flapping against the bars until we feared he would injure his body or his excited heart would explode. Unlike most birds, whose beaks wield considerable clamping strength—especially when my finger is involved —a starling asserts its jaw muscles by opening its beak and prying things apart. It's a handy skill for enlarging a hole in the soil to access hidden insects or for widening the spaces between stitches in a woven placemat. And while Weaver lacked a parrot's talent for picking up small items and throwing them on the floor, he compensating by whacking them croquet-style with the same end result.

Even when standing in one spot, Weaver was constantly in motion, exercising a repertoire of tics and twitches that aided his deliberation over a tabletop project. Cocking his head and scissor-ing his beak, he would unhurriedly study a situation from every possible angle before getting down to the business of toppling a saltshaker or shredding a paper napkin. Whenever I felt especially generous, I would place a few curls of adding-machine tape beside his cage, and he would arrange and rearrange them obsessively, lifting a loop and stepping through it, positioning it vertically into a wheel, or grabbing the tape by one end and tugging it behind him.

Even though I saw nothing of Stanley Sue's white-hot intelligence in his actions, Weaver had the most soulful eyes I could ever imagine a bird possessing. Neither judgmental, like a parrot's eyes, nor as innocent as a turkey's, they spoke of emotions every bit as lively and deeply rooted as the fat, luscious grub of his dreams. Whenever I brought Weaver's cage into the back room at night, just before covering him, I'd sit down for a moment in the chair at Linda's desk and talk to him while I marveled at his eyes. "You'd better start flying soon," I'd tell him. "You need to stop pooping on the kitchen table." He'd hop to the perch closest to me to give my suggestions the deliberation they deserved.

A bird looks directly at you by looking at you sideways. It's an odd thing to get used to, and I can never help but wonder how Stanley Sue, Howard, or Ollie's brain simultaneously integrates an image of me with a completely different panorama on the other side of the bird's head. But a starling's eyes are positioned just above the base of its bill and shoved slightly forward toward the front of its head, the better to study the patch of ground that the bird is probing. Because of this, whether Weaver turned the side of his face toward me or squinted at me down the length of his beak with both eyes, I received the full weight of his attention. And I couldn't shake the impression that his eyes held a nagging question. I seldom studied his face without encountering the query.

If only I could figure out what Weaver was asking me.

"Where's my food?" was my best guess, based on his voracious appetite. Weaver's lifeblood coursed with a current of sheer joy. When Linda or I would walk into the dining room, he was so pleased to see us, he would literally hop up and down with happiness. His exuberance was greatest when we came bearing food. He ate each and every meal as if it were his one and only meal of the day. Never mind that we might have filled his dish three times in a single afternoon with a dollop of canned cat food sprinkled with avian vitamins, or with minced red grapes, or with several wriggling mealworms. He would still attack the treat with all the ferocity of a child tearing the wrapping paper from a birthday present. His passion for his food dish became the most effective means of engaging his interest. This soon became important. Two months of Weaver's unflagging devotion to eating yielded a healthy set of flight feathers and the ability to elude us at will whenever we set him free in the dining room.

Weaver was smart enough to discriminate between our trips into the room on rabbit business and our ostensibly nonchalant visits aimed at surprising a roaming starling and returning him to his cage. If we were lucky, he might light on my hand at first sight of the purple plastic feed dish I was carrying and ride the dish to the kitchen sink for a brisk cleaning, to the refrigerator for replenishing, then back inside his barred enclosure. But if we needed to pen him up before his hunger got the better of his penchant for flying free, we were forced to chase him from the dining room table to the window sill, from the top of the refrigerator to the curtain rod over the sink, and from the antenna of our portable TV to the summit of another birdcage before he might finally decide to surrender by hopping onto one of our heads.

"What's that little sound you're making?" Linda asked one evening during dinner.

"I don't know, I guess I'm chewing too loud."

"Not you. Weaver. It sounds like he's trying to talk."

"He's saying 'buzzy buzzy.'"

"'Busy busy.'"

"Whatever it is, it isn't talking," I insisted. "He's just making buzzing noises. We might as well be keeping a bumblebee."

But a few days later I walked into the dining room while Weaver was in his cage indulging in his favorite noneating pastime of splashing around in his water dish. He took more baths than any bird I had ever seen and would probably have loved living outdoors with the ducks and geese, though he wouldn't have given them a chance to use the pool. I was toweling up the floodplain at the far end of the table when I distinctly heard him interrupt his happy twittering to greet himself with a hearty, "Hi, Weaver." Unlike shy performers Stanley Sue and Ollie, who refused to vocalize if we were in their field of view (and that applied to Stanley Sue's whistles), Weaver flaunted a bold stage presence. He excelled at ventriloquism by keeping his beak neatly closed as he repeated the phrase for me again, "Hi, Weaver. Buzzy buzzy, hi, Weaver."

Linda shared my elation at having a readily talking bird in the family. "Maybe he'll tell us what he wants, like Arnie." Occasionally, Margarete's starling would pipe up with a prescient comment in an appropriate context, but Weaver's commentary was a far cry from including pithy observations. Within another few days, he had picked up, "Whatcha say, Weaver?" from me, raising doubts as to which I should improve first, my grammar or my diction.

"You hear that?" I asked my parrot Stanley Sue accusingly, as Weaver practiced his repertoire. "Are you going to let a starling show you up? You could talk better than that if you wanted to. I've heard you do it."

I should have known better than to even jokingly pit Stanley Sue against another bird, especially when the other bird's affectionate hitchhikes on my head, hands, and other body parts had begun kindling the parrot's jealous side. If I walked around the dining room with Weaver clinging to my shirt, Stanley Sue would race behind me on the floor biting my shoes as an attention getter. Why she never exercised her own talent for flying was a riddle, since she could easily have flapped up to my shoulder and shoved him off. The closest she came to taking to the air was launching a snapping leap in Weaver's direction whenever he foolishly decided to share the top of her cage. Such aggressiveness raised our fears of another Stanley Sue–Howard-type rivalry and resulted in our decision not to let the parrot and starling out together.

One afternoon, while slowly emerging from an extended winter afternoon nap, I heard an unfamiliar trilling from the dining room. Weaver was flying free, and Stanley Sue was shut in her cage where she shouldn't have been able to cause him any harm. But the shrill cry alarmed me, and I hurried into the kitchen and dining room area only to find blood spattered across the top of the refrigerator and puddled on the table next to where Weaver stood forlornly on one leg. One toe on his right foot had been neatly amputated just above the toenail, and the presence of said joint with toenail in front of Stanley Sue's cage implicated the parrot, who must have been hanging upside down from the top bars just waiting for Weaver to land within reach of her beak. The incident also solved the mystery of how Elliot, our canary, and Howard, our dove, had managed to sustain foot injuries from time to time. Within an hour of losing his toe, Weaver was briskly chatting away in his cage, but three full days passed before he resumed using his right foot. From then on, we always draped a towel across the top of Stanley Sue's cage when the other birds were loose.

Weaver's escalating friendliness toward us was matched by his increasing restlessness. If I were working upstairs on a writing project and needed a cup of coffee in hope of jogging a few brain cells into action, I was forced to weigh my craving against undergoing a pestering blitz from the starling. When I walked into the kitchen, Weaver would land upon my head and gleefully begin drilling for dander and sebum. Brushing him off only glued him to my arm, and from there he would migrate to my hand and peck at whatever task my fingers attempted to accomplish, knocking coffee out of the measuring spoon or dipping his beak into the stream of water from the faucet. Meanwhile, the confined Stanley Sue protested every moment that Weaver flew free, with squawks that reached upstairs and defeated whatever concentration benefits my dosage of caffeine had conferred. As soon as I returned home from work, Stanley Sue insisted on prancing around the dining room climbing the drawer pulls or bothering the rabbits. She loathed the briefest imprisonment in the afternoon, especially if it was for the sake of the starling. For his part, Weaver thrashed around and squealed inside his cage whenever Stanley was at large. Two incompatible birds clamoring for simultaneous freedom presented us with a problem.

"He needs a flight cage," Linda informed me, as we tried eating lunch one Saturday while a caged starling fussed at us from the other end of the table. "This one's way too small. If he had a big cage he could fly around in, he'd be a whole lot happier."

"I'll build him one," I said.

Actually, I said no such thing, though the potential cost of buying a large cage made me seriously consider expanding my carpentry skills to include making straight cuts with a saw and springing for a powered screwdriver. For the moment, I dodged the issue by asking her, "And where would we possibly put a flight cage?"

Linda had no ready answer. Stanley Sue's cage and a beat-up chair consumed one wall of the dining room, while three rabbit cages and three birdcages lined the windows of the adjacent wall. The opposite wall was out of the question, because it didn't exist—a countertop divided the kitchen and the dining room instead. The fourth and final wall, a short and stubby run of Sheetrock across from Stanley Sue's wall, struggled to accommodate a Jurassic-scale hanging fern and required space for a door to the outside to open, but it was the most logical spot for a cage. That door eventually provided a solution to Weaver's housing problem.

All eight of our birds regarded the dining room, the top of the refrigerator, and an area around the kitchen sink as the extent of their territory. Only Howard occasionally flew into the living room to perch on a coat rack and hoot derisively at Grapey, Linda's purple stocking cap. On the extremely rare occasions when another bird blundered into the living room, the bird considered itself lost, abandoned, and easy prey for passing eagles, even though the brightly lit dining room beckoned loudly through the doorway. Similarly, our birds expressed zero interest in the great outdoors. Any activity that transpired just beyond the quarter-inch thickness of glass that dominated two walls may as well have taken place in Capistrano, for all they cared. But Linda and I still exercised great caution whenever we used the dining room door to step outside when any of our birds were loose. One day, though, Weaver was just too fast for Linda. As she darted outside, he accompanied her and, without the slightest hesitation, disappeared into the open sky.

I was devastated when I learned the news. Next to Stanley Sue, Weaver was my favorite bird, and I couldn't accept the fact that he had simply flown away. The situation was eerily reminiscent of a scene in *Arnie, the Darling Starling*, where Arnie slipped out into the yard just as a monstrous storm was brewing. As ominous clouds swirled above our heads, Linda and I combed our property calling for Weaver, the wind gulping up our pleas until a drenching rain drove us inside. A sorry and soggy Arnie had eventually returned to his owner Margarete. I hoped Weaver would do the same, and to help him find his way back home, I revived my owl-calling trick. The following day, I made a tape of starling vocalizations from a birdsong CD and walked around the nether borders of our property broadcasting them from a portable boom box. I even drove through the trailer park a half-mile away from us, cruising past green areas where starlings gathered, calling, "Weaver, Weaver, Weaver," from the car window until I feared the residents would call, "Police!"

Day after day, whenever I went outdoors to change the pool water for the ducks or visit our turkeys, Hazel and Lizzie, in the barn, I trailed pleas for Weaver behind me. I was stubborn about the loss, furious that Weaver would have chosen a perilous existence for which he was ill prepared over the pampered life that we had given him. "You'd think he would at least let us know that he's okay," I insisted illogically to Linda. "You'd think he would show a little gratitude."

Eventually, it dawned on me that perhaps the question that had loomed so large in Weaver's eyes was, "When can I go free with the others?"

Raising and releasing him had been our original intention, after all, and I felt better once I began to view his escape as the realization of our interrupted plan. I also loved the thought of unleashing a talking starling upon the world. I pictured a groggy resident of the trailer park stepping out of her front door early one morning in a terrycloth bathrobe. Bending down to pick up the newspaper, her hand would twitch, and she would spill her coffee as her body stiffened at the sound of a small, shiny black bird that looked identical to every other small, shiny black bird. But this one would interrupt his gleeful pecking at the ground to observe in a clear voice, "Pretty boy, Weaver. Pretty boy, nice nice."

CHAPTER 15

The Parrot Who Hated Me

A s an unexpected side effect of pet ownership, I would find myself getting seriously puffed up from time to time. Physically I remained as skinny as a Weimaraner. That wasn't it. And allergies to bird dander, cat hair, and rabbit fur along with mold and spores from poultry pens swelled nothing more visible than my nasal passages. But my self-importance was known to inflate to the dimensions of the Hindenburg should any keeper of a mere half-dozen animals recklessly raise the topic in my presence.

If no ready victim sought me out, I might sucker some blameless shopper I observed in the bird supplies section of PETsMART. I'd watch for a middle-aged woman selecting cockatiel food, and I'd saunter up to her while conspicuously holding a bag of parakeet seed.

"You must have some kind of fancy bird at home," I'd comment wistfully.

"Well, we've got a little cockatiel named Joey," she'd tell me.

"A cockatiel! You've got a cockatiel?" I'd exclaim, as if she'd claimed guardianship of a cassowary. Then I'd lower my eyebrows in deep thought and venture, "That's the one with the crest on its head, isn't it?"

"And the orange circles on the cheeks. And loads of personality."

"I've thought of getting a cockatiel," I'd reveal with an undercurrent of profound sadness. "My wife says they're probably too much trouble compared to—" I'd raise the seed bag I was clutching and, while forcing a quivering smile, point to the color illustration of a parakeet on the wrapper.

"You tell your wife to let you have a cockatiel," she'd insist and pat my bag of parakeet food sympathetically. "They're no trouble at all once you get the hang of owning a bird. And if you already keep a parakeet, you're probably ready for a cockatiel."

"But added on to caring for our African grey," I'd suggest with a shrug.

"Oh, well if you already have a grey—"

"And then there's the ring-neck dove. He's really no big bother, but he chases the parakeets and canary and likes to tease our pocket parrot, Ollie. He used to go after my pet starling, Weaver, too." Here I'd heave a mighty sigh. "At least the turkey's no longer in the basement and the bunnies have gotten their play area back again, plus the goose fully recovered from aspergillosis and we put her out back with the other goose and a bunch of ducks. But we're so busy raising a batch of baby robins right now—we did bluebirds earlier in the summer and released them—that I don't think we could squeeze in time for one of your little cockatiels. But tell Joey I said hello."

SATISFYING AS THIS WAS, I wanted more. I haunted the pet-bird newsgroups on the Internet and freely dispensed half-baked information to novice parrot owners, carefully avoiding encounters with breeders who possessed actual scientific knowledge. Whenever a poster to the group complained about a bad-mannered parrot that bit their spouse or shrieked incessantly, I rattled the keyboard with a rapid-fire answer that politely heaped blame upon the poster's ignorance of avian psychology, as if our own Ollie wasn't guilty of the same bad behavior.

My comeuppance was devastating once Linda brought home Dusty, a Congo African grey parrot she had spotted in the classifieds.

"Sweetheart," I remember her informing me one evening as I sat on the sofa basking in the glow of a *Wheel of Fortune* "Las Vegas Vacation" episode as it faded into a junk-food commercial. "There's an ad in the paper for a parrot that's supposed to be a really good talker. He's an African grey."

"We don't need another parrot. We couldn't possibly stand another parrot."

"I know," she told me. "But I'm still going to call the people and find out what kind of cute things he says."

Though I hid in the bedroom with the door sealed shut and the BBC world news cranked up on the headboard radio, Linda's explosions of glee still reached me as the bird's owner regaled her with endless anecdotes. I shivered under the sheet in the early July heat as a damp chill foreboding my inevitable fate wracked my body. "He sounds like a wonderful bird," Linda exclaimed as she burst into the room. "His name is Dusty. Can we go see him?"

"We're not getting another parrot," I insisted through the pillow.

"There's no harm in looking at him. You like looking at birds."

"I don't want another parrot. I really don't want another parrot. We've got our hands full caring for the birds we've got."

"The owner's a real nice lady, and she said we could come over on Saturday. We don't have to buy him if you don't want to."

"Buy him?" I groaned to Ed, the sock monkey, who snuggled against my chest trying in vain to comfort me.

We'd been down this road many times before. Linda was driving

a steamroller and nothing more substantial than a plywood cutout
of a husband stood in her way. I might have succeeded in kidding
myself that I had gained vast knowledge of animals over the years,
but clearly I didn't have a clue how to say no to my wife, particularly
when the question involved a new pet that part of me secretly
wanted, too—and that part was the knot inside my pine head.

We weren't allowed to see Dusty right away when we visited
Becky in Kalamazoo. The three of us sat in the living room. The parrot sat in the den. "He won't talk sometimes if you're in the room,"
Becky explained in hushed tones while her nineteen-month-old son
whacked the walls and furniture with a plastic baseball bat. "Especially with strangers."

"That's too bad," I said to Linda, raising my eyebrows. On the
hour-long drive from Lowell, I had raised every objection that
came to mind against taking on another parrot. "He'd better be absolutely perfect, or he's staying right where he is," I said.

"Oh, don't worry, he talks all day once he gets used to you,"
Becky said. Then she was silent for a moment as her son's bat
ticked off the seconds. "I sure hate having to sell him." Her words
caught in her throat. "I'm afraid Brandon's going to stick his hand
into the cage and lose a finger one of these days. And Dusty's used
to walking around on the floor after breakfast, and I can't watch
them both every single minute. Not that he would mean to hurt
Brandon." She moved her knee to avoid a blow from the vinyl
slugger, whose wielder had shifted from bopping the coffee table
to raising wisps of dust from a couch cushion. The little boy's enthusiasm made me wonder if the bird wasn't the family member
who was actually in peril. "I brought up Dusty from a little chick
years before I ever thought of getting married. I've listed him three
times in the paper and shown him to several people, but I haven't
been able to let him go."

"You haven't?" I asked, brightening with hope. "Maybe you should keep him."

"I just haven't found the right home for him, I guess. But you seem like a really nice person," she concluded, turning to Linda. "And you definitely have the right experience with parrots."

I had counted on the bird refusing to talk as the ultimate deal killer, and time seemed to be favoring me until a barrage of noise and speech erupted from an unseen source. "Wanna peanut?" said an excellent imitation of Becky's voice, followed by a squeal, apparently from the very same child who now sat tight-lipped on his mother's lap, wondering why she had confiscated his cudgel.

"That's Dusty," Becky told us. That was our cue to see him.

"Quack, quack, quack, quack, quack," said Dusty. That was Linda's cue to buy him no matter how he looked—and he looked impressive. In fact, I had trouble reconciling the female persona he had voiced with the bruiser of a bird we confronted in the den. Almost half again as large as Stanley Sue, Dusty carried the lighter plumage, solid black beak, and bright red tail feathers of a Congo African grey, along with a wild expression in his eye. His gorilla-proof stainless steel cage backed up Dusty's implicit show of strength as he snapped his beak with an audible click that set my teeth on edge.

"He seems a bit aggressive," I murmured, as I moved in back of Linda.

"He's a sweetie," Becky insisted. "But he's not too good with my husband. That's because Kenneth is allergic to birds and doesn't pay enough attention to him," she added.

"Can people touch him?" Linda asked.

"He lets me cuddle him. When he's walking on the floor, anyone can pick him up."

We didn't even try to pick up Dusty's cage, which was clearly too large to fit inside the backseat or trunk of my Ford Contour. "Too bad," I sighed to Linda, in a last ditch effort to avoid buying the bird. "I guess this just wasn't meant to be." But two days later, she and her friend LuAnne unloaded the mammoth cage from LuAnne's SUV and installed Dusty at the far end of the dining room between the hanging fern and the door to the backyard—the spot where Weaver's flight cage would have stood.

Almost immediately, Dusty began assailing us with voyeuristic sonic montages of his old life with Becky and Kenneth. It was as if a tape recorder that switched on and off at random had been secretly planted in their house. He mimicked the chirpy ringing of their cordless telephone, the declamatory buzz of a dot-matrix printer, clinking glassware, a small dog yipping, followed by what sounded like a volley of swats with a newspaper, and the *beep-boop* of an electronic toy. He captured the full harmonic complexity of toddler Brandon's laughter. He even staged miniature dramas, such as Becky brightly and cheerfully calling, "Kenneth!" and her husband replying, "What?" in a sour, put-upon tone that reminded me of myself. He turned us into reluctant window peepers, and I began guarding my own speech for fear of what Dusty might absorb and spit back later.

The first week or so that Dusty spent with us, he displayed warmth toward Linda and bland indifference toward me. After dinner, Linda would open Dusty's cage, and he'd step onto the hinge of the drop-down door and let her scratch his head with an index finger. Some nights I'd beat her to the draw, hoping he'd let me do the honors, but he would hang around his seed dish until I gave up and left. Once when he descended to the floor to explore the kitchen at ground level, I managed to scoop him up with my hand and nervously return him to his cage as I cried, "Oh, what a good boy he is." Another time when he strutted into the living room, I flopped down on the rug beside him and wiggled a shoelace for him to bite. I even carried off the trick I liked to practice with Stanley Sue, touching my nose to his beak as a familial way of saying hello.

Our relationship hit the skids the day that Dusty decided Linda was the family member with whom he would bond. As he sat on his cage top waiting for Linda to return from feeding apples to the turkeys in the barn, I approached to try the old nose-and-beak touch routine. He replied by pecking me soundly on the cheek. Determined to give no quarter to the massively intimidating bird, I hesitantly raised my wrist and commanded him, "Step up." He sank his beak into my forearm. He held on so firmly that when I snatched away my arm, he stayed stapled to my flesh and rode along, crashing harmlessly into a pinecone-and-evergreen floral arrangement on the dining room table that had somehow survived the many months since Christmas.

Rushing into the side yard, I confronted Linda and cursed her new parrot as a criminal, a monstrous animal who had no business living in our house with decent people. "No animal has ever treated me like this," I howled in indignation. "I've never been anything but decent to that bird."

I had recently weaned myself from Zoloft, and the entire world seemed as sharp and steely as Dusty's beak. The medication had lost its effectiveness over the years, and since I didn't want to suffer through the high-voltage emotional jolt of another dosage increase, I had decided to cut the chemical strings instead. Despite my dislike for Dr. Rick, his admonishment about the lack of information on the long-term effects of Prozac, Zoloft, and related drugs had begun to gnaw at me. To mitigate the Zoloft vacuum, I swallowed a couple of capsules of St. John's wort each morning to slightly pad the edges of my nervous-depressive personality. But it wasn't particular effective against parrot jaws.

I decided to give Dusty a wide berth and leave the touchy-feely aspects of his care to Linda. Unfortunately, my newfound cautiousness only emboldened him. Wandering around downstairs while Dusty was at large invited aggressive lunges at my shoe that quickly turned into an ankle attack if I didn't immediately shake him off my foot. Eager to regain the psychological ground that I had lost, I took to donning a pair of daunting winter boots and affecting an attitude of vexed forbearance.

"What's the story here?" I'd ask him in a sleepy tone of voice, as he exercised his beak on the impenetrable leather of my boots. "I don't think that's going to get you anywhere." It took him exactly three futile assaults before he learned to climb the laces and strike at my vulnerable calf.

"Get this bird off me!" I'd holler to Linda while hopping up and down on one leg. "Get him off!" To her credit, she never exactly laughed out loud, though an hour or so later, while reading an Emily Brontë novel, she might lapse into a snicker and refuse to discuss the reason.

I wasn't the only person who had problems with parrots and feet. In her book, *The Parrot Who Owns Me,* ornithologist Joanna Burger reported that her fiercely loyal Amazon parrot, Tiko, loved giving painful bites to her husband's toes. And a woman on a parrot newsgroup told me, "Don't take it personally. African greys have a thing about shoes." I didn't even need to be wearing them. One day I came home from work and noticed that a pair I had left under the coffee table sported a fresh coat of black polish.

"Thanks for shining these," I told Linda. "What's the occasion?"

"Dusty chewed on them this morning," she confessed. "I don't think you can notice the damage now."

Linda's shoes he left alone.

My sole defense against embarrassing foot attacks was to carry a heavy towel whenever Dusty was free and interpolate it between his beak and my fleshy parts. His response was to climb the towel toward my hand. That left me with the choice of dropping the towel and beating a hasty retreat or trying to reach the open cage door with the dangling bird and pop him inside before I sacrificed a digit.

WHILE I SAT UPSTAIRS at my computer, I considered myself safe when Dusty was on the prowl. However, my sense of security was punctured one afternoon when a piercing pain to my ankle interrupted an e-mail session. Using his beak to help him climb, Dusty had quietly scaled twelve carpeted stairs and crept up to greet my foot in his inimitable way. A few days later he tried reprising the stunt, but this time I spun my head around and caught him at the entrance to my office. "I'm sorry," he announced in my voice, then proceeded to clamber up my quickly vacated chair with unthinkable mayhem in mind. From then on, whenever he was loose and I was working upstairs, I barred the steps with the plywood board that kept the rabbits out of the living room during more tranquil hours. He could, of course, flap his wings and sail over the board at will, but like Stanley Sue, his odd reluctance to fly trumped most other concerns.

I decided I had better fix the situation before I needed a bodyguard. My only recourse was changing my behavior. Maybe at some level he was afraid of me and acted aggressively out of defensiveness, I reasoned. Or perhaps he had transferred his dislike for his former owner's husband to me and didn't understand that I wanted to be his friend. In an attempt to win his trust, I began demonstrating my value to him. Whenever I woke up in the morning before Linda, I humped to the kitchen to shower kind words on Dusty along with the more tangible treats of fresh parrot seed and water. At first I only dared unlatch and slide out his bowls if he was perched on the opposite end of his cage, safely beyond biting distance. But once he began associating my actions with a benefit, he permitted these incursions with a mild look in his eye. During meals, I could even get away with poking table scraps through the bars into his dish, mere inches away from his beak.

Dusty loved wooden chew toys. I almost never bought them, because fifteen dollars seemed pricey for an item he would be reduced to splinters and sawdust within a few hours. Calculating to endear myself to him, I bought scrap pieces of pine from Home Depot. I brushed the cobwebs off my power tools and cut, drilled, and strung the shapes on leather thongs. I was hesitant to thrust my arms into his cage to hook the limp kebabs to a top bar. But my hands darted and shook with impunity as he stood marveling at the gift.

At the various stages of toy demolishment, I'd saunter into the dining room and praise his progress with exuberant cries of, "Dusty!" His delight in my reaction was obvious. "Dusty!" he'd repeat in my voice throughout the day. I made him a new toy at least once a week. Soon I could walk past his cage without earning a bloodthirsty lunge at the bars in my direction.

The situation had definitely improved, and so I boldly proceeded with phase two of my plan. My friend Ron worked for a hi-fi products company for which I wrote catalog and Web site copy. Early in his marriage, he had owned an African grey Timneh named Franklin, who threatened to carve him into tiny pieces whenever Ron tried to pick him up.

"I finally decided that I was just going to let him bite me and put up with the pain no matter how bad it was," Ron explained. "So I stuck out my hand, said, 'Step up, Franklin,' and sure enough, he bit me."

I nodded in sympathy.

"It hurt like a bitch, but I kept doing it, and he kept biting me. My wife was disgusted and called me a masochist," he laughed. "She said, 'You're one sick puppy!' But finally, one time when I put out my hand, Franklin decided, 'Oh, well, what the hell,' and got up on my finger. And he never bit me again."

Unlike Ron, I had zero tolerance for pain. But there was a solid core of sense to his strategy. I would also essentially be following standard wisdom for dealing with a parrot that's partial to one spouse. Take the bird into a neutral room on the hand of the person that the bird is bonded to. Then have that person hand off the bird to the other poor sap. Stoking my bravery was the realization that the bites I had received from Dusty so far had intimidated me more through surprise than actual injury.

That Saturday, I returned from my weekly visit to the feed store for duck food and bird seed to find Dusty engaged in his favorite morning pastime of standing on the rim of a ceramic dish on my dresser and throwing loose change down the floor register. Our heating duct concealed more dimes and quarters than a row of slot machines. When Linda picked him up to return him to his cage, I met her at the bedroom door, extended my arm, and told her, "Let me take Dusty back." She shook her head, but I insisted. Without a fuss, the parrot stepped onto my hand. Bird and man glared suspiciously at one another. I quickly handed him back to Linda. "He feels more comfortable with you," I told her breezily. "You'd better take him."

Buoyed by my success, I tried the stunt again the following Saturday. This time when I reached for Dusty, Dusty also reached for me, clamping his beak on the fleshy bit between my thumb and forefinger with such intensity that my eyes rolled up into my head and flooded my brain with crimson light. I had no notion how long he hung on or how many times he bit me. The pain transported me to an extra-temporal dimension where a dozen episodes of *The Honeymooners* fit into the space of an aspirin commercial and where embarrassing incidents from my college dating years unfolded in excruciating slow motion.

Once Linda had convinced Dusty to let go of me, I sat silently on the edge of the couch staring with concern at the vivid pistachio-shell outlines he had embossed on my hand. I could hardly move my fingers and wondered if I'd ever be able to type, tie a knot, or drum my fingers ever again. He had meant to hurt me. He knew exactly what he was doing, intent on causing the maximum amount of pain while barely breaking the skin. Forget the branding irons, whips, and lack of indoor plumbing. The Inquisition could have done without its fiendish dungeons and managed quite nicely with an African grey parrot.

Instead of erupting in anger at Dusty, I simmered in perplexity. After almost a decade of close relationships with animals, I had finally come full circle — kicked back to the starting point by a feathered reincarnation of Binky. Years before we had transformed our house into a full-fledged petting zoo, I had pitted my weak will against a belligerent bunny in fruitless hopes of altering his nature. I was doing the same with Dusty. The difference was, I genuinely liked the parrot. Or did I? I liked the idea of a talking bird. I liked it that Linda liked him. But in my heart, I probably didn't actually like Dusty, and that difference proved to be crucial.

Time and time again, I had noticed a huge change when I had moved from simply being nice to a pet to actually doting on it, and the animal always knew when that change had occurred. No matter how gently I would hold our Checker Giant rabbit, Walter, when carrying him from his cage to the basement pen, he would start kicking his powerful legs at a crucial point midway down the stairs, gouging parallel red lines across my stomach with his toe-nails as he sent me tumbling into the bag of potatoes on the landing. Not until he'd had a scary run-in with Pasteurella, a bacterial infection that frequently kills bunnies, did I actually crack open my heart to Walter. And that change changed everything. He suddenly relaxed when I held him in my arms. He sought me out to stroke his head. It had gone like that with our dove, Howard, too. And with Muscovy duck Hector. And rabbits Bertie and Rollo. Each could distinguish genuine affection from mere goodwill.

But you open up your heart to an animal at your peril. On the positive side are the purrs, licks, contented quacks, the gleeful hops onto your lap, and the electricity that leaps between their eyes and yours. A dove flies to a chair to bow and coo his love for you. A duck roosts on your shoulder. A starling hangs from your hand. A parrot drinks from your juice glass, and a parakeet nibbles your cheek. An injured turkey struggles to her feet when she hears the sound of your voice. The goose on the porch that may not make it through the night honks softly because she wants you near, while the rabbit in the living room tears across the carpet. He jumps straight up, spins around in midair, and runs off just because he can. Just try and put him back into his cage.

On the downside are the disappointments—not to mention the inevitable deaths. It's the parrot that hates you, of course, and the cat that hides under the bed. It's the trust that never comes, and it's the other broken bonds. The pampered turkey blinds her sister. The gentle parrot slashes open a dove. The starling you saved leaves without a glance good-bye. And the ducks and geese you cherish, feed and water every day, nurse through sickness, and try to keep safe still shy away as if you were a predator, simply because you tower above them. These misunderstandings can never be re-solved. But find a clump of grass the ducks haven't flattened, plop down on it, and speak with a soft voice, and you might be rewarded with the close approach of a goose. She might even let you touch her. And you had better treasure the gift. Too suddenly and too often, they leave us. It's then that we realize most sharply the subtle comfort of our animals' companionship. It's then that we know that we can't live without them, even though we sometimes must.

THAT SUMMER, LINDA and I took a break from the pets to visit her cabin in northern Michigan. We hadn't been up there in over two years, and I had forgotten the intimate details of the two-room cabin overlooking algae-choked Morley Pond. Walking into her tiny kitchen evoked an overwhelming sense of nostalgia as palpable as running nose-first into an ancient wall. At first I thought I was pining for the last bloom of my youth, but I had met and married Linda in my mid-thirties and had already been a crotchety old man in spirit for decades. So that wasn't what I was feeling. Stepping out her back door, I nearly tripped over the remains of a chicken-wire pen where Linda had occasionally kept Binky during the first few weeks we had owned him. I remembered buckling the struggling bunny into a purple harness, carrying him out to Linda's field, and trying to take him for a walk with no understanding of how poorly he would do on a leash. Those days marked the end of a kind of innocence about animals. The comings and goings of so many pets added richness and complexity to the years that followed. Our enslavement to ducks, geese, rabbits, parrots, turkeys, cats, starlings, parakeets, doves, and canaries helped teach me a smidgen of patience, tolerance, and respect that I even applied to people from time to time. But this gain came at the expense of a certain lightness of being. We became wiser but sadder, and not really all that wise.

But I couldn't turn back time—especially if it involved diddling with a digital clock. As a realistic alternative, I decided to stop taking Dusty for granted as an adversary and start noticing his finer points. An example was quick in coming. I strode into the dining room late one afternoon while Howard was chasing the smaller birds from the plant hanger to the refrigerator top and noticed to my horror that our parakeet, Sophie, had squeezed between the bars of Dusty's cage. She flitted about like a moth touring a chandelier, flicking against him with her wing tips until she finally settled on his bowl and helped herself to his exotic seeds. As we had learned from previous unpleasantness with Howard, Stanley Sue would have made mincemeat of any intruder in her cage. Dusty was generous about the visit, however. He gazed at the yellow parakeet with avuncular affection and never made the slightest move in her direction.

He seemed to demonstrate similar fondness for the starlings we raised that summer. "Aww," he would coo in Linda's voice, when she brought the baby birds to the dining room table for feeding. Once we had released the batch, a few of them hung around our yard to beg for food at regular intervals. "They're here," Dusty announced one morning. We hadn't heard him use that phrase before, and we hadn't mouthed it ourselves. A glance out the window revealed three birds on the backyard gate clamoring to be fed. "They're here," he told us again and again over the next few days. Then the starlings left us, and the phrase flew from Dusty's repertoire, never to be repeated.

More than any other factor, Dusty's keenly honed sense of humor was what finally won me over. He loved exploiting his talking and mimicry talents to lord it over the other animals and make fun of us. Whenever we released Howard from his cage, immediately after lighting upon the back of a dining room chair in front of the parakeets' cage, Howard would hurl his swaggering *hoo-hoo-hoo-hoo* call at them. The unvarying nature of this event wasn't lost on Dusty, and neither were the intricacies of timing. One day when I opened Howard's cage door, Dusty waited patiently for the dove to spring into the air, arc across the table, and flutter toward a landing on the appropriate chair. An instant before Howard's feet touched the wood and while he was still gearing up for an impressive hoot, Dusty beat him to the draw with a louder version of the dove's own call. *Hoo-hoo-hoo-hoo!* Deflated, Howard was forced to face the parakeets in silence. Later he hooted at them, but a parrot had already tarnished his perfect moment.

Within a half hour of finishing dinner, we always rounded up the birds that weren't hand-tamed by clapping and shooing them into their cages. Dusty contributed after his own fashion. "Time to go back," I would remind the three parakeets and our canary, Elliott, as Ollie watched from Linda's shoulders. They typically snubbed my request. "Go on!" Dusty urged them in Linda's voice, followed by an imitation of our bird-herding handclaps that came just as I was about to put my hands together. *Hoo-hoo-hoo-hoo,* I felt like telling Dusty.

He showed the same sarcastic consideration for our cat. Before I could even clomp all the way down the basement stairs to call Agnes into the house for her after-dinner treat, Dusty would anticipate my routine by unleashing the mocking cry, "Agnes!" with perfect mastery of my dulcet tones. Later in the evening, after we had switched off the lights in the kitchen and dining room, we always kept the noise level low lest we disturb the sleeping birds. The penalty was facing a domino effect of complaints. If I crept into the kitchen and inadvertently crinkled a bag of tortilla chips while removing it from the cupboard, the caged and covered Howard would emphatically hoot his disapproval. Annoyed at being awakened by Howard, Stanley Sue would raucously throttle her bell, prompting Dusty to exclaim in my voice, "Stanley, be quiet!" The only thing missing from this chain reaction was a salivating dog.

Linda and I were away from the house during Dusty's most outrageous verbal performance. While we vacationed in Tennessee, our pet-sitter Rhonda was having trouble convincing Dusty to return from his constitutional across the living room rug. Following the instructions Linda had left her, Rhonda dropped a towel over the parrot to minimize the chance of falling foul of his beak, picked him up, and deposited him inside his cage. As she closed his door, Dusty shot her a piercing look and cursed her with the epithet, "Bitch."

"That's what he said," Rhonda reported later. "He said it loud and clear."

"He's never heard that word from us!" Linda exclaimed. "He must have heard it at his previous owners."

"Don't look at me," I insisted.

"Well, I just froze when I heard that," Rhonda told us. "Then I burst out laughing, he imitated my laugh, and we got along just fine from then on."

As I became more appreciative of Dusty, Dusty became more tolerant of me. He stopped making a beeline for my feet when he crawled down from his cage in the evenings. While I sat in a battered dining room chair rubbing the head of Stanley Sue, who crouched beside me on the cushion, he would often strut right by without so much as a threatening glance in my direction. The pillow on the floor blocking my feet might have helped, though no armor had ever dissuaded him in the past. I still couldn't follow Linda's lead and feed him lukewarm licorice tea from a coffee mug without inviting a lunge for my hand. But once he was back inside his cage, Dusty would accept a peanut from my fingers with such ethereal delicacy, I was rarely certain it was the same beak that had tattooed my flesh. En route through the dining room to take care of our backyard animals, I'd pause at the door, turn, and talk to Dusty, only to find myself favored with his soft eye peering back at me.

Outside in a burst of clear grey light, as clouds lingered between gathering and dispersing, I sloshed dirty water out of a plastic swimming pool. Ducks and geese nibbled noisily at the lawn. Across our lot and behind the barn, one-eyed turkey Hazel and her former tormentor, Lizzie, sat together on opposite sides of a fence. A mosquito threatened my neck, as flecks of mud and manure accumulated on my pant leg. A goldfinch sang a song that celebrated his freedom from the burden of keeping pets. I breathed hard walking up the hill to shut off the hose. I lumbered back down carrying two pitchers of scratch feed. I just wasn't built for manual work. But still, I could be seized by the mindless certainty that I was doing exactly what I should be doing with my life, and for a little isolated instant in time, everything felt essentially right about the world. Even if another animal disaster lay just around the corner, clacking its beak.

Acknowledgments and Culpability

MY POOR WIFE, LINDA, was forced to hear about this book on a daily basis for the past three years, and I thank her for her unflappable enthusiasm. She could easily have written her own book with herself at the center of events, and it would have been truer than mine.

My agent, Jeff Kleinman, and my editor at Algonquin Books of Chapel Hill, Kathy Pories, both bear the blame of contributing ideas that helped shaped my narrative. My good friend Bill Holm joined me frequently at a sparsely inhabited Chinese restaurant and helped me work through story ideas. I would compliment him as an excellent sounding board, but that's unfair to boards in general. He also read every chapter and made seemingly endless suggestions.

My sister, Joan Smith, and her husband, Jack, are among the many animal lovers who have helped Linda and me with our menagerie. Their ferrets, cats, dog, fish, and house sparrow are even more spoiled than our critters. Peg and Roger Markle gave us valuable bird-parenting advice, and their wildlife rehab work is awe inspiring. The veterinarians who have provided lifesaving care for our animals include Richard Bennett, John Carlotti, Alice Colby, Edward Farnum, Owen Fuller, Michael Hedley, and Raymond Leali. Extraordinary pet-sitters Jamie Beean, Betty MacKay, Mary Vaught, and Rhonda Delnick allowed us to escape from it all once in a while. Ron Biermacher gave me excellent, if not amusing, parrot-keeping advice.

A special thanks goes to Wayne Schuurman, president of Audio Advisor, Inc., who generously provided a flexible work schedule that allowed me time to write this book. A chain of gratitude is due my friend Rhonda Lubberts, who introduced me to Mary Jane Pories, who introduced me to Kathy Pories, who introduced me to Jeff Kleinman, who sold my book to Algonquin through Kathy Pories, who lives in the house that Jack built.

CC Smith, editor of *The Beat* magazine, encouraged my writing over the years as did my *Beat* co-conspirator, Dave Hucker, and his wife, Kim. They all commented on various chapters, as did Carol Holm, John Storm Roberts, Lorraine Travis, John Brosky, and Mike Bombyk.

Thanks also to my supportive sister, Bette Worley, her husband, David, my mom, Linda's mom, and my late dad. And to everyone who buys a copy of this book, thanks for keeping the memory of our animals alive.